THE AUTHOR

Saddlebags for Suitcases

by
Mary Bosanquet

The Long Riders' Guild Press
www.thelongridersguild.com
ISBN No: 1-59048-071-6

To the Reader:

The editors and publishers of The Long Riders' Guild Press faced significant technical and financial difficulties in bringing this and the other titles in the Equestrian Travel Classics collection to the light of day.

Though the authors represented in this international series envisioned their stories being shared for generations to come, all too often that was not the case. Sadly, many of the books now being published by The Long Riders' Guild Press were discovered gracing the bookshelves of rare book dealers, adorned with princely prices that placed them out of financial reach of the common reader. The remainder were found lying neglected on the scrap heap of history, their once-proud stories forgotten, their once-glorious covers stained by the toil of time and a host of indifferent previous owners.

However The Long Riders' Guild Press passionately believes that this book, and its literary sisters, remain of global interest and importance. We stand committed, therefore, to bringing our readers the best copy of these classics at the most affordable price. The copy which you now hold may have small blemishes originating from the master text.

We apologize in advance for any defects of this nature.

CONTENTS

CHAPTER		PAGE
I	AFTER AN ADVENTURE	1
II	THE ROAD AT LAST	12
III	TO THE SNOW-LINE IN JUNE	23
IV	FROM CACTUS TO JACKPINE	29
V	NOTES FROM A HILL-SIDE	37
VI	DAYS IN THE DOUKHOBOR COUNTRY	41
VII	OVER THE SELKIRKS	52
VIII	CAMP ON THE KOOTENAY	60
IX	LAST OF THE MOUNTAINS	66
X	PRAIRIE WINDS	75
XI	LANDS THAT WAIT FOR WATER	84
XII	WAR	96
XIII	INTO WILDERNESS	113
XIV	WINTER ON OUR TAIL	122
XV	GREAT LAKE	137
XVI	WE DROP ANCHOR	151
XVII	ACCIDENT	162
XVIII	WINTER DAYS	172
XIX	SPRING AND SPY MANIA	184
XX	RIVER-DRIVE	194
XXI	LAST DAYS AT DAYTON	208
XXII	THE ROAD AGAIN	220
XXIII	NEW FRANCE	230
XXIV	END OF AN ADVENTURE	234

ILLUSTRATIONS

The Author	*frontispiece*
	FACING PAGE
"Douglas Lake is One of the Largest Ranches in Canada" .	8
"Camp on Some Pleasant Flats"	24
"Where the Dry Wind Rolls the Tumbleweed Across the Dusty Range"	32
"The Columbia, a Lovely Temperamental River" . . .	54
"Steamed and Ate Bacon and Eggs"	58
"The Weathered Selkirks"	58
"The Young and Precipitous Rockies"	64
"Forest and Mountain and Cloud"	72
"Curving in Long Bright Lines Among Its Dark Islands" . .	144
"At Nightfall They Would Come Back, Secret and Satisfied"	152
"My Irish Canadian 'Mum' "	176
"I Soon Found That I Could Milk with the Best" . . .	180
"The Gordons Boil Down Right Out in the Bush" . . .	180
"We Had One Favourite Trail"	192
"Moored Beside the Cook Tent Lay a Long Heavy Boat" .	200
"One May Ride from Dawn till Dark Without Ever Touching a Highway"	240
"Jonty's Temperament Has Not Suffered from the Ride" . .	244

Chapter I

AFTER AN ADVENTURE

It was on the tenth of May, 1938, before the second Great War drew a line across our lives, that I was bucketing down the Bayswater Road in a number eleven bus.

Past the windows streamed a dark and windy London evening. On one side of our way slept the black shadow of Hyde Park; on the other the lights of the big Bayswater houses broke into changing stars as the rain lashed the glass. The bus was villainously overcrowded, and its badly packed cargo steamed morosely, saying nothing, seeing nothing, inwardly hurrying, tensely preoccupied in the all-important business of getting home.

I swayed at the end of my strap, bouncing in an uneven rhythm between the lean back of a man in a mouse-coloured mackintosh and the plump resilient shoulder of a dark, much-decorated lady in bedraggled fur. I was ridiculously encumbered with parcels and bothered by the certainty that my hat was crooked. I steamed and dripped and scowled with the rest; and somewhere, inside me or outside, serenely detached from the muddy tiredness of my body, burnt the steady vitality, the undeniable, undramatic ability to do, which leaves no peace to the people whom it inhabits. And then, like a stone falling into a pond, the idea dropped into my mind.

To ride across Canada. Just that. As simple as that, and as easy and as difficult as that. Before the ripples in the pond had died away, I knew that the future life of the idea depended entirely upon my mother and father. Mummy and Daddy are simple people, and big, and they see things, not from angles, but straight. If they said "Yes," it would not matter who else said "No." But if they said "No," then the stone should slumber on the floor of the pond forever.

That evening when Mummy came to say good night, I asked her, "How would it be, do you think, if I rode across Canada?"

Mummy looked at me with her calm eyes. "I think," she answered, "it might be a very good idea."

So I asked Daddy. "Well," he said, "I should hate to do it myself, but if you want to, you'd better go ahead."

Then the project was folded up and put away in the back of my mind, but I knew that early in the following spring I should set out for Vancouver.

Meanwhile I went on with my job, met my college friends, drove Mummy in the car, went away for week ends, and forgot Canada. One gift which I possess is the inability to worry beforehand about anything which I am going to do, but the defect of this quality is an equal inability to make accurate plans.

I knew well that I ought to be studying the geography of Canada, estimating expenses, designing saddlebags, securing expert advice, and all the rest of it. But personally I find the study at long range of physical features and climate a dreary occupation at best. As for expenses, I had about eighty pounds; if the journey cost less than this, well and good, but to persuade myself in advance that it was likely to cost more would have been merely an unnecessary discouragement. As for saddlebags, I knew no more about them than any other girl whose equestrian experience has been confined to hacking, horse shows and the hunting field; so I decided to let the problem of luggage take care of itself.

I made only one definite decision, viz. (as Robinson Crusoe would have said), that I would cross by train to Vancouver and begin my ride in the West. I was under the impression that all Western horses were strong, full of quality and cheap; and it occurred to me that if, as most people predicted, the horse and I broke down before we reached the half-way mark, we should at least have had the journey through the mountains. At first I did try to secure advice, but as my advisers almost all confined themselves to attempts at dissuading me from my foolhardy escapade, I soon gave up even this. Thus it was with the shameless optimism of almost complete ignorance that, on March 31, 1939, I boarded the C.P.R. liner, *Duchess of Bedford,* bound for my unknown continent.

I remember one thing above all about that voyage—the night of the gale. Till evening I lay like the majority of the passengers and abandoned myself to misery. But at last a companion of the voyage came in to visit me. Ted was a young pan-god, brown as a hazel-nut, and the points of his ears quirked up into his curly hair. He looked down at my invalid form and laughed like a satyr. So, stung to action, I crawled from my bunk of suffering and staggered up with him to the third-class deck. We were all alone up there, and ropes had been stretched across to keep any one from going out, but we scrambled under and clung on panting, while our feet slid from under us on the washed decks. Moving mountains, lashed by the rain, came surging towards our little ship. An army of lost souls shrieked in the wind that tore across our quarters. I forgot my panting body and was translated by the exaltation of the sea. My heart whirled in the storm; for a little while I rode life bareback, with my hands in the tangled mane.

Well for my happiness, well for my exaltation, that I did not know what future was rushing towards us, that I could not see into the fire and darkness of 1940, when, on so many nights like this, so many ships went down. Thank God I did not know that, before I saw him again, my brother would be threading the maze of mines and running the gauntlet of submarines over this same relentless sea. . . .

On April the seventh we landed in Halifax, to find slush on the ground, sleet in the wind and no sign of the sadly lagging spring. A little *froissée* by such a reception from a climate which I had always believed to be superior to our own, I piled on plenty of clothes and climbed into the trans-Canada train. At once I was forced to strip almost to the skin again by the temperature of the carriages, which were maintained at over eighty degrees by the air-conditioning system. This temperature suits Canadians very well, but I, being used to the windy cool of English houses and the draughtiness of our little English trains, sat sweltering in depression. I must confess that my four-day train journey did not dispose me to take a particularly rosy view of the country I proposed to discover.

Having traversed the Maritime Provinces by night, our train set out into the rich farming country of southern Ontario. But in the second week of April, with the virginal mantle of the snow already gone, but with no hint yet of Ontario's swift vivid spring, even this fine rolling landscape looked stark and unprepossessing. After interminable hours we bent north-west and began to climb up the map into northern Ontario, soon losing ourselves in the wilderness. I had hardly realized there was so much forest anywhere in the world. At every station I would get out and walk along the train to look at the great romantic engine which stood steaming and panting at its head.

These are real adventure-engines with their snow-ploughs in front and the great bell clanging before the driver's cab. Best of all is the wild mournful hoot which they make in place of a European engine's whistle. There is all the soul of Canada in the sound of their hooting; there are prairies and precipices and seaboard cities; there are grizzly bears and mountain goats and caribou and eagles flying; there are storm and snow and forest fires and flooding rivers, darkness and dawn and the sea. And now, as I lie in bed and hear the trains go hooting by in the night, I can feel all Canada again, the Canada whose wildness and wonder I was so soon to discover. But in these first days what most impressed me was still the heat of the carriages.

As we bored deeper into the forests, I was astonished by the tiny settlements at which our trans-continental dragon would snort to a standstill. I gazed at the little wooden houses, many of them apparently built of bare boards, and had to tell myself, like one repeating a lesson, that Families Lived in Them. I had not then learnt to know the wealth of simplicity, warmth and kindness which can make of these packing-case houses homes indeed.

We saw little of the Great Lakes, leaving them to the south, but my companions of the journey discoursed at length upon the subject of their immensity, informing me with relish exactly how many times the British Isles would go into Lake Superior. I have since observed, on looking at a map of the world, that the British Isles would not go into Lake Superior even once; however I accepted the statement at the time with the unquestioning awe of the ignorant traveller.

We left Winnipeg in the morning. All day and all night we crossed the prairies. I had known, of course, perfectly well beforehand, that they were as wide as this and as flat as this; but it is impossible to imagine, before you have seen it, such interminable expanse. At daybreak on the fourth morning we hauled out of Calgary and began to climb up into the snows.

Owing to the efficiency of the newspapers, pretty nearly every one on the train knew by this time who I was and what I was going to do. My natural reaction to reporters is unfavourable, and at first I received them with a quite unjustifiable hauteur; but in point of fact I had some cause to be grateful to them, for, as the result of a paragraph in the Vancouver papers, a lady from Kamloops, in the interior of British Columbia, had kindly invited me to stay with her while I searched for a suitable horse. So at midnight, in the bewilderment of darkness and broken sleep, I bundled out at the little station and was met by a fair-haired, friendly young man in a car, and whirled in the dark to a small house, where my hostess welcomed me and tumbled me into bed.

Next day was Sunday, and I awoke alone while Mrs. Lewis and

her son were still at Mass, for they were Catholics. I dressed and went out into the warm garden, to find that the little house was perched upon a mountain side. Below me the town of Kamloops nestled in the valley, and before me the broad North River of the Thompson came curving through strange flat-topped hills to join the main stream. In the bright, brittle Sunday silence a man was singing a cowboy song and yodelling between the verses. There was a twitter beside me. I looked—and it was as though some one had grasped a handful of sky and moulded it into a bird. I had felt, as I passed out into the suspended stillness, that I was walking into an opera set. Now I knew it—Maeterlinck's *Bluebird*, bluebird of happiness—flying wild in the wild mountains.

As I watched, there was a sudden flash of wings and the lawn was empty; and I heard Mrs. Lewis calling me from the porch. So we three sat down to breakfast. The Lewises possess the western gift of making a stranger instantly and completely at home. Before I had been a day at Kamloops I had met and been taken to the hearts of the entire neighbourhood. There was only one notable exception to the rule of friendliness. This was Polly, Mrs. Lewis's highly intelligent and house-trained parrot, who took an instant and unalterable dislike to me. To the day of my departure, Polly would come tripping and stumbling the entire length of the house, expressly for the pleasure of biting me in the ankles.

Kamloops lies in the so-called dry belt of British Columbia, and dry it certainly is. I spent the first days there basking in the sun and gazing at the river, climbing up the strange hills to the edge of the receding snow, and watching the wild sunflowers come out to clothe the southern slopes of the range in a sheet of gold. Splendid and strange and lonely is this half-discovered Canada. At night I would lie in bed and watch the northern lights go arching up the sky, then leap broad awake at four in the morning, creep out of the house, and climb up the arid shoulders of the range into the sunrise. At breakfast I would be dog-tired, and Mrs. Lewis would marvel at my absurdity and put me back to bed till lunch-time.

But soon a more serious business had to be undertaken—the business of finding a horse. The Lewises and their friends rallied round like heroes. We visited every kind of horse imaginable. We saw heavy horses and light horses, red and grey and spotted horses, lazy horses and lively ones, thoroughbreds and cow-ponies —with none of them would I be content.

It was when I had already been searching for ten days that a friend of Mrs. Lewis's took me out to visit the Douglas Lake ranch. Douglas Lake is one of the largest ranches in Canada, covering, with the grazing, five hundred thousand acres. Its borders lie about seventy miles south-west of Kamloops. We drove over the ranch for nearly an hour before we reached the ranch-house. There it stood at last, between two lakes, with the bunkhouse beside it, and beyond that the whitewashed barns with the high corrals behind. As we drove up to the house, there was a thunder of hoofs and I saw a dark herd galloping down the range in a cloud of dust.

"The boys are running in a few horses to see if we can find one that will suit you," said Mr. Ward, the owner of the ranch, coming out to meet us.

It was not long till I was standing in the middle of the corral, watching the horses run round and round. They had just come in after wintering on the range. I never ceased to be amazed by this Western practice. In autumn, when an English horse comes in to be fed and cosseted through the winter, these little Western broncos are turned loose on the mountains to feed themselves by pawing through the snow. No wonder that now, when they came down with the shaggy remains of their winter coats straggling under their bellies, and with their lean bodies pitted by unexpected hollows and ridged by mountain ranges of bone which my unpractised English eye had been accustomed to see smoothly overlaid with muscle—no wonder that I seemed to be confronted almost with a new breed of animal.

Nor was their physical condition the only surprise which awaited me. Never having seen a cow-pony except on wild west films, I had innocently believed that the high carriage and delicate collection which these film star ponies exhibit was typical of Western horses. Nothing could be further from the facts. The cowboy, when travelling on horse-back, encourages the pony to hang his head and go uncollected, as thus he can walk with the maximum of speed and the minimum of effort. As for the rider, he sits in any way that pleases him, leaning into the high cantle of his stock saddle and propping his arms upon the horn. If they stop, the horse seems to go peacefully to sleep, while the rider slumps in his saddle as though endeavouring to do likewise. It was not until I saw one of these ponies in action that my disappointment was turned to wonder.

The job which had to be done was to round up a bunch of horses who were running on the range and drive them into a fenced field. The pony and his rider came sauntering along as usual, wandering vaguely over the grass with their eyes half shut. And then the miracle happened. The cowboy sat up; he made a low whistle through his teeth; he loosed the rope from his saddle-horn and began to swing it round. The little horse leapt into the bit; his body drew up like a coiled spring; his ears cocked and his eyes sparkled. Like a shot from a gun they went to it. That pony was an artist. He galloped full out; he stopped in his tracks; he wheeled on his little hocks a dozen times in a minute. A dozen times a lean black filly, who was the brains of the bunch, would double and try to break back. Always the little horse was too quick for her. He was everywhere at once—holding the bunch together, watching the leader, watching the gate through which they must pass. In less than five minutes they were in the field. The cowboy shut the gate. The little horse went to sleep again. I realized that I had everything to learn about the West.

And now, at Douglas Lake, I felt again how little I knew.

"DOUGLAS LAKE IS ONE OF THE LARGEST RANCHES IN CANADA"

Round and round went the horses. One or two I began to like. But none of my chosen ones were suitable. Some were too young; some were not broken; some of the mares were in foal. And then I saw her. She was a bay, blooming neatly in her complete summer coat, fat as a seal, set on four perfect legs and with bright, anxious eyes in a little wild western face, instantly captivating. The men were dubious. "Hasn't been rode much," they said. However, they roped her, saddled her, and she went well, swinging over the range with a long easy stride, breaking neatly to a canter, bounding lightly over the irrigation ditches. But she was terrified in the stable. She would kick and bite and rear sky-high. She stood in the stable for several days, while I enjoyed the generous hospitality of the ranch, but the somewhat belligerent attitude of the cowboys did nothing to reassure her. At last the edict went forth; they did not feel they could let me take her.

Then it was that Timothy came on the scene. He was the exact opposite of the horse I had imagined. He stood nearly seventeen hands high, with a noble Irish hunter head, tremendous bone in his rather common legs, and a phlegmatic disposition unhampered by temperament. I did not much like him. But the cowboys were unanimous in his praise. He was a good age (nine years old), in good shape, strong, sound, sensible, and above all he could "single-foot." The single-foot is a remarkable shuffling gait, fairly common among Western horses, in which the horse puts down every foot at a different instant. It is comfortable to both horse and rider and can be maintained for long periods at a rate of about six miles an hour. As for Mr. Ward himself, he was anxious only for me to have the horse I wanted, but he considered that Timothy would be a wise choice. I chose Timothy.

So I went to Vancouver and made arrangements for the horse to follow. It happened that, at the time of my arrival, there was a large horse show in progress, and the organizers of it were so kind as to make a great fuss of me, so that I found myself suddenly caught up in a perfect whirlpool of social activity. I was hastened in large cars from lunch-party to tea-party, from dinner-party to horse show to supper-party. The last night but one before my departure, the show ended. Its successful prosecution was duly celebrated, and I spent the longest night of my life in valiantly keeping awake, among an enormous concourse of people whom I did not know but all of whom knew me from the newspaper articles.

In endless procession, as it seemed, eminent authorities from the world of horsemanship came forward to shake hands and explain to me why I could not possibly succeed in what I was undertaking. To begin with, there was the horse to consider. If he did not break his leg in the mountains or go lame from a stone bruise, he would undoubtedly fail from leg-weariness plodding through the prairies. There was the difficulty of time—I should never reach Montreal before winter. Did I properly realize, they asked, that the distance from Vancouver to Montreal is over three thousand miles? Yes, I realized. No, I did not see any reason to think it too far. But deep in my secret mind I was suddenly aware of the map of Canada, and of the Great Lakes looking so small along the boundary of Ontario, and I remembered what they told me about the British Isles going two or three (or was it four?) times into Lake Superior. And my inside tightened, but I said nothing. Expenses would be heavy, my advisers continued. Again I blenched inwardly, knowing that I possessed in all a little over three hundred dollars. In any case, they would state with finality, for an ignorant English girl to start out to ride alone through the mountains was nonsense. Rock slides, windfalls, creeks in freshet—the frightening unaccustomed words were hurled at me almost menacingly. "If you ever get so far, come and see us," said one army officer from Winnipeg, "but you'll never get through the mountains."

I made one real friend while I was in Vancouver, a tall, willowy woman, with three horses and a beautiful seat in the sidesaddle. She had come from a ranch in Alberta; she was simple and witty and loved people better than parties, and horses than horse shows. I surrendered to her at sight. It was she who sustained me through my last frantic day in Vancouver, when, weak with lack of sleep, tense with the knowledge of essential preparations not made, bewildered by reporters and telephone messages, and so sick from parties and mental pandemonium that I was unable to eat, I listlessly began to pack for the journey. Everything I thought I should not need, I put into my suitcase to send to Montreal.

I had brought with me a sleeping-bag, a rain-coat, a ground sheet, a pair of grey saddlebags, designed to sling over the cantle of the saddle behind my legs, and a pair of oblong brown ones to hang over the pommel in front. Into these receptacles I insinuated, with difficulty, a jersey, two clean shirts, a set of warm underclothes, stockings, slippers, writing material, toothbrush, comb, powder-puff, a brush for Timothy, a hoof-pick, a jack-knife, some string, a Bible and Stevenson's *Travels with a Donkey*. I did not doubt that I had forgotten innumerable essentials, but I was past caring. At nine that night I had to go to the C.B.C. to broadcast. My Alberta friend drove me down in her car. On the way she had to stop for me to get out and be sick. So the last day in Vancouver ended.

I read a little of Stevenson before I went to sleep. Inimitable Stevenson; he knew. Ever since the trip began, all through the voyage, all through the train journey, all over Vancouver, people have been asking me WHY? Why do I want to ride across Canada? Why do I think it will be fun? Why am I not afraid of danger? Why am I not afraid of hardship? Why on horse-back? Why alone? Why Canada? Why anything? Why, *why*, WHY? I am paralysed. I know why myself, but I do not know how to tell them. And now I find that Stevenson has said it:

"I have been after an adventure," he says. "I have been after an adventure all my life, a pure dispassionate adventure, such as befell early and heroic voyagers."

Chapter II

THE ROAD AT LAST

So Timothy and I, so Timothy and I, alone and unencumbered, are on the road at last. Unhurried we jog along the highway towards the Fraser valley. My plan is to follow the Fraser Canyon as far as Hope, then strike into the mountains.

At present we are still considerably hampered by publicity. Constantly people stop me to shake hands, slide a knowing eye over the horse, and observe the inexpert arrangement of the pack. Nearly all the motorists who pass us toot and wave their arms, to the discomfiture of Timothy; and I suspect that school teachers have been informed of our approach, for whenever we pass a school, a hooting mob of children stream out of the door and festoon themselves along the railings of the playground to observe our progress. I wonder a little wistfully when our dispassionate adventure is going to begin.

This country between the mountains and the sea is voluptuously fertile, and, coming direct from the scant simplicity of the dry belt, one feels almost smothered by such a prodigality of growth. To be suddenly transferred from the dry belt to the coast belt is like switching over from a diet of brown bread and butter to one of chocolate cake.

I rode through the sunshine with my eyes half shut. Grass stood high beside the road. Rich fields ran back to the feet of the nearer hills, up the sides of which lush trees went billowing. The horses at pasture were all fat and soft as butter, and I contrasted them, not altogether to their advantage, with the wild, wiry herd who came galloping down to the corrals at Douglas Lake; and with Timothy, who went striding under me up the highway, lean and strong.

But as I looked between his golden ears I only half saw the riches which surrounded me, for beyond the broad fields' fatness and plenty, beyond the smooth highway, beyond the cushioned trees, stood the mountains—the beautiful, bitter mountains, crowned with ethereal snows. Towards their white-headed majesty, Timothy and I plodded unromantically enough.

Upon the first night it had been arranged for me to stay with a Scotch lady in Langley Prairie. She received me in some trepidation, having been teased into believing that I was Chinese, and was much relieved by my satisfactorily Anglo-Saxon appearance. She charged me only a dollar for my night's lodging.

"My husband wanted me to charge nothing at all," she said truthfully, "but I felt I could not do that!"

On the second day of our journey I made the acquaintance of another Scotch couple. About four o'clock in the afternoon a lean, elderly man and his pleasant, plump lady came running out of a small house and begged me to stop for tea. So I led Timothy into their orchard, unclipped the bit from his halter, and gladly went in with them. They were from Inverness, half a century ago; but, oh, how they remembered! We talked of Inverness and Lairg, of Thurso and Cape Wrath, and of the lonely coast which looks upon the Hebrides. And as they spoke, I could almost feel the salt mist in my eyes and see the bare, purple hills of the North running in long lines down to the sea.

That night I stayed in Abbotsford with a family who had come out forty years ago from Somerset. The father and mother were as English as I am, and their sons were Canadian as maple leaves—brown-faced, beautiful boys, built body and mind for the new world. Their mother watched them, loving but bewildered, with the quiet of the Somerset lanes still sleeping in her heart.

I think it was when I sat down to supper in her little kitchen that the "dispassionate adventure" really began. Brown bread and eggs, cherries and cream, she gave me, while Timothy munched crushed oats in the barn.

So ended my second day, and, as I went to bed, I considered how we had fared so far.

First of all Timothy: As far as I could make out, his phlegmatic disposition was standing him in good stead, for he was settling down to the road without the smallest fuss. He ate his oats, drank plenty of water and lay down at night. As for me, although he was not the kind of horse who made my heart beat with the adoration which I reserve for light-built, high-crested perfection, I found I was beginning to fall in love with this large, lean power and his stately aloofness.

As for the pack, contrary to all expectations, it appeared adequate, and was giving very little trouble. I had invented an arrangement of straps which crossed under the belly and held the bags in position. Over the pommel I slung the rain-coat and ground sheet, over the cantle the sleeping-bag, and, having deftly inserted myself into the small space which remained, I was compact and ready for the road.

My own physical condition was satisfactory. I had recovered in the twinkling of an eye from the *malaise* which had assailed me at Vancouver and was neither tired nor stiff. One small trouble only I experienced. My underside, which I had always believed to be singularly well upholstered, had by this time revealed a deficiency, and two totally unexpected bones had made known their presence, and had rubbed against the saddle until they wore two neat holes in the skin at their points. However, I patched these holes temporarily with sticking plaster, and nature subsequently overlaid them with good saddle-proof hide. This trifling discomfort was the only one I experienced.

Next day just at dusk, we struck into the Fraser Canyon. The great river was in spate (freshet, the Westerners call it) and came racing down the canyon wrenching rocks and trees in its course. On either side of the stream, forest-laden precipices climbed into the sky. Very tiny at their feet, we began to walk up into the gorge. And then, with the suddenness of a drop-curtain, night fell. The effect of darkness on the trail is a curious one. It does

THE ROAD AT LAST 15

not matter how little one has exerted oneself during the day, or how early the hour may be, or how energetic one may have been feeling a short time before—horse and rider are instantly overcome with exhaustion. So it was at any rate with Timothy and me. Wearily we toiled along the forsaken highway. The pale face of the river brooded on our left; on our right hung the side of the gorge, a solid wall of darkness.

I knew that somewhere within thinking-distance there was a tourist camp. On we plodded. At last we turned a corner, and before us loomed a power house, lighted with eerie-looking flares. Beside it was a collection of bedraggled shacks—could this be the tourist camp? Pressing the unwilling Timothy, I rode in among them. In one there was a small light. The others were dark. I called. The echo came back to me across the water. Timothy was trembling a little. He snorted uneasily. And then, all alone, out of the darkness, trotted a little horse in a pack-saddle. I cantered out on to the road and caught him, rather deftly I thought, by the flapping haltershank. Whereupon, sauntering behind him, there appeared a short, broad young man. I rode up to him leading the pony.

"Is this your horse?" I inquired rather unnecessarily.

"Why sure," answered the young man. "You needn't have bothered catching him, though; he was going home anyway. But what are you doing here?" he inquired, peering at me through the darkness.

I replied that I was looking for the Restmore tourist cabins.

"Aren't you afraid?" he asked, staring round-eyed.

I answered "No," quite truthfully. For now that he and the pony had come, I wasn't.

So we tied Timothy beside the pack-horse, and while I rubbed his legs and slapped his back, the young man fetched hay for them both.

"He'll be all right here," he said, "the pack-pony will be company for him."

So we left them and set off together in the young man's aged car, for I found that he lived at the Restmore cabins, working as a guide, or "packer" as they call them in the West. He was evidently still overcome by the romance of my sudden appearance out of the darkness. Where was I going all alone, he asked. "Into the mountains," I replied vaguely. With a sigh of contentment, I realized that here, for the first time in many weeks, was some one who had not heard of my proposed journey. I asked if he had always been a packer. On the contrary, he told me, till six weeks ago he had been a salesman in Vancouver. "A good job too," he remarked without regret. I asked him why he had left it. I knew I was being every bit as bad as the people who asked me why I wanted to ride across Canada, but the words were out before I could hold them.

"Oh," he replied airily, "got fed up on wearing a white collar."

Then I saw the large liberty of Canada. How the Wild waits at the gates of her cities, and how unhampered the Canadians are to choose—success or freedom, city or wilderness, what they will.

So we jolted to a standstill before the tourist camp, and, dazzled by sudden lights, I stumbled out of the car. There seemed to be one big central chalet, highly ornate, and around it, among the trees, the little one-roomed huts in which the tourists slept. The chalet was filled with American fishermen, large, kindly, drawly-voiced men, with a new pattern of laughter and solemnity. I watched them under my eye-lashes and listened. They laughed when I should have been serious, and when I was amused they saw no joke whatever. In its sense of humour, before everything else, every country is alone. The Frenchman's delicately *risqué* witticisms are lost upon the Germans. To read the Canadian funny papers is for me a labour inexpressible, and any one who has watched an American's face lengthening over *Punch* can appreciate the perplexing effect of our own somewhat recondite wit.

Next morning, very early indeed, two of the fishermen kindly gave me a lift back to the place where I had left Timothy. There he was, tied to a tree, ready-saddled and polished to perfection. A minute later my friend of the evening appeared and I asked him diffidently how much Timothy owed for his lodging.

"Oh, nothing," said the packer, looking at me as though he were seeing Joan of Arc. "It was wonderful."

So away we trotted into the morning. Timothy's neck shone golden, and there were silver streaks in his mane. I was so much possessed with healthiness and high spirits that I galloped Timothy along the grass edge of the road, singing at the top of my voice. Then I jumped down and ran and skipped on my own legs, with Timothy jogging behind me. Then before us the sun rose and struck slanting into the canyon, and we settled down seriously at last to the business of reaching Hope.

We entered the little town about midday. It consisted of a collection of frame houses, set wide apart on some flats low down by the roaring Fraser. There were generous tracts of grass between the houses, and upon these the cows and horses of the village wandered in unrestricted possession. I found that Timothy and I were eagerly awaited. All was arranged for Timothy to stay with Mr. Richmond, the principal packer and storekeeper of the village, and for me to stay with the postmaster and his wife. Kindness lapped us round. But there was disappointment in store. From Hope I had firmly decided to follow the pack-trail which runs over the Coast Range to Princeton. However the villagers now hastened to inform me that this was out of the question. There was still far too much snow on the summit, and the rivers were in freshet. Anyway, concluded the sages, wagging their heads with finality, the trail was never open till July. I drooped. The only alternative was a long weary ride up the Fraser Canyon to Lytton—beautiful scenery and everything, but rock-bound and hard for Timothy. One hundred and fifty miles longer, besides. But I did not know then the genius and vitality of my little hostess Anna. From the moment I mentioned the Princeton trail, her mind had been working.

It worked in secret, however, and while I endeavoured to resign myself to what appeared to be inevitable, I was tucked into a car and whirled away up a mountain to visit a family of whom the inhabitants of Hope spoke with such respect that my imagination invested them with an awe-inspiring magnificence. I was relieved therefore to find a simple and charming English household, with nothing more formidable about them than unusual intelligence and an encyclopaedic knowledge of Canadian birds. What I principally remember about that visit, beyond the charm of my hosts and the magnificence of the view from their house, was the lyric experience of finding a white goat in the outside lavatory.

It was not till we came down from the mountain that Anna set to work. It seemed that next day Mr. Richmond's son Billy was starting out for a ranch in the mountains, to take in a French Canadian care-taker and stores. The first thirty miles of the way to the ranch led over the Princeton trail. Anna now set to work to prevail upon Billy to take us with him, so that we might see for ourselves at least the first part of the trail. After considerable persuasion, Billy was converted to the plan.

So, early next morning, four riders and two pack-horses set out for the Whitworth ranch. At first we climbed gradually up a wide easy road, with the mountain torrents which crossed our way passing decorously underneath corduroy bridges. But soon the trail grew narrower and steeper, and at last we rounded a corner to find a naked creek hurling itself across our path with a melodramatic roar. I drew Timothy behind, imperceptibly I hoped, and watched. Billy went first, smashing through the water without so much as a look sideways. Next went Anna and the Frenchman, driving the pack-horses before them. By this time it looked so easy that Timothy and I plunged through with an equal *sang-froid,* and by the end of the day the snowy creeks held no terrors. Meanwhile we climbed slowly on and on through the majestic forest. Before us wound the tiny trail and above our heads the trees towered into vaults of distant green. Sometimes for a moment their density would break and hoary peaks would dazzle into view.

"See that snow?" Billy would say then. "The Princeton trail is higher than that at the summit; it'll be five feet deep up there." But nothing could dishearten me, for we were riding into the mountains, and even if we had to turn back, I did not care.

About five o'clock we reached a clearing, in the middle of which, beside a creek, stood a small shack. This, Billy informed us, was Bert Robinson's place, and here we were to spend the night.

Bert was not at home. So we tied the horses to trees, unpacked and fed them, and were just going into the house when Bert appeared. He was walking slowly down the trail with a bunch of scarlet wild flowers in his hand, so much absorbed in his thoughts that for a moment he did not see us. Then, without haste and without surprise, he took in the circumstance of our arrival. His face slowly wreathed itself in smiles; approaching with an easy stride, he drew us all into the cabin. He took down an empty jam pot from the shelf and arranged the flowers in the middle of the table. Then he threw logs into the big furnace-range, and soon had a fire roaring under the lids. In a surprisingly short time he had fried us bacon and eggs, and stewed a mighty pot of tea. For our part we unpacked butter and a new loaf of bread and opened a tin of peaches. Soon we were all sitting down to a hearty supper. When the meal was over and cleared away, our host walked over to a ricketty cupboard, drew out a home-made violin and played us all the tunes he knew, singing sometimes in a musical, husky voice.

Billy had told me that Bert was a trapper, and I watched him a little disconcerted. With the hatred I have for trapping, I had vaguely imagined a rough, tough hulk of a man, not this slim dreamy person, putting flowers on the table and sitting down to play us Dvořák's *Humoresque*. . . .

Next morning, very early, we set out for the ranch, leaving the Princeton trail before it began to climb steeply, and heading south-east. Early in the afternoon we reached our destination. Quite suddenly we came out of the forest into about fifty acres of cleared grass-land, in the middle of which stood a fine log house with a barn at a little distance. Here, in Selkirkian isolation, the French Canadian was to spend his summer.

We unpacked the horses and turned them loose in a water meadow, where, after having enjoyed a hearty fight, they settled down to graze contentedly. I did not ask Billy whether he would take me on to Princeton. I knew. All around us soared the peaks, deep in snow. But Billy put me out of my pain.

"Not a hope, Mary," he observed laconically. So Anna and I decided we would stay one day at the ranch and then go back to Hope.

The day had seemed to be in its prime when we reached the ranch, but soon night began to fall. And it was then that they came—step by delicate step, their ears cocked cautiously, their great eyes luminous—the deer out of the forest. We watched them moving in the dusk, daintily eating the tit-bits we had put out for them. Then, silently as they had come, they went; and we were alone again on our meadowy island, with the mysterious ocean of the forest whispering along our shores.

Next day we occupied in exploring the woodland trails, and in teaching the horses to jump. They were inexperienced, but they did gallantly, and Billy was much delighted with the unexpected prowess of his pack-mares. Every now and then he would say, "Mary certainly can ride a horse," and I would sit up straighter and press down my heels importantly, intoxicated by this praise from a Westerner.

Next day Anna and I rode down to Hope. Forty miles, through sheets of perfectly unmitigated rain. I said to myself, "If I don't mind this, I couldn't mind anything, and I don't mind this." At last, shivering and in the dark, we were back again.

That evening I prepared for my trip up the Fraser Canyon. I had done all I could to escape the highway, and now I felt I must accept failure with a good grace. But again fortune and unknown friends were with me. For that night a certain Mr.

THE ROAD AT LAST

Grainger, who knew every creek and rock slide on the Hope-Princeton trail, was so kind as to telephone from Princeton to let me know that he believed the summit could be reached in a week or two at the outside. Upon the strength of which I changed my plans again, and decided to wait ten days until Billy came down from the ranch where we had left him, and then ask him to take me over.

So next day I caught a bus and went speeding north to spend the two weeks with my friends in Kamloops. It is a majestic journey up the Fraser Canyon. The road, perched upon the side of the precipice, has been smashed out of living rock. On the one hand sheets of titanic forest sweep down to the water's edge, on the other they climb into the sky. In May the dogwood trees are mooned white with great, surprising blossoms, which leap into dazzling relief against their shadowed background. And through the valley the furious river goes tearing to the sea. As I watched it I thought with shivering awe of Simon Fraser, for whom the river is named, who founded Fort George and who, setting out to explore the course of the stream, went forth in a birch-bark canoe and rode this torrent down to the sea. Such are the men who have made Canada!

All this I watched and thought about through gaps in the conversation, for my fellow passengers on the bus were extremely talkative and friendly, and I remember how one girl gave me my first stick of chewing gum. I accepted the small packet with interest and masticated the contents with a certain amount of enjoyment, until the point was reached when I ought to have spat it out, whereupon I became paralysed with embarrassment. I watched the other passengers covertly, hoping to seize a moment when the whole company's gaze was simultaneously averted. But fortune was against me. Nothing of particular interest appeared upon the road. Conversation buzzed. The regard of the passengers was turned sociably inward. Finally with a distracted gulp, I swallowed. I have never ventured upon chewing gum since!

The days in Kamloops flew, and it seemed that in no time I was travelling south again. I reached Hope the day before King George and Queen Elizabeth—who were then engaged upon their tour of Canada—were to pass through on their return trip. Ten minutes the train was to stop, and the village was in ferment. What to wear, where to stand, what to say, what to do, whether to look all the time or devote a few minutes to taking photographs—over such all-important problems controversy raged in every house in the village. The momentous day dawned fine and fulfilled its early promise, and in the evening, as we assembled at the railway, the air glowed. Smooth and punctual, the long blue train drew into the station; and there they stood, upon the gallery of the observation car, radiant in the radiant evening. I do not know what the magic is, but I believe they gave every one of us in that crowd the feeling that we had received their personal greeting. Together we glowed in the wonder of experience. What we saw was not only the beauty of the Queen and the fine simplicity of the King, for through these and above them shone the love for their people, deep as their life itself.

So we went back to the village warm and excited, and I began to pack, for we were to start the next day, and Anna oiled her saddle and told her long-suffering husband where to find the sardines, for she was to go with us.

And here my journal begins.

Chapter III

TO THE SNOW-LINE IN JUNE

The day is bright with June sunshine and white clouds as our party of three prepares to set out. The people of Hope regard us pessimistically. "Too early yet," they say. "Creeks high; snow on the summit, the trail blocked with fallen trees." Even Bill, who is to lead us, and who knows the trail like the back of his hand, says, "Don't be disappointed, Mary, if we have to turn back." Only Anna, optimistic as myself, says, "Don't worry; we'll make it." Anyway we shall not starve, for Billy has brought a pack-mare laden with food, besides a tent for Anna and me, which we scorn extremely.

So at last we are winding again through the woods, up and up the stony path, under rugged firs and slim, distinguished cedars. Soon we come out on to bare, rock-strewn hill-side, with the dark summits of the pine trees below us, the creek shouting through the valley, and, beyond, the shadowed mountains, roughing their fir-tree-fretted edges against the sky; then into the forest again to lose the blue and white day in the green twilight of the trees. An hour in the dreaming dusk, then out again for a moment, with the sunshine glinting on Timothy's red-gold neck, and below us a tiny lake, curled like a green water-snake in its nest of trees. Again we plunge into the forest; and so we travel all day between shadow and sunshine, till early in the evening we reach Bert Robinson's camp, where we are to spend another night.

The horses are watered, fed, and tied up in the forest. Anna and I sleep in a shack by the creek. We seem to have been asleep about five minutes when a knock comes at the door. Simulating a gratitude we by no means feel, we shout "Thank you," and, staggering out into the unfriendly grey of five o'clock, we roll up our sleeping-bags and wash ourselves hastily in the windy creek. The horses are fed—breakfast—the horses saddled.

"Gosh darn you women," says Bill to the pack-mare, roping down the pack with a diamond hitch; "quit foolin'. Come here, some one, and take up the slack. I guess that'll do. All right, get going!"

Higher and higher through the forest; and now, when we come out on to the open hill-side, there is a two-hundred-foot drop below us, and the horses grow solemn and pick their steps cautiously. Just where the trail rounds the shoulder of the hill there has been a slide of rocks, and the track is obliterated by a pile of logs and loose rubble. Bill looks at it seriously, and my heart stands still with the fear that he may tell us to turn back. But he simply tells us to wait, and leaving his horse, he scrambles carefully on to the rock slide, and disappears round the bend. Anna and I listen in suspense while loosened stones go crashing ominously down the hill-side.

At last, to our relief, Billy returns. Taking our horses by the bridles, we scramble carefully on to the shifting edge. Billy goes first, then I, then the pack-mare and last Anna. When we have rounded the bend and the open trail is already in sight, I hear a sliding noise behind me, then crashing and thuds, as a great weight goes avalanching down into the creek below. Feeling perfectly certain that it is the pack-mare, I go straight ahead, not daring to look round. But finally I snatch a fearful look over my shoulder, and there she comes, picking her way daintily under the ungainly pack. Behind is a new gap in the slide where a rock has just been dislodged. I am thankful when we regain the solid trail.

After this we climb more and more steeply. Once Timothy, who is leading, jumps forward, and looking back I see a brown bear disappearing into the forest. A tiny deer peers at us, fascinated, and goes bounding away between the trees. Squirrels and

"CAMP ON SOME PLEASANT FLATS"

TO THE SNOW-LINE IN JUNE

chipmunks chase about among the roots, not deigning to be afraid of us. The horses are labouring, and we stop to rest them.

About noon we come to a scene of the most appalling desolation, an area recently devastated by fire—a fire started (with an irony of which even Thomas Hardy would feel proud) by last year's Sunday School picnic. Great trees stand up charred and lifeless or lie piled across the trail. For three hours Bill hacks a way through, step by step. As suddenly as we came to the area we come out of it—into fresh green forest and the first signs of snow. We are within thinking-distance of the summit. Soon the patches of snow grow thicker, and the horses slow down and begin to flounder.

"Tiny," comes a menacing voice from the rear, "you'd better leave that creek alone and climb the hill. You can have your bellyful of water when we get there. You mind, or I'll take a club to you!" The pack-mare, well aware that these threats carry not the smallest animosity, comes waddling fatly after us. We scramble on. Soon we have to dismount and lead the horses. Once Timothy falls over a hidden root and drops his quarters into a drift; then his forehand goes in up to the neck. He grunts anxiously, and I think he is going to panic, but with a big effort of the powerful quarters he wrenches himself free and goes on again cheerfully.

The summit, when we reach it, is disappointing—wide, snow-covered plateaux, surrounded by peaks, and providing no particular view of anything. But the summit it is, and I could dance for joy at the sight of its gloomy expanse.

We climb down out of the snow-line and camp on some pleasant flats where there is a little grass for the horses. In less time than it takes Anna and me to wash our faces, Bill has the tent pitched and a fire blazing up into the evening sky. We make tea and fry strips of delicious bacon. The forest keeps guard behind us; the horses graze the flats; and, as I watch the sparks crackling into the dusk, I hate very much the thought that Anna and Billy must go back tomorrow and I must go on alone.

Anna and I go early into our tent, put on all our clothes and snuggle into our sleeping-bags. Silence. Then a scrambling noise in the forest.

"Anna," comes Bill's voice, "I hope that's not a grizzly."

"I hope not."

"If it is, the horses will stampede."

"Yes."

"Well, good night."

"Good night." And we are soon asleep.

Some hours later I become aware that I am no longer completely asleep; next that the ground is like an iceberg; and finally that I am broad awake and shivering from head to foot. Anna is also awake, but we make no comment. From now on we get steadily colder all through the night. At half past four we hear Bill shouting to the horses, tearing about and making shivering noises. We thankfully abandon the pretence of sleep, crawl out of our tent and find Bill lighting the fire. The horses stand round looking gaunt and unhappy with staring coats. I rush to poor Timothy and begin to groom him, thinking it will warm us both. But his coat refuses to lie down and he continues to shiver reproachfully.

Breakfast is soon over and the horses packed. After a farewell stripped of all vestige of emotion by the intense cold, we start out—Bill and Anna to ride back to Hope; Timothy and I bound for Princeton.

About seven o'clock it begins to rain. Very little at first, so as to fool one into not putting on a rain-coat; and when one *does* put it on, one is already much wetter than one realized. By eight o'clock the rain is pouring steadily. The mountains swathe themselves to the feet in a blanket of cloud. Timothy's irremediably wavy mane goes into a mass of hideous convolutions. My hair does the same, and the raindrops run off the ends, deftly inserting themselves between my coat-collar and my neck, and finding their way down as far as my waist. Timothy and I, curtained with rain, go on mechanically, shut up in the forest, which

TO THE SNOW-LINE IN JUNE

hangs suspended, dead to everything but rain . . . rain . . .

At last, when I am beginning in spite of myself to fear that we are on the wrong trail, and shall go on and on through the mountains and never come to Princeton, we find our way on to a handsome road, cross a bridge, and all of a sudden there are cars passing, and lo and behold, a lady on a black horse followed by a man on a bay, and they are Constance Swartz and Bob Thomas, and I find that Timothy and I are to stay with Mrs. Swartz in her cabin on Bob Thomas's ranch.

Timothy walks up, the country looks interesting again, and even the rain no longer seems to matter.

In about two hours we are home. And this is the right word. For Constance is one of those rare people who can give one the feeling on a strange continent, half across the world, that one *is* coming home.

Constance comes from Vancouver. She belongs to two countries, for she is an Englishwoman, born and brought up in Canada. She has smooth hair and a cool, educated voice. She talks of plays and books that I know, and English north-country families, whose very names send my mind wandering back over the dark Northumberland moors. She feeds me on brown bread and vegetables and salad, and absently hums a Wagner *leit-motif* as she scrapes the carrots.

On Sunday I get up late, groom and admire Timothy, borrow a black plug from the ranch and ride in to Princeton to church. Arrive late and acutely conscious of aged slacks, dirty riding mac and small handkerchief round head, my only apology for a hat. The congregation, magnificently caparisoned, are filling up the back pews, so I am faced with the alternatives of clumping up to the front or squeezing somebody out of a place at the back. I select the latter solution.

When I recover from all this, I discover that the service is being very well taken by a fair-haired young man with a good English accent. He and his wife ask me to lunch afterwards. They are a delightful couple, just married—very much in love and very busy not being sentimental. The young lady assures me that she hates housework, and her husband adds that he never gets enough to eat; then he gives her a small slap on the behind, and they laugh radiantly.

After lunch I regretfully decline the offer of a picnic on a local mountain called the Elephant, mount Nigger and trundle home. Mrs. Swartz is not in the least surprised at my having stayed out to lunch; nor when, a few minutes after I get back, some people called Gregory arrive in a car to take us both out to tea; nor even when, late in the evening, Mr. Leir, a sawmill owner from Penticton, comes in to see me. He has a white moustache and eleven children (not with him), and is a perfect dear. He makes all sorts of plans to help me over the next bit of the way. He says that, when a person does a sporting thing like this, it's up to the rest of us to help them—what? (Especially, he rather indicates, when they are a female and young.)

Chapter IV

FROM CACTUS TO JACKPINE

Now Timothy and I are in the midst of the dry belt. These days in the stony valley of the Similkameen River are in astonishing dramatic contrast to the first days after leaving Vancouver, when I rode into the Fraser Canyon.

At last I am learning a little of the nature and extent of the dry belt. It seems that between the Coast Range on the west and the Gold Ranges on the east, there lies a mountainous central plateau, upon which the annual rainfall is some twelve inches only, whereas in the stormy lands along the Coast, sixty inches is not unusual. For the rain-laden winds driving in from the Pacific beat out their moisture against the first range of mountains they encounter. And so it happens that one climbs up through the lush vegetation of the coastal belt, to drop down from the height of land into this frugal country where the dry wind rolls the tumble-weed across the dusty range and cactuses stab your ankles as you pass.

For two days we never lost sight of the Similkameen. Bright, stormy, rainbow days they were, with the shadows and sunshine chasing each other across the firry hills and the white road winding away ahead of us on the banks of the river. Mr. Leir was as good as his word and has been a positive fairy godfather to us, arranging places for us to stay the night, and turning up at midday in a car stacked with hay and oats.

The first night he arranged for us to sleep at a little farm belonging to some people called MacRae. Mrs. M. ran out beaming, crying, all in one breath, "We're delighted you must excuse the mess we're in this is my husband Jimmy you really should have shaved you look like a ground-hog!" Mr. MacRae, not in the least abashed, came out and showed me where to put Timothy.

He and his wife were both from Skye. We talked of the Cuillins and the Kyle of Lochalsh; and I remembered as if it were yesterday a summer in my childhood when we stayed on the West Coast of Scotland, and at evening looked across the sunset sea to the dark little island of Skye, while the lady of our cottage brought home the cows, calling in Gaelic to her white-haired child. At that time the MacRaes were still living at Skye, upon those very shores which we saw shadowed against the sunset. And now we were sitting down together to supper beside an evening river, seven thousand miles across the world. In such intricate patterns do the lives of men go winding and crisscrossing over the earth!

The next night I spent in a spotlessly perfect house at Keremeos, with a sheep-farmer and his wife. We got there rather late, and Timothy very tired. For a little while nothing happened. Then a pretty, white-haired lady wandered round the corner of the house, looking vague and saying:

"Are you Miss Bosanquet? You must forgive my not coming out before; it's the children; they scatter one so."

At that moment round the corner rushed three astonishingly energetic little boys, shouting in discord:

"Mum, may I ride him?"

"May we ride him one behind the other?"

"Why not?"

"May I ride him first?"

"Does he buck?"

"Does he kick?"

"Why mayn't I ride him first?"

Before I could say "Knife," the eldest one was up and whirling poor Timothy down the drive, with the middle one whooping at his heels on a bicycle and the smallest one yelling because he had to stay behind.

Mrs. Graham explained through the hubbub that the boys were

taking Timothy up to a ranch a mile away, and we would join them in the car.

I suppose I looked a little harassed, for she took me and the smallest boy into the house and turned on the radio to distract us. . . . "Dark-haired English girl," the announcer was just saying, "left Hedley this morning, and hopes to reach Keremeos tonight. She has had a good trip so far." This had such an electrifying effect that the small boy stopped crying, and getting out the car we drove up to the ranch in comparative peace.

We found Timothy already unsaddled and tied in a stall, but while I was rubbing his back and legs, a young man appeared in a dilapidated car, saying forlornly that he had been driving about all day to find us and take a photograph.

So poor Timothy had to be all dressed up again and paraded outside, while his likeness was secured from every imaginable angle. The same young man returned the next day, waited patiently for two hours while I was delayed, and then escorted us out of the town on his pony, taking photographs all the way. He said he had had a wonderful time lately—first he had had quite a close view of the King and Queen, and now an even closer one of Timothy and me. He indicated that it would take him weeks to recover from such an orgy of experience.

There is one aspect of the dry belt which surprises me a good deal. One will come all of a sudden to islands of luxurious vegetation, blossoming untended and unirrigated among the hills. Thus on the day when we left Keremeos, we climbed up off the range into leafy woodland with banks of crimson briar roses and syringa and masses of lupins growing right down to the path, so that Timothy could bend down his ill-mannered head and haul up great mouthfuls as he went along. And then down we came again on to the range.

I spent that night at Oliver with the district nurse, a large, sporting person who welcomed me gladly to her small and already densely populated house, folding me on to her living-room sofa with the heartiest unconcern.

From Oliver there was a forty-five-mile trail over the mountains to Rock Creek, and after copious inquiry I elicited the information that it was believed to be open, that there was a ranch ten miles up, but after that no human beings of any sort except a gang of workmen working on a mine. Accordingly I set out early next morning, weighed down with feed and looking forward to my first night out with Timothy.

The day was brilliantly fine. The range quivered with heat, and great clumps of cactus at the side of the trail were flowering exotic yellow. The hot dust billowed up under Timothy's feet, coating us with grey. And then we began to climb into the mountains and were plunged once more into leafy woodland. The air grew languorous again with the scent of roses and wild syringa, and the range might have lain burning a hundred miles away. We met no one all the morning except one Indian to whom I said "Good morning," and he said "What?"

About midday we reached (as predicted) a pleasant little ranch, so I went in to ask for some hay for Timothy. We were welcomed by a solitary cowboy who had been left all alone in charge and had not seen any one for many weeks. It was some time since he had shaved or cut his surprising ash-blond hair, and how it bloomed above his freckled face like the syringa in the valleys. He hustled me joyfully into the little ranch-house, apologizing for the mess, and it certainly did look untidy even to me, who am myself very nearly as untidy as it is possible to be. He had been carpentering, and the floor of the living-room was covered with chips and shavings. In the corners of the room, unwashed dishes were piled high. In the kitchen stood pail upon pail of milk, provided, with unappreciated generosity, by the solitary cow.

"Drink all you want of it," said the white-haired boy. "I hate the stuff." So we carried out the freshest looking pailful on to the sunny front steps, where I unpacked my provisions—brown bread, butter, cheese, chocolate, oranges—and we made an excellent dinner.

"WHERE THE DRY WIND ROLLS THE TUMBLEWEED ACROSS THE DUSTY RANGE"

Then I lay down and stretched my limbs happily in the mountain sunshine, while the boy watched me in wonder, and told me, with evident intent to please, that I looked much older than twenty, nearer thirty in fact, which was the age of his betrothed.

"She's quite a bit older than me," he explained, "but I don't like young, flippity-gippity girls—Fyrla's a wonder!" His eyes sparkled, and I hoped rather wistfully that she was all he thought; for women of thirty who marry white-haired boys with tip-tilted noses are apt to be—well, strong-minded, anyway.

"She's wonderful with horses," he continued, beaming, and my heart warmed to her a little. "She's the only woman who's rode my bronc," and he jerked his head in the direction of a small chestnut mare, picketed in a near-by field. Only two months before, he told me, she had been running over the hills, wild as an antelope. "She fought like a wild cat when she was roped," he remarked reminiscently. I watched her now grazing, plump and lethargic, alone in her rich field. Then in the open spaces of my mind I saw her forgotten companions streaming over the range. The galloping rhythm of their untamed feet beat through the sunshine and was gone.

My companion continued to regard his mare complacently. "She's broke now," he said.

"Yes," I answered, "she's broken now."

Then I realized with a start that, while I lay in the sunshine, time had crept away, and already the hours were hastening on velvet feet into the afternoon.

"I must go," I cried, jumping up.

"I'll go with you," said the cowboy. So quickly he saddled the chestnut mare while I packed Timothy, and soon we were riding together up the mountain side. The little mare hustled along busily, with her head down, and big Timothy had to single-foot to keep up.

So I jogged on and watched the mare's range-bred muscles under the new layer of fat rippling back from her fine shoulder. I watched the trail winding before us and the chipmunks scuttling among the roots. Then I would look up at the towering trees and wonder at the contrasts of this country, where one can ride in one day from the naked range to the flowery woodlands, and from the woodlands on into these titanic forests. And I listened half in a dream as the boy talked of horses and the trees and Fyrla whom he loved.

It was not till the sun was sinking that we passed over the summit and reached a clearing beside a creek. Here, said my companion, would be a good place for a camp. So, obediently, I unpacked Timothy and arranged my sleeping-bag. Then the cowboy said good-bye and rode slowly away, with his surprising hair glimmering white against the shadows of the forest.

I sighed and prepared to have supper—and it was not till then that I became aware of having left my entire stock of provisions at the ranch! Well, there was nothing to do but to forget about it, in which resolve I was unwittingly assisted by Timothy, who being broken-hearted at parting from the mare, was now engaged in dancing round and round the tree to which I had tied him, looking powerful and passionate and tangling up his rope. For a while I allowed his antics to distract me from the vanishing thoughts of supper, but at last I spoke to him with considerable severity, when he gazed at me in astonishment and horror and at once became perfectly decorous again.

So I gave him his oats and, closing my mind to thoughts of human food, lay down in my sleeping-bag, and prepared to appreciate the poetry of my first night alone in the wilds. I knew, of course, from copious reading, exactly what to expect.

Slowly the colours of the sunset would fade, while I lay beside the stream and listened to the whispering of the forest behind me, whose furry denizens (romantic, but not dangerous) I should soon hear engaging stealthily in their nocturnal avocations. As for me, I would watch the vault of sky above my head and wait in rapt expectancy for the virginal appearance of the first star.

So certain was I of all this that it never even occurred to me to consider that I was lying in the open, and that the trees immediately surrounding my clearing were too small and scrubby to afford any shelter, should such be needed. I lay and watched. Surely by now the first star was considerably overdue? But no star appeared. Instead the little pink and yellow clouds, which only an hour before had been grouping themselves so artistically around the setting sun, now swept together into a scowling array of sooty black bogies and whirled up into my vault of private sky, with a screaming wind on their tails.

At nine o'clock the rain began. "Just a passing shower," said I to myself, regarding the scudding bogies optimistically. After I had inwardly repeated this for over half an hour, I put the saddle over my feet and regretfully pulled out the mackintosh from underneath me and put it over the top. Soon the rain was drumming on it like a percussion band. I found that by lying perfectly still I could keep fairly dry, and for some time I slept, but woke in the very small hours to find that the underneath half of me seemed to have died, all except the point of my hip, which created the impression of being about to poke its way out through my skin.

The rain had not even slowed down. Holding everything, and knowing well how unwise I was, I turned over. It was a greater mistake than I thought. I moved off my dry patch of ground on to a wet one, the rain sloshed off the mackintosh and came trickling in underneath, and, to crown everything, the sack of oats which I was using as a pillow came undone and spilt its contents within a few feet of Timothy's head. Immediately a tremendous pawing and snuffing began and continued unabated till I had, with much labour and wetness, returned as much of the grain as I could to the sack and put a few handfuls within reach of the imperative snorts.

At half past two the rain got thinner and stopped. I put my head out, snuffed, and thought, "Heaven be praised; it's over!" But my pæan went up too soon, for in a very little while the clouds rolled back, and soon the percussion band was again beating its unremitting tattoo on my saturated mackintosh.

It went straight ahead till a quarter past five, when I decided it was never going to stop, crawled out and gave Timothy the rest of his grain. At five-thirty, when the one or two parts of me left dry by the night had got thoroughly wet, the rain stopped. I regretfully put the streaming saddle on Timothy's streaming back, festooned my goods and chattels around it, and, wringing out my hair, started off down the trail.

We had not been going more than an hour, when we came to a little shack. Thinking this must belong to some of the workmen from the mine, I went to the door to ask the distance to Rock Creek. It was opened by a man with a thin face and an educated American accent, who told me he was a Government research-worker, and invited me to go in and have some coffee. A minute or two later a plump, pretty woman came out of an inside room and said, Goodness, why hadn't I come to them for the night? They had a spare bed.

Drawing my body up tight to escape the embrace of my sodden clothes, I looked at Timothy dripping under the dripping pack; there was nothing to say.

Chapter V

NOTES FROM A HILL-SIDE

ALREADY we are half way through June. I am writing this dangling my legs over a precipice, high up in the Cascade Range, while Timothy picks up some straggly mouthfuls of grass along the road.

I can look down six hundred feet and watch the river and the road I have been following, winding away together along the Kettle Valley. Directly below, and looking like a toy village, lies Little Cascade, with the garage where I asked the way and the store where the owner gave me five bananas and six postcards as a present, while his daughter-in-law invited me in to have coffee. To the north lies the sun-bright sheet of Christina Lake, and all before me stand the fir-tree-freckled mountains.

Well now, I must do some catching up. On the day after my rainy night, which was Saturday, we came down the mountains into Rock Creek. I have never seen one of Canada's famous and tragic "ghost" towns, but I have already seen several with one foot in the grave. They are born quickly, but they die slowly, these sad little mining towns, springing up like mushrooms in the night at the whispered word "Gold," living for a few years with feverish intensity, then slowly, slowly decaying, dying down dully, back into the earth. This seemed to be to some extent the fate of the little town which we now discovered. But glad I was to be in a town at all, with a hotel and a fire to dry my clothes, and a hot dinner to come steaming out of the kitchen.

The next day we set out again, down the valley of the Kettle River, which runs east toward the main range of the Cascades. It was a pleasant road through neat farming country, between wooded hills; but light rain was falling and depression sat heavy upon the day.

At about eleven o'clock, I was stodging along, realizing, as one always does sooner or later on an expedition like this, that I had muffed the whole show. I had chosen the wrong continent, started not only too late in the year but also too late in the development of civilization, chosen the wrong route and the wrong horse—in short, muffed it.

While I was still sunk in these gloomy meditations, I came round a corner and found a little grey lorry standing by the road. As we approached, two girls leapt out, and my cool and discouraged inside warmed suddenly with the hope against hope that it might be a pair of Miss Hazel's Sunday School people. Now I had heard of Miss Hazel's Sunday School before I left England. Her girls go out in pairs and travel about the lonely parts of British Columbia in these small lorries (or trucks as they call them here) holding classes for the children. Well, Miss Hazel's Sunday School it was! And as delighted to see me as I was to see them. Near by was a farm, and before I had properly grasped everything Timothy was tied in the barn, munching hay and nickering happily at the imminent prospect of oats. The "Missionary Ladies," as they called themselves, took me back to the lorry, where we pooled our picnic lunches and were soon talking nineteen to the dozen, while the rain battered on the roof and the mountains began to disappear again into the clouds, my own depression disappearing with an equal rapidity.

The Missionary Ladies were holding their Sunday School that afternoon in Rock Creek, so we decided that I would leave Timothy at the farm and return with them for the rest of the day. We rattled back into the village with great hilarity, and when the Sunday School was finished we went to a rather dismal little conventicle in the schoolroom, which was the best Rock Creek could offer in the way of a service.

After this was over we were drifting companionably down the road when a very old car came clattering up. As it drew alongside, the lady-driver yelled, took both hands off the wheel, stamped on the brake and, just in time, remembered to get into neutral. She and her husband appeared to be close friends of the Missionary Ladies, and in no time we had all piled in behind them and were whirling away up a precipitous road to have dinner, with the driver talking and laughing gaily, and the car bouncing from side to side with a positively miraculous immunity from disaster. At last we reached a little house perched on the side of the hill, with a superb view of the Kettle River and stormy mountains swathed in sinister cloud. The grass sloped away like the side of a roof, and one felt if one stepped off the veranda one must be careful not to fall into the valley two hundred feet below.

We found the house rocking with the antics of a large gang of hilarious young men. Soon we were in a whirl of conversation about Timothy and the trip; suggestions, advice, encouragements and discussions tumbled over one another in an avalanche. Next began descriptions of apocryphal-sounding adventures with grizzly bears, mountain lions and outlaw broncos. Finally the "side-hill-gouger," that mythical animal who is forever being described for the delectation of gullible Easterners, made his impressive entry into the conversation. Instantly an earnest solemnity clothed the entire assembly. In point of fact I had already made my acquaintance with the side-hill-gouger, but I listened politely round-eyed, while the remarkable disparity in the length of his legs was explained to me in detail. "It's handier for him when he's running round the side-hills," my instructors pointed out. Then sheets of laughter went up, and grizzly-bronco stories continued as before.

Meanwhile our hostess ably made use of us all to prepare and arrange a lordly supper, of which we heartily partook. Then the girls and I tore ourselves away, and I skipped after them down the darkening hill-side, once more completely convinced of the rightness of this adventure. For swiftly as the geography of British Columbia leaps from the Pacific belt to the dry belt, so swiftly will my own absurd temperament leap from depression to delight.

That night I slept curled up in my sleeping-bag in an empty house kindly lent me by some friends of the Missionary Ladies, and in the morning regretfully said good-bye to them and set out again. And this I think is the moment when I must say good-bye to Cascade and Christina Lake, close the journal and set off again up the mountain. As I take a last look down the distance at the tiny village, I can see the storekeeper's daughter, infinitesimally small, come out of her house and hang some clothes on the line. A cloud is sliding a fine mantle over Christina Lake, and upon my hill-side Timothy has wandered nearly out of sight in his search for dinner. I must go and saddle him and set out in earnest to climb the mountain.

Chapter VI

DAYS IN THE DOUKHOBOR COUNTRY

Four days have passed since I sat on the mountain side above Cascade, and nearly a week since we left Rock Creek. That morning I was intent upon a difficult search, that of finding a blacksmith to shoe Timothy. The West is poorly equipped with blacksmiths, for here men nearly all buy the shoes ready made, and tack them on their horses themselves. However, I had been told that in Midway, a village some twelve miles from Rock Creek, a good blacksmith could be found. He now kept a garage.

About noon I reached Midway—a collection of shacks scattered with abandon over some wide flats. Among the buildings dull tracts of grass lay empty in the sun. Across one large expanse a very old man on a very old horse was riding, silent and slow.

Having wandered vaguely through this vague encampment, I finally came upon the garage and a woman somnolently in charge of it. Her husband, she said, was up at the house, sleeping off some late nights. What he could conceivably find in Midway to give him late nights I was at a loss to imagine. However, at Mrs. Bush's instigation, I went up to the house to see if I could wake him. After I had knocked some time at the front door, a very grumpy face, with its eyes three-quarters shut, appeared at an upstairs window and asked what I wanted. The owner of it turned out to be deaf, and it took me some time to acquaint him with my desire, whereupon the discouraging reply was, "I don't shoe no horses."

"Oh, dear," I cried, in an ingratiating bellow, "Mr. Wilson said you were *such* a good blacksmith."

"I haven't," replied the face, "shoed no horses in years."

"Oh, please," I yelled, "the horse has to go such a long way. In fact," I added in despair, "he has to go to Montreal."

"I don't," repeated the face, completely unmoved by this intelligence, "shoe no horses."

"Oh, well," said I, preparing to retire in good order, "perhaps they'll do him for me in Grand Forks."

"There's no one in Grand Forks," replied the face with scorn, "that could lift a hammer."

"Oh, well, never mind," said I with resignation, getting as far as the gate.

"Wait!" said the face. I waited. Long pause. "Guess I'll have to come and do him," said the face.

Ten minutes later a handsome car drew up at the garage and Mr. Bush, with his eyes wide open and a pleasant smile on his face, climbed out. "What you want to wake me so early in the morning for?" he inquired, looking me a dig in the ribs. After three quarters of an hour spent in collecting his tools, he set to work on Timothy and did a very good job.

Early that evening we left the highway and climbed up a rose-clad hill-side into the forest. For hours we followed the lonely trail. It was not till night was falling that I came upon a clearing with a small house at its edge. I knocked at the door and was accepted without surprise by the occupants—a frail old lady and her son. Sylvester was the most superbly handsome man I have ever seen. He had sombre blue eyes, the colour of deep water under the bows of a ship, and there were strong lines round his wide, steady mouth. He observed me with dispassionate amusement and said I should go to Hollywood. He wanted to cut off Timothy's mane, and I let him, being as putty in his hands, though afterward I deeply regretted it. Splendid Sylvester! I wonder whether he will ever leave his mountain retreat and discover how magnificent he is.

Next day, armed with a sketch map and copious directions, I set off through the forest for Grand Forks.

Have you ever come down a valley with a thunder-storm behina you, when the lightning grows brighter and brighter and the thunder louder, and they come closer and closer on each other's heels, and the birds are silent and the trees stand up dark and menacing against a grey-green sky, and you hurry on, fearing and yet hoping that the storm will catch you up and fight out its battle above your head? That is how is was, going down the trail to Grand Forks; and then, when the thunder and lightning were nearly on top of each other, the rain burst and the storm veered off down a neighbouring valley. And I went on, drenched, and somehow a bit disappointed.

We left Grand Forks at five o'clock, walking out into the fragile, tear-stained radiance which belongs to sunlight after a day of storm. Suddenly, into the delicate evening broke a surprising old man. He was brown, with a grey beard and long grey hair tied in a knot on top of his head. Stately he was and smiling and, craning his neck over a hedge, he began to speak to me. His speech was slow, emphatic and for a long while completely unintelligible. At last it became apparent that he was inviting me to supper. With words, which he did not understand, and with "nods and becks and wreathed smiles," which he did, I gratefully accepted.

So, after feeding Timothy, we set off together up the hill-side and climbed till we reached a small creeper-clad house, from which, at my companion's knock, there issued forth an assortment of anxious-looking women and children. Soon the old man and the women were conferring at high pressure in a variety of language which was intelligible neither to me nor, as it seemed, to the participants. Once or twice I endeavoured to make my escape, but the old man grasped me by the arm and instantly increased the volume of his argument.

How long this state of affairs might have continued I do not know, for, after I had at last abandoned my attempts to withdraw, a little girl came whirling down the stairs and dived in among us, quickly reducing the situation to order. She spoke excellent English and soon had us all explained to one another.

The old man, she said, was an East Indian (or Hindu as they call them here), and it seemed that he had invited me to sup, not with him, but with this totally unprepared family of Doukhobors. No wonder they had been somewhat at a loss! But when little Katja explained the situation to them, their attitude changed at once to one of friendliness and welcome. Quickly they drew me in, set me down at the table, and began to prepare a meal. I looked with interest at the downstair portion of the house. It consisted of a small kitchen and a large living-room, clean as paper and surprisingly empty, containing in fact, a table, a bench and half a dozen chairs—nothing else whatever. The women brought me my meal—boiled eggs, boiled potatoes, piles of asparagus and a pot of black tea. While I gladly set to, the oldest of the women, a flat-faced grandmother with a white handkerchief over her head, sat before me and asked questions, using little Katja as interpreter.

The old lady was amazed at my undertaking. "Why was I not afraid?" she asked over and over again. She was greatly exercised by the fact that I was not married. "Surely you are pretty enough?" she marvelled. She asked me where my parents lived, and when I told her far away in the old country, she said that surely they must weep every day at the thought of me. "Are they not terrified," she pursued, "at your being here all alone in a strange country?" I told her I believed not, but she continued to shake her head over them and sigh for their anxiety.

When I had finished my meal, she invited me to stay the night, but next day Timothy and I had to cross the Cascades—a small undertaking compared with the crossing of the Coast Range, but nevertheless, I felt that I should ride up as close as possible under the mountains before nightfall, so that Timothy might not have too long a trail on the day when he must make such a heavy climb.

So, bidding a reluctant farewell to my kindly friends, I set out once more and rode steadily for an hour. About sunset I saw before me, some way back from the road, a handsome farm-

DAYS IN THE DOUKHOBOR COUNTRY

house. Here, I decided, I would ask to stay for the night. But as I drew nearer I became aware of a dozen or so young men, playing ball in the stable-yard, and as I drew nearer still they stopped playing to watch me and began to hoot and whistle in the manner of young men; and, almost before I knew it, I had hustled past and was around the next corner. It was not till I was safely out of earshot that I realized how foolish I had been. Behind me lay a comfortable farm-house, before me lay the darkening country, billowing into the distance entirely innocent of habitation. There might be another farm-house just out of sight. But on the other hand I might ride for hours without seeing so much as a shack.

So, realizing that, in this instance, discretion and valour were inseparable, I turned Timothy's head, rode up to the farm, ran the gauntlet of the young men, who had stopped hooting and were now staring impassively, and knocked at the door. Why, yes, was the kindly answer, sure I could stay the night, there was lots of room. At once the embarrassing and indistinguishable male crowd broke up into a company of smiling individuals. They helped me to unpack Timothy, made room for him in the barn, watered and fed him. Then they stood around, cheerful and loquacious, while I rubbed his legs, slapped his back, and lovingly groomed his golden coat.

I found that my hosts were from South Russia and had thirteen children. The whole family spoke such good English that I took them to be Canadian born until, as I came in from a last visit to Timothy, my ears were saluted by a stream of high-pitched German and I found that one of the twins had upset a pail of milk and his mother was upbraiding him in the language which came handiest. It seems they are from Odessa, and German is their language.

We sat up a long time that night, talking of their far-off home, till I could almost hear the sleigh-bells jingling through the winter streets, almost see the strange little troikas with their horses, one set in the middle, trotting under his steel arch, the others cantering beside him in loose traces. Then we talked of the solemn Lenten festival of the Greek Church, of the long last vigil of the Passion, and at length the greeting called from man to man on Easter morning like a release: "Christ is risen!"

At last when hours of the night had already slipped away, they showed me to my room. It was empty of furniture but for one bed. They turned two children out of this bed on to the floor, which left two more in it, and remarked dispassionately as they bade me good night: "Push them up to the wall when you get in. They won't wake."

Next morning, very early, I set out for the mountains. One of my little bedfellows came with me some way up the road and, hearing that I had spent the evening before with some Doukhobors, began to talk about them. They are a fanatical sect originally from Russia, and the strict ones refuse to send their children to school or go to church or pay taxes.

"Oh, yes," said Mary, in a conversational tone, "every spring they burn down schools and blow up bits of the railway and churches." There was a family just across the river, she told me, whose daughter married a man they did not like. The man came to see them, and he and the father fought all night. In the morning the girl went and drowned herself in the river. "Gee," said Mary, "they're queer."

So far goes the journal. Since then I have learnt a good deal more about this remarkable people.

It would seem that the company of the Doukhobors grew up in Southern Russia in the eighteenth century, amid toil and tribulation. They accepted stoically, flogging, starvation and banishment to the Caucasus, believing it to be the unavoidable persecution meted out by the world to those who followed God.

For they sought to live wholly in the spirit of Christ—owning all they had in common, admitting no temporal authority, eating no meat in order that they might not have to kill. They believed that no man had a right to be a leader or a judge over his fel-

DAYS IN THE DOUKHOBOR COUNTRY

lows; and, for this reason perhaps, since they were unable to get on without one, many of them invested each leader as he arose with the divinity of Christ, in order that they might believe themselves to be following the leadership not of a man but of a god.

When in the early nineteenth century a Doukhobor colony emigrated to Canada, to be joined a few years later by their leader Peter Verigin, the expedition prospered. They were clean-living, honest and excellent farmers, and the land gave back the love they gave it. But they were soon in conflict again—in conflict with the government, in conflict among themselves, in conflict within their own minds. The supposed divinity of their leader threw them into confusion. The cool common sense of some was in constant collision with the fanaticism of others, who followed him blindly. The question: How to do right? absorbed the attention of all alike, and the search for a solution of the problem of life externalized itself in some extreme instances in the undertaking of pilgrimages which were to end in the discovery of some vague and unspecified promised land. In other cases it would lead to the pushing of religious beliefs to the point where the logical became the absurd. Some men, believing that it was wrong to enslave animals, turned their stock and horses loose in the hills. Some believed all education to be wrong, since we must live by the guidance of God alone, not by the ingenuity of man, and so in protest they burnt the schools. Occasionally they would discard their clothes and go naked, believing that thus they were returning to the perfect state of man as God made him.

Meanwhile they raised heavy crops and strong children and were as healthy as the birds.

A strange, fine, contradictory people. Without: solid, hard-working farmers, loving the land, belonging to it, bringing forth the best it has to give. Within: souls in travail, striving and losing, struggling and forever frustrated. What will they achieve as the years go on? Are they working their way at last, as fanaticism subsides, toward the wisdom they have been seeking?

I was struck by words spoken not long ago by one Doukhobor:

"Pravda, we have one horse. You saw that the horse was fat. Also, when I took you close to his head and asked you to look into his eyes, you saw happiness shining in those eyes? Da, it is necessary to feed the horse well and not make him work too hard, and also it is necessary to think of him always as a brother and never as a slave. Some farmers give their horses much food and not too much work. Yet those same horses will not have happy eyes if the ignorant farmers are thinking of their horses as slaves and not as brothers." *

There, I believe, is wisdom. And here, in the manifesto signed by the Doukhobors in 1939, is steadfastness:

"War will cease only when all men and women turn from violence . . . refuse to fight, no matter what provocation. . . . Christ said turn the other cheek. Some among humanity must begin, must set an example. Our ancestors did not give way to the Cossacks. We will lead the way, will suffer for our principles—come what may." *

So these are the Doukhobors, a peculiar people indeed, but one to be respected.

Now to return to the journal: In the little village of Cascade, at the foot of the mountains, my small friend left me. After collecting my lunch from the village store, I climbed for an hour up the hill-side, then sat down to write and to look my last upon the Kettle Valley.

After this Timothy and I set out again and climbed for twenty miles. For ever and ever the road went winding up, up, into the trees. I walked and led Timothy, then I rode, then I walked again. Up, up. We did not reach the height of the pass until dusk was falling. To the east the mountains fell away so steeply that looking down through the tree-tops one could catch glimpses

* *Slava Bohu*, J. E. C. Wright. Farrar and Rinehart.

of the road, winding down like an interminable snake. Dismounting to save Timothy's forelegs, I led him slowly down into the gathering evening. After we had followed the convolutions of the road for about ten miles, we came out upon some broad water meadows, and there in the midst of them was the black outline of a farm.

My heart stood still, for it was in total darkness. They had told me in Cascade that I should find this farm; they had told me, moreover, that there was no other habitation until I reached Rossland, which must be fifteen miles further on. What if there were no one at home? Anxiously I tied Timothy to a post and knocked. To my relief I was answered by the bark of a dog, and a minute later a woman came to the door and replied to my shy inquiry that I might certainly stay the night.

Having made Timothy comfortable, I went in with some curiosity, to find that the house was now lighted adequately enough. The occupants were two women who had evidently been sitting contentedly in complete darkness. Now they bestirred themselves hospitably and made me some supper, then pulled out a sofa bed for me in the living-room, upon which I was soon so deeply asleep that the men came clumping in later without my so much as hearing them through my dreams.

Next day they told me I had better stay, for it was going to rain, but I said no, that I was used to rain, and moreover I did not believe it would be much. But they were right, for it *was* going to rain; it was going to rain and rain all day.

I have reached the conclusion that rain simply does not matter if you know where you are going. But when there is absolutely no certainty of getting feed for the horse or dry clothes for oneself, and hardly even a possibility of a bath, the effect on morale is considerable. Any mackintosh soaks through after five or six hours, and the luggage and ones legs are soon a sodden mass. If one gets down to walk, the saddle collects the water like a dew pond. If one does not walk one grows numb with cold. I shall never forget that ride, with the clouds driving up the mountains like smoke, and not one single sign of life except once a deserted mine standing in grim desolation on the side of a hill, in a perfect misery of cloud and rain.

At last we got down into Rossland and passed through the streaming village on to a paved road, and thereupon came over a hill, to see a completely unexpected factory town fuming up at us. This was Trail, and any one who had heard of the Consolidated Mining and Smelting Works should have known it would be like this; but, with the mountain fastnesses so lately behind me, it seemed like something in an absurd play. The prospect of any one in the whole town's knowing what to do with a horse seemed unspeakably remote. I crawled down the hill towards it, dragging Timothy behind me in dejection.

When we were so near that we began to smell the smoke, a car stopped and a pleasant elderly man climbed out. I knew what our conversation would be almost word for word. "Are you the girl?" etc. "Yes," I replied dismally, with the rain trickling down my nose. Without much hope, I asked him if he knew any place where they would take in the horse.

"Why, yes," he replied, "go to the Company's model farm. Bill Forest will look after you both." He little knew, bless his elderly heart, what a herald of Peace and Joy he was.

There was the farm, sure enough, just a mile or so further on. Although Bill Forest was not at home, they took us in perfectly as a matter of course, and, after Timothy was settled, a nice-looking young man, who knew exactly who I was without even asking, packed me into a car, with another young man, and sent me up to his wife. A girl about my own age came to the door and accepted me, streaming hair, filthy boots, soaking wet luggage and all, without even looking bewildered. In no time at all her pretty kitchen was strung from end to end with clothes-lines and rendered completely impassable by the presence of every single one of my steaming possessions. And I, Oh ultimate luxury! was piled into a hot bath.

Today I am allowing Timothy and myself a "rest up." The

peace and relaxation of the Moffits' little house is utterly delicious, and Hermy is one of the easiest and most unexacting hostesses I have had the luck to encounter. Timothy meanwhile occupies a model stall in the model farm with cold water bandages on his legs and more hay and bedding than he knows how to use.

I know well that today I ought to be getting myself shown over the Smelter, and in general taking an intelligent interest in this perfectly gigantic mining concern. Instead of which I am slacking about the house, writing and mending my clothes and talking to Hermy's friends, who are happening in, one by one, to see what I look like. The last to look in was a pleasant, plump little woman with an autograph album and eyes as round as moons. She asked me, as they all do, whether I was not afraid. Then, after much thought, she asked if I wore stirrups. And finally, whether my parents knew what I was doing. This "does-your-mother-know-you're-out?" attitude always amuses me, as it is almost entirely due to her quiet encouragement that I am doing this at all.

I am worrying a little about Timothy. He is in good heart and condition, but his legs are not perfect. He is straight in the shoulder and straight in the pastern, and jars the tendons as he walks. Today they are puffy and hot, after his climb over the mountain. I hope I may be able to keep him sound.

Chapter VII

OVER THE SELKIRKS

AFTER a day's rest we left Trail and followed the Columbia River to Robson. It was a pleasant ride, undistinguished except by one escapade of Timothy's.

About noon I was invited to stop for lunch at a filling station, and gladly accepted. Timothy thought poorly of this idea from the beginning, having a curious mistrust of filling stations, so we tied him on the other side of the road, under a small tree; and, against my better judgment, for he is also afraid of a rope, we tied him long, so that he could eat some grass, and left him feeding happily enough.

Five minutes later, as we were going in to lunch, there was a crashing noise in the bushes, and Timothy came tearing out as though the fairies were after him and disappeared up the road, kicking his heels and dragging the tree behind him on the end of the rope. We leapt into a car which was standing outside the garage and, after driving for half a mile, caught a fleeting glimpse of the red horse, speeding round a distant corner. We renewed out efforts and finally saw him not so very far ahead, still in full flight, with a car coming fast towards him. We waved our arms beseechingly; the car slowed down across the road, and Timothy stopped. When we had reached him and disengaged the tree, we found him much agitated but hardly blown and sweating very little, which shows the condition he is in.

We reached Robson in a red and yellow evening, to find our hosts all ready to receive us. They had heard me speak over the radio from Vancouver, and had written to invite me for the night. They have a neat house on the shores of a lake and a beautiful dog whom they found last year starving in the woods. The Doukhobors are forbidden by their religion to kill, so they drive away their unwanted dogs to die in the mountains. "God will look after them," say the Doukhobors.

We left Robson on Sunday afternoon, and about eight miles along the road we passed the grave of Peter Verigin, the famous Doukhobor leader. They have erected a splendid monument in his memory and value highly the farms in its immediate neighbourhood, so that the road is bordered for many miles with Doukhobor holdings. At the time of our passing the owners embarrassed me a good deal, for they were all doing nothing, because it was Sunday, and were therefore at liberty to stare at us from the moment we hove in sight until we disappeared over the horizon, of which opportunity they fully availed themselves. However, I observed them in return, and a solid-looking company they were. The older women wore long full skirts and had white handkerchiefs over their heads. The young men were clean and brown and handsome, with buxom girls beside them. A fine sturdy people, peculiar or not.

Early in the evening we reached South Slocan, where there lived a cousin of the North Country Bosanquets, called Jim Craster, who had most kindly arranged for hospitality for me and Timothy. I stayed with some delightful friends of his in a little house belonging to the West Kootenay Power and Light Company, which concern is the reason for the existence of South Slocan. Here, owing to heavy rain, I spent a whole day. In the afternoon Jim lent me his car, and I drove my hostess and her children into Nelson. As we came over the last stretch of the mountain road the weather was clearing, and there below us lay the little town, in a burst of sunshine, and behind it the clouds rolling off the mountains, and the lake in exquisite transition from storm to brightness.

The next day, still through showers and sunshine, Timothy and I travelled the same road, with the river below us frowning and dimpling in vivid caprice and crashing into snowy cascades at the Power Company's dams. A lovely river, the Columbia, a lovely temperamental river, and I was sorry to leave it.

The only incident of the day was provided by Timothy. I rode him into a small shallow-looking pool, thinking he needed a drink. He did not, but there was an unexpectedly deep hole in the middle of the pool, and when Timothy felt the water under his belly, he lay down gracefully against the side, depositing me in the mud. That horse has no respect.

One serious business which I had to perform in Nelson was to make up my mind how to cross the Selkirks. The highway turns south at Kootenay Lake, and pursues a lengthy and decorous course, running down almost to the international boundary, then north again to Cranbrook. But I knew that a pack-trail ran over the mountains to Marysville, over a hundred miles shorter and inestimably more fun. There have been the usual array of local authorities adjuring me not to go, asserting with confidence that there will be snow slides, rock slides, great piles of trees across the trail and creeks so high that the horse and I will undoubtedly be drowned. When I mention bridges they are forced to admit that there *have* been some; but no doubt, they add, these have been washed away. One kindly man, who had crossed the trail himself ten years ago, sent messages to the newspaper, the bank, and the post office, begging me to pay him a visit; and when I went, he told me that he could not reconcile it with his conscience to allow me to go, assuring me repeatedly that the pass was over eight thousand feet high at the summit, and I knew nothing whatever of what I was attempting. However, one or two younger and more enterprising people have given me more optimistic accounts of the trail. As for my cousin Jim, he advises me not to go, but adds that, if I do go, he is coming with me. I have decided that I will, so Jim joins me tomorrow.

Today I rode up a finger of Kootenay Lake and crossed by the ferry from Fraser's Landing. We reached Gray Creek, on the east side of the lake, in the early evening, and I set out to

"THE COLUMBIA, A LOVELY TEMPERAMENTAL RIVER"

find the home of an English family to whom I had an introduction. After a short ride I reached a pleasant house standing in a rolling English garden, in which I am now waiting. The family are out, so I have found a patch of rough grass for Timothy to graze, and now sit writing the journal and hoping my unsuspecting hosts will be pleased to see me.

That was two days ago, and soon after I finished writing, my host and hostess, with their little boy, came home and made me welcome. Next day Jim arrived, and we went on up the lake shore to the foot of the trail by which we were to cross the mountains. Here we stayed the night with a young couple called MacGreggor. These two took a more hopeful and considerably less ·melodramatic view of the trail than did the inhabitants of Nelson. They secured a good saddle-horse for Jim, helped us pack our provisions, and set the alarm-clock for four-thirty, in order that we might be away in the morning with the birds.

But we did not start in the morning. For we awoke to find that it was raining, raining with the dour insistence which seems somehow peculiar to rain in the mountains. Perfectly straight it falls, pouring off the branches of the firs and cedars, pelting down their trunks, pounding upon the roof of the cabin where you huddle. Down the hill-side rush the creeks, muddy and tempestuous, and other creeks, new-born, stream down the trails which you had thought to travel. So we did not start in the morning. Instead we lay about the house, slept and read the funny papers.

When I was first introduced to a funny paper, it left me at a loss. I read it through and through, completely unable to discover anything funny about it. But I must now confess to a growing affection for "Li'l Abner" and his family, a mild admiration for the achievements of Joe Palooka, and an increasing interest in the frustrated life of Jiggs. Perhaps with a little more practice I may yet acquire an addiction to The Funnies. . . .

Next day we again rose considerably before the lark, to find the rain still falling, quietly and insistently, out of a leaden sky. But this time we were forced to go. Jim had to be back at work in two days; and I, after all, have to reach Montreal. So damply we began to get ready. We were joined in the gloom of our five-o'clock breakfast by a young man called Eric, who had decided to accompany us. Jim came to look after me and Eric came to look after both of us, so protectors were plenty.

At six o'clock we started out. The forest dripped mistily; its fir trees and cedars gloomed in the wet; the trail grew narrower and narrower and the branches brushed our faces and poured their raindrops with unerring precision down our necks. Eric had packed our provisions on his little mare and was walking and leading her. Jim and I sat on our horses and I think had the worst of it.

After about an hour the trail led down to the shores of a river. It was not unusually wide, but it was swift and swollen with the rains, and the waters came crashing menacingly over their rocky bed. Timothy, being the strongest and steadiest horse, tried it first. Cheerfully he walked in, feeling his steps, then took off and, with a few powerful strokes, reached the farther shore. But as I was about to congratulate him and wring out the legs of my trousers, I turned and saw Eric's little mare standing knee-deep in the waves, and too much paralysed by fear to go forward or back.

Eric had optimistically predicted that she would follow Timothy, but this had been an uninspired prophecy, and now any minute her legs might be swept from under her by the force of the water. There was nothing to do but for poor Timothy to plunge in again, which he did; and, while I caught the mare's haltershank, he made a dexterous turn in midstream and dragged her to safety on the opposite bank; then he shook himself and was all ready to go on. Jim's little horse crossed next, with much splashing and snorting, and finally Eric, going a little way upstream, clambered over with gibbon-like agility on a fallen tree, some rocks, and another tree.

Now the ascent began in real earnest. From here to the summit the trail climbs three thousand feet in three miles. We dismounted to help the horses. I held on to Timothy's tail and let him drag me up, but the men panted up bravely under their own steam, stopping occasionally to chop a way through the trees which had fallen across the path. Water squelched in our boots after the fording of the river, and our upper portions were hardly drier, since the rain continued unabated. The trail strained up ahead of us, steep as a house-roof.

About noon we reached the summit. I believe there is a view, but all we could see was a gloomy expanse of rocks, rain and sombre fir trees, circled in cloud. I suppose all this sounds fearful, but as a matter of fact I was very happy, and so I think was Jim; so were the horses when they got their oats; and Eric, being used to his own country, took anything it provided as a matter of course.

While I unpacked and fed the horses, he and Jim collected some wet wood on to a wet stone and, with the magical ingenuity possessed by Canadians where an outdoor fire is concerned, soon got going a merry blaze. We sat down beside it, steamed and ate bacon and eggs. About two o'clock we started out again. At first the trail was hard to find, for, since the pass actually *was* about eight thousand feet high, it was still deep in snow. In some places the blazes on the trees were covered, and it was a good thing that Eric was with us and knew the trail. This was the highest summit over which Timothy and I had passed, but, in spite of one or two difficulties, it certainly did not justify the pessimists' gloomy predictions.

In the early afternoon we reached the first of the wide and terrible creeks which they had described. The bridge, however, was in excellent condition, so their expectations were fortunately unfounded. In the early evening the clouds began to lift, and looking back through a clearing we saw the rain, drifting west in a silver veil, shining against the sun; and behind, a startling snow-capped peak, guarding the pass over which we had come.

About six o'clock we came in sight of the Office Camp, a small cabin where we proposed to spend the night. To our surprise, we saw smoke rising among the trees and, as we drew nearer, the solemn, inquisitive face of a horse was raised from the grass to peer at us. We reached the cabin to find a boy and girl already in possession. They regarded us in sombre silence. Fearing that we might have burst inadvertently upon a honeymoon trip, we started a one-sided and somewhat embarrassed conversation, only after a long time discovering that the boy and girl, hearing that I hoped to cross the pass, had ridden out to meet me, and were in fact delighted to see us, but so completely paralysed by shyness that they could not get a word out.

We cooked our supper out of doors (bacon and eggs again) and then hung up our saddles and spread out the pack to dry as best it would. Inside the shack were bunk beds with straw mattresses and some old blankets. There were cooking-utensils too, besides a knife and some cups and plates. For a trapper leaves his cabin open, and he leaves his possessions behind him. He knows that those who travel the mountains are more likely to leave some token behind them than to carry anything away. So the girl and I made ourselves comfortable in the hospitable little house, while the men gallantly spent the night on the damp porch.

In the morning we woke to sunshine and snow-capped peaks. After an early breakfast (bacon and eggs!) Jim and Eric set out to return to Crawford Bay and Ralph and Alma and I rode away down the east side of the mountain. . . .

The brother and sister were still almost completely silent, which I liked, as it gave me a chance to watch the trail winding through the woods, the whisking squirrels and chipmunks, rare sudden birds, and snowy peaks flashing between the trees. In the late afternoon we reached my companions' home, a settle-

"STEAMED AND ATE BACON AND EGGS"

"THE WEATHERED SELKIRKS"

ment in a little clearing, girdled by the mountains. They lived in a one-roomed house built by themselves. Alma and her sister shared a bed behind a rug at one end, and Ralph and his father shared one on the other side. That night Alma slept in the living-room end of the house, and I shared with the married sister.

I can never get over this kindness to strangers. These Westerners will put themselves to endless trouble to help one and bear any inconvenience to show one hospitality, as though it were not kindness at all, but the simplest matter of course. I hope that before I die I may have a chance to give back to some one who needs it a little of this wealth of friendship which has been so freely given to me.

The next day I rode down into Marysville. Here I had the great honour and felicity of meeting the Evans boys. They are famous all over the Kootenay district and their ages are seventy and seventy-five. All their lives they have been prospectors and geologists, seeking for gold and silver and finding it, but never growing rich. They possess a nine-thousand-foot mountain, solid with ore, but have never had the capital to work it. The discovery which has given them the greatest pleasure was of a rare pine tree with an exquisite grain, and now Bill Evans spends all his time carving and polishing the beautiful wood, while his brother looks after their tiny shack.

I wonder who will mine Mount Evans, how big a fortune he will make, and whether he will remember the two old men to whom the mountain first belonged, and who lived and died without riches and without regret, while their wealth slumbered untouched in its virgin snows.

Chapter VIII

CAMP ON THE KOOTENAY

It is Sunday again, and Timothy and I have reached a deserted logging camp on the Kootenay River trail. I picked curved spruce-branches for a bed and laid them in one of the empty huts. After that I bathed in the creek, and I can feel now the aching-cold water passing my naked body. Afterward I ran in the clearing to dry; then I caught Timothy and put the bridle on him, leapt up and cantered round the edge of the forest. Never have I ridden a horse like this, with nothing, not even a layer of cloth, between me and him, with his salt hairs pricking my naked thighs and the smooth muscles rippling under my very skin. So must the Indians have ridden, in the old days of their freedom; and so, since we are imagining, might Adam have ridden, if he had stayed only a few more years in paradise!

Now I am dressed again, for the evening is shivering up the valley; and before I go to bed, I am sitting to write the journal. Where was I? Yes, at Marysville. Well, here I had to make a decision which I had been putting off for the last week. It was: whether to ride direct east to Macleod and Lethbridge, much the shorter and much the duller route, or whether to strike north through the national park to Banff and thence to Calgary. Personally I would not walk round a block to see Banff, and even Lake Louise, "Most Beautiful Spot on Earth" and all that, has been so insistently advertised that one could not look at it with the thrill of any kind of discovery. But the thought of the national park, wild, precipitous, netted with trails and alive with animals, would not let me rest, and I did want to ride down the mountains and see Calgary, first great city east of Vancouver, spread out on the edge of the prairies.

The morning dawned when I had to start. If it had been a rainy day, I should undoubtedly have gone to Macleod. But the day was brilliant, and there was the vivid line of the Rockies, running up north and drawing my eyes like a magnet. In vain I thought of the extra distance. In vain I concentrated my mind on the banffish-ness of Banff, and the prodigious size of the Lake Louise hotel. By nine o'clock I was riding up the range due north.

I did not get far, however, for about noon I reached a pleasant little farm, from which two girls came running out and besought me to come in, saying that they had followed Timothy's and my progress in the papers all the way along. So in we went, and once in the house they set about persuading me to stay the night; and at last, partly because they were so charming and partly because they promised to try to get me permission to see over the famous lead and zinc mines of Kimberley, I decided to stay.

In the afternoon we set out for Kimberley and, with some trepidation, presented ourselves at the office of the mine superintendent.

"I don't see how you can," he said, when he heard what we wanted. "The three-o'clock shift is just coming off, and there'll be no guards, and you've no appointment." We looked crestfallen.

"I know you're crazy," he added, "to want to ride across Canada, but you're crazier still to expect to go down the mine at this hour and without an appointment."

"Please," said I.

"Don't say pretty please to me," said the mine superintendent, ruffling up his hair. Silence. Superintendent registering distress.

"Aren't girls awful?" demanded the mine superintendent, seizing the telephone. "There," he said after a few seconds' conversation, "go up to the minehead and ask for Fred Waldie and see what you can do with him." With profuse thanks we made for the door.

"I think you're crazy!" shouted the mine superintendent as the door closed.

Fred Waldie was all ready for us. He dressed us up in mining-clothes and electric lights and we plunged into the cool depths of the mountain. The passages are high and well ventilated, and working conditions seem good; there are showers and artificial sunlight treatment for the men, and they look well. We saw some of the great caverns where the ore has been dug out; we shot down to the lowest level in a skip, and once took cover in a little antechamber while a terrific explosion of blasting took place. After an hour and a half we came out again into the sunlight, having seen an infinitesimal portion of the enormous mine.

Very early next morning Timothy and I set out. All day we rode up the valley between the two ranges. I was struck by the contrast between the weathered Selkirks and the young and precipitous Rockies, the effect of whose spectacular outline against the summer sky was positively operatic. We made about forty miles that day, over a lonely range trail, through cactus and sage-brush and burning heat. In the evening we came to a dude-ranch. The trail led up to the brow of a hill and there lay the little ranch, nestling among trees on the shores of a lake.

"They'll be delighted to have you," I had been assured; so, certain of our welcome, I led Timothy thankfully down the winding drive. But I had forgotten that this was no ordinary ranch. As we trailed wearily into the yard, the difference became apparent. On the lawn beside the lake lay an assortment of the dudes, arrayed in bathing-dresses and sun-suits, cool, serene, and exquisitely sun-tanned, beautifully groomed as to the hair and hands. I became aware of myself and Timothy, drooping wearily and covered with dust and sweat. Pushing back the tangles of my hair, I remembered that my nose was peeling. Diffidently I inquired of the nearest dude whether the owner of the ranch was available.

"You'd better go over to the office," he replied, looking at me with faintly supercilious curiosity. I discovered the office, and in it a militant lady in highly ornamental cowboy boots, who found the sight of me quite manifestly repulsive, but said that I might stay, and that I had better take a shower. The dudes were evidently surprised to observe at dinner-time that there had been a reasonably presentable girl under all the dirt.

Dinner over, I hastened up to the stables to see Timothy, and was relieved to find in charge an honest-to-goodness cowboy in battered chaps and an aged ten-gallon hat. We were soon happily engaged in looking over the horses, and, deciding that Timothy needed a reset, took him down to the forge. One by one the dudes came drifting by, and I found that the position had undergone a subtle reverse. For now the cowboy and I, in our shabby old clothes, were the real people, and the nicely dressed dudes were shy and out of place.

Lovely as this ranch was, I was glad to be on the road again next morning. That evening we made Canal Flats, and here my plans changed again. I find the best way to run this trip is to work out the route a hundred or so miles in advance, but be all ready to change it over night. For at Canal Flats I heard that, instead of taking the highway to Windermere, as I had supposed from the map I must, I could follow a trail up the Kootenay River and thus strike directly into the national park. To my surprise not a voice was raised this time in gloomy prediction, so joyfully I awaited the morning.

That night Timothy and I stayed with an elderly Swede, who seemed to be the only person with a good barn and hay. Mr. Jonson and I decided that, in view of his being a bachelor, convention demanded that I should sleep in the hay-mow. So the old man made me a bed in the hay with Hudson Bay blankets, advised me to shut the door of the mow for fear of bears, bade me good night and departed.

For some time the darkness was silent. Then something began noisily eating in a corner of the loft. I knew well it was not a bear, and anyway I had shut the door. But nevertheless I listened with considerable concentration. Animals in the day are enchanting, but an animal at night, making eating-noises and sounding rather large, is a little disconcerting. I was thankful when it withdrew and allowed me to go to sleep.

Early in the morning I heard Timothy stamping about below, so, collecting an armful of hay, I went out into the bird-filled silence of four o'clock, to find a great moon setting in a path of gold over Columbia Lake, and beyond it the long, quiet line of the Selkirks, serene and snow-capped and very far away. Timothy was delighted with the hay and I lay down again, to the pleasant accompaniment of munching, and slept till the sun was high. After breakfast I set out along the trail, which begins in a wagon-road and follows the line of the wide, swift river. It was a day delicious with sunshine and cloud, splashing creeks and red Rocky Mountain lilies.

Dreamy with forest lights and aloneness, I was jogging on, singing songs and thinking how far we were from every one, when I was startled by the grind of brakes behind us and turned to see a small car groaning to a standstill. Out of it climbed a young man whom I had met some time before in the course of my travels. He had come to ask whether I would marry him. He accepted the inevitable reply with fortitude, but I continued my journey in some bewilderment of mind!

That night I slept at a logging-camp. Quite a little village it was, perched on the mountain side, with the Kootenay River, far below, swirling through the valley. They have logged the Kootenay River out to this point, driving the timber down the stream. Some years ago they were working at the camp where now I am sitting, and before that they were even higher. Next day, laden with oats and food, which I meant to buy, but which the foreman has given me, I set out for this deserted camp.

So here I sit in the wide clearing, with the group of huts behind me, and east of me, at the forest's edge, the old corral still standing, into which I shall put Timothy before I go to bed. The setting sunlight slants across the clearing. Timothy now is grazing at the edge of the forest, shining red as amber against

"THE YOUNG AND PRECIPITOUS ROCKIES"

Courtesy Canadian Pacific Railroad

the shadow of the trees; I must go and catch him before it is too dark.

From here on, they tell me, the trail is narrow and hard to find. They say they hope I shall not get lost. The foreman of the logging-camp has lent me a little gun, in case we do get lost and I have to shoot birds to live on while we are wandering in the forest. I almost wish that this may happen. I expected difficulty, and I should not be sorry if difficulty arose.

Chapter IX

LAST OF THE MOUNTAINS

It was next morning, a few minutes after we left the deserted camp, that we met the grizzly. I might not have seen him, for he was very still; but Timothy suddenly stopped dead, sweat broke out on his shoulder, and in the silence I could hear his heart beating. Then I looked between his ears and there was the bear, six feet of him, upright beside a cedar. Proud as Lucifer he was; the mountains were his; he knew it and I knew it. Timothy and I did not run; we walked slowly past the king and never turned our heads, but I could feel his eyes in my back. I can feel them now, and my spine prickles. . . .

The bear opened a morning for us which was magical with animals. We had not left him long when we came upon a tiny fawn lying asleep in the grass. About the size of a hare he was, curled up as neat as an egg, with his legs tucked underneath him. As we came near he raised his head and looked at us quietly with his baby eyes. Soon we met another young deer, stepping delicately through the forest; he was not much bigger than the first one, and just as neat, complete, and faerie as he. He walked carefully up to Timothy and me; it was not till he could nearly touch Timothy with his inquisitive nose that the horse made a movement, and the youngster went bounding away with his white flag set behind him. It was some hours later that we came upon the nine-pointer buck, stalking among the trees in perfect self-possession. He watched us solemnly as we passed. Last of all a timber-wolf bounded on to the trail, a great grey creature with a ruff round his neck and all the fear of the wilderness behind his lonely eyes. But he did not seem greatly afraid of us, for he loped ahead of us up the trail for several paces before he slid into the forest.

Any one riding a horse finds a strange acceptance with these animals of the wilderness. My own theory is that the smell of the horse is more powerful than the smell of the human, and that therefore they accept one to some extent as one of themselves. Certain it is that they observe one with interest rather than fear.

All this time I had been keeping a sharp eye open for the trail; for by this time it was very small and wound among the trees almost indistinguishable. Once I had gone astray, but found my way back again, and about midday we came upon an encampment of men who were laying a cable across the river. I was somewhat disconcerted at again being surprised by human life when I had imagined myself and Timothy so far from any one but the animals. However, I went in and was delighted to find that I had arrived in the nick of time for dinner—roast beef and carrots and apple pie—and the more delicious for being unexpected. Late in the afternoon I reached the Banff-Windermere highway, and tonight I am staying at an auto-camp, a settlement of little huts run for motorists which are very common on the Canadian highways.

All day through the park. Forest and mountain and cloud; forest and mountain and river; sun and storm and rainbows down the hills. So many fir trees and mountains that it is difficult to believe that there is anything else in all the world. But deep in the forest-laden mind lies the aching knowledge of another crisis in Europe—Hitler yelling for Danzig, England bluffing, Germany bluffing, and no faith, no security, no rest for our restless lives.

Today we went on again through the park, more and more and more of it, with the forest running in spurs up the mountains, and the snow running down to meet it. But already Banff is beginning to insinuate its barely perceptible tentacles. The motor cars which pass us are beginning to have a solemn, sight-seeing look. At noon I stopped to walk up the far-famed Marble Canyon and found a very beautiful little river, rushing between rocks hewn deep by the water; but the place was so much dressed up, with little paths, crazy steps, rustic bridges and what-not, that one felt one was walking into a picture postcard.

At sunset we passed over the border into Alberta and saw the strange battlements of Castle Mountain rising before us. As we were going down the valley in the dusk towards the mountain, Timothy turned, and I saw behind us a great bull-moose, looming enormous in the shadows. His antlers spread wide above his bumpy face. It always seems to me they must be singularly inconvenient for an animal who has to live in the forest; but Nature, one supposes, knows best. That night I slept with a ranger's family, close under the brooding mountain, and the next day set out for Banff.

Banff is exactly what I expected—large expensive hotels, small expensive shops, notices directing one to beauty spots, and flocks of brilliantly dressed visitors from cities in the South and East. They admire in chorus and exactly as instructed; the town reverberates with them. "Say, isn't this wonderful?" and "Gee, isn't this swell?" come ringing through the sound of the streets with the interminable recurrence of the hammer *motif* in *Siegfried*.

Upon the day after my arrival in Banff, came Roy and Peggy Walker, friends with whom an uncle of mine had stayed when he was on a world tour examining in music. Timothy was left behind, and they whirled me away to spend a week at their home in Vulcan. They gave me such a dazzling round of sight-seeing and gaiety that I had no time to write the journal and must now recapture those days as best I can.

Before setting out for Vulcan, we drove north-east to visit Lake Louise. Up the much-travelled road we sped and finally brought up under the cliff of the gigantic hotel. Following other sight-seers round the end of this massive structure, we came out upon a smooth lawn, and there before us lay the lake, smiling with the faint self-consciousness of a society beauty. Beyond the exotic blue of the water the glacier splayed in a white fan. The mountains running symmetrically to the water's edge framed the picture with neat perfection.

I know Lake Louise is a miracle of loveliness. To come upon such a jewel of nature unexpectedly, at the end of a lonely trail, would be the experience of a lifetime. But to approach it around the angle of a luxury hotel is to be handed the world's beauty on a plate.

Having duly admired, we climbed back into the car and headed for Calgary. As we left the mountains, loneliness sank down upon my spirit. I did not know till then how their presence had possessed me. After we left Calgary and struck south into the flat farming country, I leant against Peggy and began to go to sleep.

"See that?" cried Roy exultantly. "She can't take it. I thought she was tough!"

The Walkers had a neat little house in a perfect paradise of a garden, which Peggy kept alive by unremitting watering and care. Here I sat down hopefully to catch up with my correspondence and write the journal. But before even the most urgent of my letters was written, it was time to set out in the car again. For the Walkers devoted every minute of that week to their visitor and each day had some new plan for giving me pleasure. We drove all over the country, we picnicked, we visited.

One day we went to Turner Valley and gazed in awe upon the little town, lying dim and disconsolate under the sheets of flame which pour day and night out of the gas-filled ground. For under those blank streets, under those barren flats, boil the deepest oil-wells of Canada. Another day we made our pilgrimage to the Prince of Wales' ranch. Wistful it looked, huddled among the foot-hills, with picnickers prowling round the locked house and no horses in the corrals.

But the high light of our whole week was the visit to the Calgary stampede. Early on the first day of the great rodeo, in a stream of cars, we entered the city. In brazen heat we scrambled successfully for a good view-point, whence we were to watch the inaugural procession. After an hour's wait, the parade began. Indians, dressed in dazzling regalia, rode past on dull and disappointing horses. Next came the cowboys, handsome and happy, prancing on their wiry little broncos. This unfortunately was all that I saw, for at this point I distinguished myself by fainting, a reaction which I have always heartily despised in others.

Roy shared my opinion, for, as the rushing in my ears stopped, I heard the end of the well-known sentence: ". . . can't take it, I thought she was tough! . . . Green as a cucumber!" he added, regarding me with disfavor. I quickly recovered, but Roy continued to murmur, ". . . can't take it," at intervals throughout the day. As soon as lunch was over, we hastened to the stampede grounds and expectantly took our places upon the grand stand.

"Coming out of shoot number six," a voice was intoning through an amplifier, "Pete Nantucket on Pinto Prince."

And then into the arena hurtled a black and white typhoon; with difficulty one's eye distinguished the wheeling outline of a horse. The head was lost to view under the belly, the tail clamped between the quarters; out like star points, down like daggers shot the whirling legs; and with every leap they flung high the arched mountain of the little back. Upon the peak of this tortured eminence perched the unlucky Pete, but not for long. For, even as we applauded, his body shot from the saddle, described a graceful arc, and landed with a thud upon the ungentle face of the arena. As for Pinto Prince, he turned back into an ordinary-shaped horse and cantered calmly up the field, until he was caught and led away by one of the "pick-up" men. The announcer was speaking again:

"Coming out of shoot number four . . ." And before he had time to finish, out shot a sparkling chestnut, bent like a bow, and surmounted by a lean boy in a scarlet shirt, who, almost before we saw him riding, had ceased to ride, and was picking himself up and unconcernedly retrieving his hat. So we watched while innumerable young men described innumerable arcs, and when now and then one of them retained his precarious throne for the short but melodramatic period prescribed, we applauded in amazement.

After this the same performance was repeated upon steers, who are less agile and spectacular than the horses, but even more disconcerting to ride, since they frequently trample upon their victims after dislodging them. Next we watched various terrified calves tearing across the field, while cowboys galloped after them, roped them, and knotted them into paralysed little parcels in an incredibly short space of time. Later we watched cowboys and Indians milking wild cows, saddling and riding wild horses, and finally "steer-decorating."

The title of this latter pastime is hopelessly inadequate to convey its hair-raising nature. Down the field, snorting like a dragon, an outraged steer comes charging. Upon the off side rides a cowboy full gallop. Upon the near side rides the competitor, carrying a blue ribbon. When he feels the moment has arrived, he flings himself from his horse, seizes the steer by the horns and, flapping beside the beast as it rushes madly on, endeavours to slip the ribbon over the horn before he is flung off or trampled down.

"Oh, they're tough, mighty tough, in the West!"

At last the great day was over, and we drove back to Vulcan. I leant against Peggy and remembered all we had seen; while Roy murmured to the road which streamed to meet us:

"Can't take it. I thought she was tough!"

All too soon my short week's visit came to an end. So the Walkers drove me back to Banff, and Timothy and I started out on our last trail through the mountains. The beauty of the way that day filled me with the sadness of parting; for I found that the mountains had grown into my life, and the prairies stretched before me like an infinitely lonely sea. Then the memory of Stevenson came again to comfort me:

"I have been after an adventure all my life, a pure dispassionate adventure, such as befell early and heroic voyagers."

So we set out towards the prairies, a very little ship.

Once more we are on the road, and I have time for the journal. It was a brilliant day when we left Banff and set out to follow the Ghost River trail to Cochrane. A distractingly lovely trail it was, beside the forest-hung shores of the long, lonely Lake Minnewanka. The little path wound in and out, now deep in the trees, now by the edge of the water. The mountains hung brooding over the lake, waiting to bid us good-bye.

In the afternoon we reached a locked police cabin, on the porch of which I proposed to sleep the night. This, however, was not to be. All day Timothy had been homesick for the horses with whom he had stayed in Banff. In view of this I hobbled him (a thing I hardly ever need to do), but even so he kept starting back again; till once, when I went to fetch him and took the hobbles off to lead him up the hill, I let go of the head-collar for a moment, and he shot round and disappeared down the trail like a gull down the wind. There was nothing for it but to take the bridle and follow him. In about three hours I reached the highway and heard that Timothy had been seen trotting at considerable speed toward Banff; so I got a lift in a car, and about a mile out of town we came up with him. There was nothing for it now but to ride him back to the livery-stables; so he got his way, horrible horse! I slept at the stables on a buffalo robe, and the next day we set out again.

Today there were waves on the lake and the pine trees creaked in the wind. It was evening when we reached the cabin. I watched the sun go down behind the mountains and the lake turn from

"FOREST AND MOUNTAIN AND CLOUD"

Courtesy Canadian Pacific Railroad

blue to gold and from gold to silver-grey, with the sombre reflection of the pine-clad mountains growing blacker and blacker.

Then came the stars, and the night life of the forest began. Quiet crackling and brushings, little splashings in the lake. Then there was the rustle of paper, and I dimly discerned the humpy form of a pack-rat, shamelessly devouring my breakfast. I roused myself and hid the breakfast under my hat. I had hardly lain down again when there was a tickling round my head and I became aware that some field-mice had as usual discovered my oat-stuffed pillow. The oat-sack makes such a very comfortable cushion that I decided not to mind them. I was going to sleep when a sound of crunching and splashing made me turn over, and sitting up I saw the dim outline of a deer coming down to water in the starry lake. He turned and his antlers spread wide as arms against the pale water. At last, with the furry tickle of field-mice against my face, I slept.

I woke to cloud and sunshine and white horses on the lake. The pack-rat had had most of my bread, but I ate the remains and we started off. The trail led on to the end of the lake, then past two more, and into a faerie forest of little cottonwood trees. At last we came out on to the shores of the Ghost River, and there were the foot-hills before us and the mountains behind—the mountains suddenly and irretrievably behind.

We crossed the river and set out over the rolling green. The further we went from the mountains the more heart-breaking they looked, piling and folding away behind us, under the evening sun. After riding over the foot-hills for some hours, I came to a little shack, and, as I did not feel sure we were on the right road, I climbed down to it to ask the way. But all I found was a notice on the door saying:

     OUT TO LUNCH
     BACK SOON
     SIT DOWN AND WAIT
          (CHAIR)↘

But, knowing the latitude permitted by Western use of the word "soon," I decided to ignore the inviting presence of "chair," and ride on, as it was by this time drawing towards evening.

Some time later we came over a rise to see before us a beautiful little ranch, evidently the Bar C (called after its brand), and the one for which I was looking.

And now I sit in the Bar C's bunk-house, snatching half an hour to write the journal, while Timothy grazes in solitary splendour in a grass-grown corral.

All today we have been running horses. We had to round up a wild bunch and chase them into a corral, preparatory to running them off the ranch, back on to the Indian reserve from whence they came. For many hours we hunted them, but saw never a horse. We pushed through the scrub; we scrambled right down to the shores of the Ghost River, and up again into the bush; we climbed to the top of every rise and gazed over the range—no horses. Then from a cowboy on the edge of the bush came a low whistle. Quietly we joined him, and there they were, grazing below us in a grass-green hollow.

Then the chase began, and the herd were away like a streak. Crashing through bush—leaping over timber—bucketing down banks as steep as the roof of a house—up the other side full gallop—plunging through creeks up to their bellies—then on the open range swinging to break back, so that our horses spun on their hocks to intercept them—they led us a wilder chase than fox ever led the pack. But at last they were all in the corral, and, wiping the sweat from my face, I came in to write the journal.

The Bar C people want me to stay a week; I wish I could. But here we are, half-way through July, and I must hurry on to Calgary.

Chapter X

PRAIRIE WINDS

It is the end of July. Much has happened in the last weeks.

During the latter part of the trip through the mountains I was worrying over Timothy's legs. They filled at the base of the tendon, and I was afraid that he was going stiff. He has not a good front. He is straight in the shoulder and a shade top-heavy. So I took the advice of experts in Calgary, sold him and bought a little dark bay horse. This pony has a good front and is well sprung, with good bone and a short back. He is by a thoroughbred out of a range mare. He is lean and ewe-necked, not a beauty, but he has the Look. A horse either has it or he has not, and the pony has. So Timothy went to his new home, and I set out with the new horse into the prairies, the widest wheatlands of the world.

Into the north five hundred miles, into the east a thousand, another sowing of grain is rising under the chances and changes of another prairie summer. Beneath our feet lies soil rich enough to make an Eden blossom, and above us blazes the capricious prairie sky, blank and blue. What would not the prairies yield to the cloudy skies and the rain-laden winds that are England's!

Some two miles out of Calgary we left the highway and took a small farm road which ran east and west, perfectly straight, as far as the eye could see. At intervals of two miles it was crossed at right angles by roads running north and south. Apart from this, there was no incident whatever to mark our progress. At sunset I began to look over the unfamiliar country, wondering where I would present myself to ask for a night's lodging. In the mountains selection had not been difficult. When I did not reach a village by nightfall I was glad to knock at the door of any habitation which I was lucky enough to encounter. But now, any time I liked to stop and look round, there would be at least half a dozen farms in sight for me to choose from. Curiously enough, this, instead of making matters easier, seemed to complicate them in my mind. For, since there were so many farms available, I felt I had no particular excuse for thrusting myself upon any one of them. Finally, however, I chose a large and prosperous-looking house with extensive out buildings, deciding that here they could hardly fail to have room for us.

I knocked. After some time a middle-aged lady—grey hair, grey eyes, grey dress, and straight as a pine—lifted the latch and looked at us through the screen door. What did I want? she inquired. Diffidently I asked whether the pony and I might stay the night. She regarded us. "No," she said finally; "I have men in for the haying, I hardly think I can keep you for the night." I wilted. Had she any friends who might keep us? I wondered. She continued to hold me with her unwavering eyes. There was an emphatic silence. Finally she gave judgment.

"Yes," said the steel-grey lady, "I have a great many friends around here. But I don't think any of them would want to have *you*." I retreated with my pennant in the dust.

The next house upon the road was very small indeed. I felt more than ever ashamed to trouble its occupants. But dark was falling and the pony tired. I crept to the door and knocked faintly. Only then did I catch a look through the window, and there in the tiny living-room were at least a dozen people talking and laughing. Instantly I knew that there could not conceivably be room for me in such a sorely over-burdened little house. Hoping that my knock had not been heard, I turned tail and fled back to the pony. But I was discovered. A perfect avalanche of people came streaming after me.

"Come right in!" they cried. "Stay the night? Why sure! Lots of room." I could sleep with Mary and Jinna, they said. Plenty of oat-sheaves for the pony. Supper just starting. So they took us in.

The next night I underwent a surprisingly similar experience. Again, as evening came on, I chose a farm which looked large enough to accommodate us without inconvenience, but the farmer's wife, evidently of foreign extraction, would have none of us. Disheartened, I trailed on over the sunset road. The next house on our way was smaller even than our last night's lodging. But the family would not hear of our going further, and, since this time there was literally not a square inch of room in the house, we decided that I would sleep with the pony, in the feed-alley behind his manger. So at bedtime they shook me down a bed of hay and I curled into my sleeping-bag close under the pony's head, with a row of young turkeys disposed in a feathery pattern along the rafters above. I was soon deeply asleep.

I do not know how long I had slept before I was hauled up again from layers of alfalfa-scented oblivion into horrified consciousness. I opened my eyes to see a square of pale light at the barn-door; powerful black forms were milling among the stalls; there was the sound of blows and squeals and thundering footfalls. For a moment I blinked stupidly, then, leaping over the back of the manger, I was in the fray. Five work-horses had forced a way into the barn and were engaged in a furious fight with my unlucky pony. Seizing a mercifully adjacent pitchfork, I beat and stormed at them until they retreated. Then I slid the heavy barn-door into place and lay down again under the pony's head, to an accompaniment of anxious snorts.

But I was not to sleep. Just as quietness was stealing over me, a crack of light appeared at the barn-door, and a black head insinuated itself, pushing. Seizing the pitchfork I went storming out again, slammed to the opening, and hung a chain across it. But to no purpose; soon a fresh crack appeared. I issued forth. There were the horses, working busily upon the door. I roared and laid about me. They trotted to a little distance and stood there, black and wilful in the moonlight. I gave up. Flinging wide the barn-door, I untied the pony's haltershank, and, holding the enemy at bay with brandishing and execrations, I led him through. Into what field he went I did not know or care; it looked endless, billowing away faint and faerie under the moon. But I closed up the gate, wiring it securely, hit the nearest work-horse, and retired thankfully to sleep.

"We *thought* we heard the horses in the night," remarked my family next morning. . . .

It was as I set out into the third prairie day that misery overcame me. My trouble was Timothy. The first day had been all right, but the further we travelled from Calgary the more passionately I longed for him. I remembered our camps together, his beautiful muscles and the lights on his red-gold coat, our long days and the many mountain trails he had carried me, never going lame. And the longer I thought the more it seemed to me that he *was* sound, and that I might be riding him then, riding him into Winnipeg, and at last riding him—perhaps—fit and fresh, into Montreal.

In vain I told myself that he was sold to a good home. In vain I tried to occupy my mind by admiring cloud-effects and puzzling over the intricacies of Social Credit. In vain I petted the new horse and pointed out to myself what good paces he had. On the morning of the fourth day I was in a bus, speeding back to Calgary. By the evening I had bought Timothy back again and was riding him out of the city.

The day I fetched Timothy is remarkable for the fact that I had no food whatever for twenty-four hours, and did not miss it. Time simply did not allow of eating, so I did not eat. Here is the schedule of the day:

6:30 A.M. Breakfast on farm.
7:15 to 9:00. Walk six miles to catch bus.
9:00 to 11:45. Bus-drive.

11:45. Rush to the Great West Saddlery and hastily buy pack-saddle before early closing.

12:10. Go to Timothy's stables and arrange to buy him back. Admire all the other horses in the stables and talk to the head groom till nearly 2 o'clock.

2:00 P.M. to 4:00 P.M. Pay visit to friends in Elbow Drive.

5:00. Have Timothy saddled and ready to start. Realize that if I go at once I can reach the little farm where the pony and I spent our first night out of Calgary.

10:00 P.M. Reach the farm and find every one in bed. Put Timothy in the barn, crawl to bed with Mary and Jinna, and am soon asleep.

7:00 A.M. Breakfast. . . .

Two days later I was back on the farm where I had left the pony. I loaded the pack on to one horse, myself on to the other, and the augmented cavalcade set forth. All seems to be going well. The horses are firm friends already, and the pack rides easily. I have called the pony Jonty, after Jonathan Langford, a whimsical and charming Irishman whom he somehow seems to me to resemble.

This flat farming country is poor company indeed, after the mountains and the foot-hill ranches. Grain and Summer fallow succeed one another in an endless repetitive pattern. The only incident in the landscape is provided by the grain elevators, which stand up beside the railway like long narrow boxes, and by the wooden farms, a few of which are surrounded by cottonwood trees, who look strained and unhappy and as though they had a hard time to grow. Wild life is provided by the gophers, rat-sized animals who sit up on end and whistle at one, then bolt down their holes. All this I observe through half-shut eyes, for the effect of a road which goes perfectly straight all day, combined with a temperature of over a hundred in the shade (though the temperature was more evident than the shade), is chastening to say the least of it. And now, to complete my discomfort, Timothy has requited my sentimental regard for him by giving me a very painful kick on the wrist.

On the second day of travelling with the two horses, I tried the experiment of driving him in front of me, so as not to need to hold the lead rope all the time. But it was then that I discovered what a pig-headed monster Timothy could be. From the very beginning he objected bitterly to being herded. His method of resistance was this: for a little while he would jog along ahead of us, meditating evil. Then he would bump down into the ditch and stop. Jonty, soon knowing his cue, would begin to caracole, and we would prance up behind our pack-horse, Jonty pitching and bouncing importantly, and I swinging the long end of the reins round and round in the manner—I hoped—of a cowboy, and whooping in a voice full of command and menace. If in exasperation I slapped the reins across his quarters, Timothy would leap ahead, registering surprise and injury, then bound into the opposite ditch, and if possible double back and begin to retrace his steps along the road. Then Jonty and I would have to gallop back until we outstripped him, when the same performance would begin again.

Finally I was reduced to riding ahead and allowing him to follow in his own manner, which was scarcely more satisfactory. For now he would graze peacefully by the wayside until we were nearly out of sight, and then come racing after us *ventre à terre*, with the pack flapping in all directions, sweat rolling off his shoulder, and his none too dependable legs pounding themselves to bolsters on the hard-packed road. Meanwhile the sun beat down upon us with merciless persistence, and he began to favour the near fore.

It was thus in considerable depression of spirits that I arrived at a small stone-fronted house, reputed to be the last for fifteen miles. But when things grow most discouraging, I find it is just the time to look out for a bounce upward, and from the moment of our installation at the Scottie Frasers', the Prairie Provinces began to be fun. For at the Frasers' we came back quite unexpectedly into a country of ranches. And instead of grain and summer fallow and more grain, furrows and fences and endless cultivation, there lay all around the house the virgin range—rolling in untold miles to the sky-line, speckled with horses and shining stock, wild and untamed and old as the world.

The house was full. But they made room, laughed and talked and were delighted to see me. I forgot the pain in my wrist and settled down to enjoy the week end.

On Sunday morning a cowboy took me riding over the ranch; and, as we cantered over the grass, with its infinite range of colour—brown and purple, red and silver, a hundred yellows and a hundred greens—it seemed to me no longer strange that a cowboy could go to the loveliest parts of the world and yet be homesick for the prairies. About noon we came to a small shack, and going in found a family of swallows learning to fly. I climbed up, with a table and chair, to put my hand in the nest; and when I came down the cowboy pushed back his hat and proposed. I laughed and he kissed me, so I boxed his ears and went and jumped on my horse, and the cowboy on to his; so we raced away together till we came to a bunch of brood mares. There we stopped, and the boy said if I'd marry him he'd give me all the thoroughbreds I could ride. As I looked at the mares with their dancing foals, I pictured the little ranch-house, the endless range, branding and breaking and running stock, sun and wind and snow, cowboys, horses, cattle, hard winters, burning summers—and it seemed to me that, of many good lives, this would be one of the best. But I did not say this to the cowboy; instead I reminded him that we were late for dinner, so we cantered home.

The next days seemed to take themselves out of my hands. I firmly meant to leave on Monday morning, but before this the Frasers put up a bar for me to jump one of their horses. He was a big buckskin and he could jump like a stag; but first, just to assert his range-bred independence, he reared and fell backwards. This little episode being closed, and the bar successfully negotiated, I was putting him in the barn when I met Scottie Fraser starting out to ride round the stock. Temptation was too great. Saying to myself that I would start later and make fifteen miles in the cool of the evening, I hauled out the buckskin and away we went. As lunch-time came on, our backs were still toward home. We went on from one bunch of stock to another, talking and talking and sharing our passion for horses.

When we reached the boundary of the ranch, Scottie said, "If we go another hour's ride I can show you a bunch of thirty pintos; our neighbours raise them." So on we went and came at last to a pretty ranch-house. Walking across the yard was a dark-haired boy, who took us up to the house, where a lady with a delicate, beautiful face met us and brought us in. We had dinner and afterwards rode out over the range to where the pintos were grazing, their round, spotted bodies shining in the sun. It seems that the principal difficulty in raising pintos is to breed enough quality into them without getting too many reversions to the straight colours.

I rode the stud, who is a well-built creature and beautifully coloured. His white body is covered with a perfect map of continents and islands, executed in the palest red-gold. We came curveting into the yard, and the Galarneaus (that is their name, French) watched us and told me that I might ride him for them in a local stampede which was to take place in two more days. So, knowing that I ought to go, I stayed.

The Galarneaus are absolutely perfect theatre. Transported, lock, stock and barrel, to Hollywood, they would go right over, without so much as a hair of their curly heads altered. Mr. Galarneau is handsome and hearty, in fine dramatic contrast to his quiet and exquisite wife. They have three sons—all tough as nails, graceful as ballet-dancers, and modestly aware that they look perfect in their ten-gallon hats. The eldest is champion calf-roper of all Canada.

The Galarneaus are exceptional, but all the cowboys I have met have this subtle dramatic instinct highly developed. By this I do not mean that they are theatrical; but I think the speed and rhythm needed in their work, the infinite distances which surround them, and the catastrophic violences of the climate, all combine to give their lives the lift, the swing, and the precarious poise of natural drama.

I rode the pinto at the stampede, and he threw me off and scratched the skin off my face—which was a pity, as the two of us must have been photographed about fifty times. The longer I watched the bronc-riding, the more it seemed to me that to ride a straight bucker could not be so fantastically difficult as the cowboys would have one imagine. For the whirling demons of the Calgary show seem to be in a class apart, and most of these local horses bucked decorously enough. Now Scottie Fraser has a good buck-jumper, and, after strenuous persuasion, I induced him to say that I might ride it. Having comforted the agitated family by writing a half-serious statement to the effect that I took sole responsibility for my own broken bones, and been encouraged by the sight of Mrs. Scottie running into the living-room to hide her face in the sofa cushions, I issued out to find Scottie and a "pick-up" man, duly mounted and holding a pretty little grey horse. After two quite good rounds of bucking, the little horse put me down, but I still maintain that with one's legs well forward and one's backside pressed well into the cantle (and *quite* a little practice) it would be possible to sit any ordinary bronc till he tires.

Chapter XI

LANDS THAT WAIT FOR WATER

WE have left the Scottie Frasers and are on our way again at last. The prairie rolls away on either side; the road goes on and on; the sun beats down; flies bother the horses; and my wrist, after the varied activities of the last few days, hurts a good deal. But I am enjoying myself again, and we jog on cheerfully.

Every one in British Columbia assured me that once we were east of Calgary all our fun would be over. But I am so happy in this ranching country that I believe I could ride forever through the changing August days. First burning heat with the brazen sun crashing down on the sage and cactus—then a day of cloud and showers with a brilliant stormy evening, the dream of a rainbow in the east, and great clouds piling up the sky, wind-tossed into a hundred arches. The next day heat again, then, with the theatrical suddenness of the prairies, a chill wind, dead black sky in the north, an eagle shrieking "Storm!" a rush for shelter, and last a deluge of rain fit to beat you into the ground.

When people were not telling me how dull I should be, they told me I should be lonely. But how can one be lonely with new friendships every day and memories of fleeting contacts to go with one all the way?

There was the plump, happy girl with a beautiful baby who gave me lunch and said: "Ooh, I should hate to make a trip like yours. Goodness, I'd be just miserable if they told me I had to!" Then we both laughed and laughed, and she lay down on the floor and put the baby boy astride her neck, and lovely they

LANDS THAT WAIT FOR WATER

both looked. There was the widow, managing single-handed two farms and seven children, who gave up her bed to me and would not take a cent, saying, as we parted, "This will be something the children will remember all their lives." Or the little lady from Basingstoke, England, who kept us on over Sunday, helped me wash my clothes and mend my saddlebags (Timothy had kicked them to pieces at the same time as he had hurt my wrist) fed me quarts of milk and piles of butter because she said I was not fat enough, and finally sent me away with a parcel of cookies and a big kiss. And last, but not least, there was the fair-haired Swede who rode with us all one morning, and at the end, turning to go home, looked at me with sky-blue eyes and said, "Come back and marry me, girl."

Just now I am particularly dependent upon the kindness of those whom I meet, for my wrist is not much use. So the men groom the horses for me, saddle and pack them and boost me into my seat, while the women wash my clothes and cut up my meat at meal times. Cowboys will ride for miles to open wire gates; nothing is too much trouble.

The horses and I are winding our way along the north shore of the Red Deer River. This strange country by the water is the most primeval I have ever seen. The barren hills, flat-topped and alluvial, the wide valley and, trickling through it, the small river, successor to an infinitely greater one—all set the mind wandering back and back into remotest ages, till at last one almost expects to see a dinosaur come stalking down the hills.

• • • • • • •

Now we have left the Red Deer, and I sit down to write this on the banks of the South Saskatchewan River, in a long, low house built of logs, with an earth roof on which grass grows, and through which the rain never penetrates.

The night before last we spent in Empress, the first town we have struck since leaving Calgary. Almost the first thing the inhabitants asked me when they heard that we had come down the Red Deer Valley, was, "Did you see the dinosaur beds?" And I found that it is famous for the discovery of great fossilized bones. So my vision of the monsters was not so far wrong; their big spirits must haunt the river still.

At Empress I went to the hospital about my wrist, and they believe there is a bone broken. So now it is all done up in a splint—fearfully awkward but much less painful. Now we are winding east along the north shore of this curly river, still through ranching country, among antelope and white-faced stock and beautiful, half-wild horses.

Through these long prairie days the mind gets filled with words; they pound in rhythm to the horses' feet, coming and going, beating in the background of all other thoughts. Last week they were from Isaiah—"How art thou fallen from heaven, oh Lucifer, Son of the morning!" The sombre words were everywhere; they climbed up into the clouds; they sang in the wind; they burnt in the sunset: "How art thou fallen from heaven, oh Lucifer, Son of the morning!" Yesterday it was a poem of Oscar Wilde's, read in quotation long ago, in somebody else's book:

> Out of the mid-woods' twilight
> Into the meadows' dawn,
> Ivory-limbed and brown-eyed
> Flashes my faun.
>
> Oh hunter, snare me his shadow!
> Oh nightingale, catch me his strain!
> Else moon-struck with music and madness,
> I track him in vain.

But as the verses skipped and danced in the mind, I saw, not clever, unhappy Oscar Wilde, not the groves and goddesses of neo-mythology, but a grass-green clearing in a British Columbia forest and a tiny deer, more beautiful, more brown-eyed than

LANDS THAT WAIT FOR WATER

any pan-god, bounding for a moment into the sunshine, then back to the shadows again.

. . . .

This has been a bad day. We had to go three miles north, and this landed us back into farming country—grain and fallow and fences all the way. The heat is considerable; there is no stock to admire, nothing to break the monotony of the landscape but occasional elevators. Finally, the sun, after burning us up all day, has gone down slap! without a ghost of a setting. But it takes, as the platitudinous will tell you, all sorts to make a world, and equally, I suppose, every kind of day to make a ride across Canada.

. . . .

Weeks have passed since I last sat down to write the journal. It seems very long ago now that we left the ranches. There has been no rain here since June, and only little then. We journey on over leaden miles of crops spoilt, of more and more good wheat burning to death in the brazen sun.

I knew, before I came, of the tragedy of Saskatchewan. Over in England we read of it in the papers; we said "How terrible," and, while our own rain swept over the emerald lawn, dripped off the eaves of the roof, beat upon the windows, we tried to imagine a land without water. I could only think of the Sahara, but the Sahara holds no tragedy. It is a bitter desert, but it has been so always. A thousand generations of Arabs have learnt to wrest life from its ungentle wastes. But the bad land of Saskatchewan is a garden dead. It is happiness and home and plenty torn from the lives of men who believed it was theirs forever. In the dead lands high barns stand empty; stalls wait in vain for the proud teams that once they knew; and no cows come in for the milking. Sand piles up at the windows of frame houses and sifts in the draft over the floors of living-rooms once rosy with fire-light and loud with laughing children.

Here in the middle of the province people are still living on the farms, still living if this can be called life—when year after year the fresh young ears wither on the stalk, when curtains and pillow-cases and shirts and skirts must be made of flour sacks, when water must be measured and carried in carts, sometimes from a mile away, when only the barren pittance of relief stands between the family and starvation. I know now what mystics mean when they say that the spirit of man is eternal. When I have stopped night after night with such families and never found bitterness, never despair, only cheerfulness and generosity, I have seen the God in man.

It is no dramatized figure of speech to say that these people of the prairies would give one the shirt off their backs; it is a simple statement of fact. For it seems that the less a man has, the readier he is to share it. The law of hospitality is unbroken. I seldom even ask now what I owe for my lodging, for I know that I shall be answered with an almost indignant "Nothing." All I can do in a few of the homes is to slip a surreptitious dollar or two into the hands of the children at parting and watch their eyes grow round as moons, incredulous at the possession of such wealth.

Burning bright and changeless, the days roll on and on. More and more and more farmlands. Fragments of Shelley, "in depression" as he would say, murmur through the mind:

> Far far away oh ye
> Halcyons of memory!
> Seek some far calmer rest
> Than this abandoned breast;
> Once having gone, in vain
> Ye come again.
>
> . . . The desire of the moth for the star,
> Of the night for the morrow,
> Of the spirit for something afar
> From the sphere of our sorrow.
>
> Oh lift me like a wave, a leaf, a cloud;
> I fall upon the thorns of life, I bleed. . . .

LANDS THAT WAIT FOR WATER

Not that the horses and I are falling upon the thorns of life in the least; there can be no greater kindness anywhere in the world than here in the prairies. But the gloomier effusions of Percy Bysshe seem somehow appropriate to the staggering heat and the quite remarkable lack of incident in the landscape.

Tonight I am particularly far removed from the thorns of life, for I have been able for the first time in many weeks to have a bath. The family with whom I am staying make use of a simple invention by which the maximum of washing can be achieved with the minimum of water. In a small outhouse a high shelf has been erected. On this shelf stands a pail with a hose-pipe affixed to it at the base. At the available end of the pipe is a sprinkler. Having made ready, one opens the sprinkler and waters oneself deliciously with the contents of the bucket. Never before have I made so wholly satisfactory a use of a pailful of water.

As we go on over the burning chess-board of the farmlands, my mind turns lingering back to the days by the Red Deer River; and I know that I cared not half enough for its liquid curves, for the willows and kindly cottonwood trees along its banks, and the herds of horses that went galloping down the valley with their manes and tails flying in the wind.

I remember now especially, as I think back, the quality of one night when we were lost. At sunset we climbed up onto the prairie to cut off a curve of the river; dark fell and we lost the line of the water. We wandered on and on; the night grew blacker and light rain began to fall. I knew there was one ranch somewhere on the banks of the river, but if we missed this, I was faced with the alternatives of goading the tired horses over another fifteen miles, on the chance of striking the town of Empress (in the middle of the night, and with every one asleep), or spending the night on the naked prairie, with rain setting in, nothing to eat and nowhere to tie the horses. As is often the way with naturally dependent people suddenly in difficulty, I began to pray—and almost immediately we came over a little rise to see black trees and water, pale in the dark. The river it was, so I hit the lost trail and turned thankfully eastward again, and before we had been going ten minutes we came upon the ranch-house.

It is fashionable, in the vaguely intellectual set with whom I naturally click, not to believe in God; but I certainly have begun to believe in Him since we have been on this journey.

So we made port after all—lights and a welcome and the son of the house taking the horses. A few minutes later I went down to see them and presently stood in the doorway of a massive barn, braced and pillared with half-hewn forest trees. A lantern hung from the roof, and there they stood, the red horse and the brown, with the kind light curving over their rounded backs and throwing shadows under their bellies dark as the night we had left. It hit me such a crack that I said, "Look!" "What at?" asked the girl who had brought me down, and I felt a fool.

The next day they lent me a wild white pony, watching I knew to see whether I could handle him, and we rode up the river and ran in some horses. A lovely day of clouds and wind, and my little mount bounding under me like a steed for the Valkyries. And I was as happy as the day, and so was the little horse. A morning to remember now, as we plod through the unending wheat fields.

Yesterday we came through a plague of grasshoppers. There are grasshoppers everywhere on the prairies, but here the whole landscape, the whole day, the whole world was grasshoppers. They crackled under the horses' feet; they crashed into our faces; they whirred up like deformed butterflies in the wind of our passing, to fall back again and lie folded by the roadside. The wheat fields were a desolation. On every head of grain hung a dull green, shifting mass. We passed a farmer, and the horror was in my voice when I spoke to him. But there was no horror in his reply, no bitterness or surprise or anger. There was nothing. Nothing in his voice, in his eyes, in his heart. Nothing but this numberless, grey-green enemy.

"Yes," he said, "grasshoppers."

Another week has passed, and today is clothed in wonder. Sitting here in the grass I am only half aware of wheat and barns, of cottonwoods and elevators. For last night at dusk we were walking along, kicking up the dust on the road between the farms, when I saw, half a mile to the south, standing on a little rise, a barn so large that I could hardly believe that it *was* just a barn; and, feeling curious, I left the road and began to climb up to it over the curving breast of a golden field, in the western end of which a fine stand of wheat billowed under the wind, while the eastern half was already cut and stooked.

Soon we were standing in a large barn-yard, among a crowd of sunburnt men, evidently the thrashing gang, who took the horses without comment and led them into the great building. I followed and was soon standing beside Timothy, rubbing his legs and looking out upon stall after stall, in each of which a huge workhorse, some seventeen hundred pounds of bone and muscle, stood stamping and nickering for oats. Behind them the great length of the barn was spotted black and white with a row of shining Holsteins, and mingling with the swish of hay came the rhythmic chuckle of milk streaming into half-full pails.

When I went into the house it was to find a long table set in the kitchen and six women, their round smooth faces glowing in the lamplight, still loading it with food. I do not think I have seen anywhere greater abundance. Steaming piles of pork, bowls full of brown and white eggs, mounds of snowy potatoes, turnips, carrots and parsnips, great blocks of butter, pitchers of cream, stewed fruit, raisin pie, plates full of fluffy new bread, and pots of steaming tea.

We sat down. Six women and sixteen men and I. I ate my supper in silence, looking at the bright-eyed women and the bearded men, and listening to their snatches of talk in English, German and some other language.

The gang finished their food and retired into the shadows to sleep and smoke and pick their teeth; then at last I began to discover the family. They were Hungarians. There were five daughters and four sons, with the quiet dignified mother, and the father, who was thin and neat as an ash plant, with a small beard and the lean lined face of that rare creation, a practical dreamer.

When the girls and I had washed the dishes, the family all sat down around the table and began to talk. I asked them how in this land of struggle they had been able to raise the great fortress of a barn and fill it with pedigree stock and horses to make the heart yearn.

"We did well in the good years," said the father simply, "and built and put away and thought ahead; so in the dry years we got by, and now things are a little better, and once more we begin to prosper." He passed on lightly, leaving me to imagine, unaided, all the genius and steadfast striving which lay behind this achievement.

Then the sons leant their elbows on the table and began to talk. It was strange as a dream, after seeing so much of loss and struggle, to be suddenly engulfed in such a flood of vitality and power and the joy of life. They were students of Communism, these boys. Not long-haired, long-fingered theorists, not tin-pan-alley agitators, but men with the earth on their hands and the sun and storm in their sinews, who, here on the prairie, remote from cities, remote from universities, had made contact with Karl Marx, had bridged the years which divided him from Stalin, and now watched in burning expectancy the bold brutal experiment which is Russia.

I watched them with the sun in their cheeks glowing and the stars shining out of their eyes. What, I asked, did they think of Russia's making a pact with Nazi Germany?

"That will hold them," I thought. But they held me.

"We do not understand this pact," they said. "To us where we stand, at this moment in time, it seems wrong. But it is in

LANDS THAT WAIT FOR WATER

the end a transitory thing, and in time to come we shall see it from other angles; and who shall say, in the years after, whether it was wrong? But this new order in Russia is not transitory; it is time itself, time present and time to come; it is life moving on, as a storm moves over the plains, as the sea comes up on the drag of the moon. It is life, yours and ours and the life of our children."

They did not say it in these words. They said it partly in English and partly in German; they said it with their hands, with their eyes, with the muscles that rippled under the sun-drenched skin of their forearms. They said it with their vitality and success.

I went to bed at last, to lie vividly awake all night, to ride out this morning along the dusty road, awe-struck before the mystery of man, and to feel slipping once more from under my hand the hem of the garment of miracle.

. . . .

There is one thing this trip is giving me anyway—a varied and instructive experience in bed-sharing.

Bed-sharers fall into three main groups. There are, of course, the rare and angelic few who curl up on their side of the bed and lie quiet till the morning. These are a gift from heaven and need no further description.

Class two are infinitely more numerous, as numerous, in fact as the mysterous religious sect known as Holy Rollers, and I think this lot might fairly be described as the Unholy Rollers. Their technique is to turn over and over with a resounding crash and an invariable tendency toward the middle of the bed; considerable play is often made with the arms. One girl, with whom I shared a bed for several nights, slept with her arms above her head and generally hit me in the face several times before the morning. The knees are of equal strategic importance. One method of attack now open to class two is to turn over with a sudden surprise movement and lie on my wrist. These tactics have been used several times lately with unconscious but devastating effect.

Class three may be described as the Pushers. Their method is less dramatic but even more successful. The art lies in setting the back against the victim and exerting an even and relentless push. Results are not manifest at first, but the victim invariably wakes to find herself balanced on the extreme edge of the bed. By holding everything and giving a gigantic heave, it is possible to force the Pusher back to the middle of the bed (class three never wakes), but this is a temporary expedient at best. An alternative method of reprisal, which I have never been wide awake enough to try, would be to climb out of one's own side and in again on the side vacated by the Pusher. It would be reasonable to hope that she might keep on pushing over till she finally fell out on to the floor. I cannot help fearing, though, that, when resistance was removed, she would begin to suspect and would range about until she discovered one's new position, and then reverse her tactics.

It is sometimes said that people reflect their waking character in sleep, but this is not my experience. One of the unholiest Rollers I ever met was a quiet, dignified girl, who sat still, walked slowly, and never made an unnecessary movement; and the most muscular and relentless Pusher was a little girl of twelve, half my size, and so charming and considerate that she would undoubtedly have given up her bed and slept on the floor had occasion demanded.

There is one thing, however, which my bed-sharing experience has never taught me; that is to which of these classes I myself belong; since when my bedfellow and I get up in the morning, we are in honour bound to state that we slept perfectly and were unaware of each other's existence. So the Pushers know nothing of their pushing, and the Rollers of their unholiness; and I too remain blissfully unaware of my sleeping egocentricities.

On the days when the weather is a little cooler, and one can open one's eyes wide enough to see them, the colours in this

LANDS THAT WAIT FOR WATER

farming country are lovely. Broad fields of ripe wheat, dark ploughed land and reaped fields flecked with shining stooks; fall wheat blue-green, and, on the waste-land by the trail, silver sage and yellow goldenrod. Then over all in a gigantic arch the sky, mostly interminable blue, but sometimes tufted white, and on the best days cool and alive with wild windy clouds.

Another good feature of the prairies, quite as pleasant if somewhat less artistic, is the fact that we always get somewhere for lunch.

Once we stopped at a house belonging to a middle-aged woman, her daughter and mother. The mother was exceptionally old, and, as her antiquity was an evident source of pride to the whole family, I asked about her age.

"A hundred and three," said the wicked old lady without batting an eyelid.

"Oh, Mother!" said her daughter reproachfully. "Ninety-three," she corrected, "but isn't she wonderful?" She certainly was in a remarkable state of preservation.

Yesterday I had lunch with three bachelors. The most talkative came from Devizes, our local market town in England! He had that typical Wiltshire roundness, not fat but just no angles anywhere, and still retained, after twenty-two years in Canada, a pleasant suggestion of soft Wiltshire speech.

This business of batching is quite an institution in the Canadian West. Men live by themselves or in twos and threes, doing all their own housework, and making a good job of it on the whole. There are exceptions, of course. One man with whom I had dinner had his dirty dishes for what must have been a week piled all over the shack, on chairs, on the table and in corners of the floor. It took me over an hour to get him straightened out.

Bad cess to Hitler! News of the Danzig affair is appalling. How I wish I had been out here forty years ago, when Canada still belonged to the Wild, and Europe left one alone to keep one's mind on the job.

Chapter XII

WAR

August 23rd

IT seems as though this time the catastrophe must come. But so many times the people of Europe have shut their eyes and waited for the blow that even suspense has not the poignancy it had at first. People become accustomed, even to crises.

Against the fantastic drama of world-events, the ride goes on mechanically. It has no longer any reality or significance but provides a way of existing, no better and no worse than any other way, while the sun is turned into darkness and the moon into blood.

August 24th

God help the peoples of the world to bear their impotence.

August 27th

So it is war! To the very last I hoped, but the last has come and gone.

Before me lies Echo Lake, and behind the hills, in a glory of red-gold, silver and green, the sun goes down. And as I sit here, German bombers go roaring toward Warsaw. So the ultimate calamity has come. Never again, as in the past five years, shall I wake in the night sweating with horror, from a dream that war is upon us. For war is here, not a nightmare, but a reality.

I shall go on. The best thing any can do who are not directly needed is to go through quietly with what they have undertaken. I am waiting for a cable from the family, but I believe this is what they will say.

WAR

September 3rd

At four o'clock this morning we heard that England had declared war on Germany, and now that France has done likewise.

Just now it seems to me that the thing of most value for us to do is to keep a civilized mind and hold fast our faith in man, whatever men may do.

At present we are aware that the inhabitants of the countries involved are only indirectly to blame for the catastrophe, and that they bear no personal responsibility for the sufferings which they will be the instruments of inflicting. Our job is to remember this.

Yesterday the cable came, telling me to go on. So we will go ahead and make Montreal. And after—? Never mind; first make Montreal; and then, whatever comes, I shall have done one thing, for which I thank God.

Today we are curving along the Qu'Appelle Valley beside Katapwa Lake. Low hills run down to the water, and the little trees are bright already with autumn. Wind in our faces, waves on the lake and great clouds racing away to the west like Valkyries to battle. An urgent, vital day. A day that says: "Live while you can, and die when you must; take all that comes and give everything you've got; only don't fear, don't waste; be alive while you can."

We have left the lake and go on along the valley. Today it is sunshine and stillness, white clouds and the trees on the hills bright gold.

Last night I stayed with some people who are moving west to Abbotsford—Abbotsford, where Timothy and I spent the second night of our trip, thirty miles out from Vancouver, with everything before us. How many wonderful miles we have travelled since then! I shall be thankful till I die for the beauty I have seen and the men and women and horses I have known. All day I have been remembering.

But as I look back and back into the West, my heart longs most of all—not for the lush beauty of the coast, not for titanic forests with rough trails winding up and up among the trees, not for shouting creeks and summer snows and little black bears, not for jumping deer and chipmunks, not even for the snow-clad mountains, which for two months wove their changing pattern into the background of my nights and days; all these things I shall remember and long for, but most of all I long for the range. The barren burnt-up windy range, bare and brown and rock-strewn, but untamed, unbroken, free as the wind, with a spirit I can never hope to describe.

One day, when I was still in Kamloops, something happened. It was a small thing and its exact nature is not important, but it had power to take the beauty out of the day and make me look at the river with eyes that did not see. That morning I went out with three people, three eager, unusual, charming people, and rode over the range. We raced and stood still; we talked and were silent; we rode and laughed, and loved the range. At last we climbed to its windy roof and looked out over the valley, to where the smooth North River came winding out of the hills. Then beauty came back to the day, and the small unhappy memory no longer had power to hurt.

And so, as I ride through the middle of Canada and remember the West, I long not for the forests and mountains, not for the eternal snows, but for the range—the burning range, the desolate range, that I may never see again.

The day ended perfectly in a lovely stretch of valley, with blue shadows on the hills, dark ploughed fields and pale stubble in the flats, and the little trees by the river green and gold and light yellow in the setting sun. I must remember this evening. I must remember all these days, later.

Tonight we are staying in a large Catholic Indian school, at the head of Crooked Lake. I think the father in charge was a little shocked at first at seeing a girl in aged slacks, with wildly untidy hair and two horses. But he was very kind and appears to like me better now.

It is a pleasant school, and the young Indians seem happy. But there are innumerable regulations against things, and I feel sure that one is a regulation against girls in slacks.

There is a big gap in the journal. Now that Europe is at war, now that hope and fear are dead, because the worst has come, I must try to go back and describe the small everyday things the horses and I were doing while all these things were happening.

On August the twenty-seventh we reached a farm north of Regina. Here I left the horses and went down by bus into the city, where I was entertained with the greatest kindness by Mr. and Mrs. Allan. Mrs. Allan is president of the Regina Riding Club, and before I had been with them half an hour, she and her husband had decided to go with me on the ride as far as Fort Qu'Appelle, about fifty miles east of the city.

The best thing I saw in Regina was the Mounted Police Barracks; good nineteenth century buildings, a magnificent gymnasium and riding school, amid pleasant watered trees, the whole greatly embellished by the presence of the Mounted Police themselves, who walk about in a stately manner, wearing scarlet tunics and dark blue breeches with a yellow stripe down the side, and looking handsome.

This paragraph was all that went into the journal, but since then I have heard and read a little of the history of this remarkable Force.

In 1883, Lieutenant W. F. Butler, sent out to report upon conditions in the newly acquired Prairie Provinces, returned with a serious story of lawlessness and disorder. As a result of his representations, some hundred and sixty officers and men were hastily recruited and sent west over the old Dawson Trail to Fort Garry, where they trained throughout the winter and in the following spring set out for the West. Thus were assembled the pioneer Force of the North-West Mounted Police. They travelled on horse-back, carrying their equipment in ox-drawn wagons; and, as I rode over the country, now pleasantly dotted with farms and ranches, I could imagine the troubles of their journey, through sun and storm, with little water and no shade, over the interminable expanse of those naked plains. It was a party of gaunt horses and weary men who finally made camp in the Sweet Grass Hills of southern Alberta, while another detachment laboured northward to Edmonton, where Fort Saskatchewan was founded.

Their first task upon arrival in the West was to suppress the liquor traffic, establish friendly relations with the Indians, and at the same time enforce the laws of "the Great White Queen" among the Indian lodges, where outside discipline had never been known. The small band of newly arrived police stood in a position of difficulty and isolation. On the one side stood the liquor traders, on the other the Indians, cautious, observant, knowing little but ill of the white man. But these were men of a new kind. Their clean-cut honesty, their fearlessness, their superb horsemanship, not unsupported by the effect of their dazzling uniforms, deeply impressed the dark children of the plains. Through delicate statesmanship, tempered by firmness, Indian co-operation was gradually secured. Tribes were protected from the debauching influence of the liquor traders and the chiefs were treated with courtesy and could count upon the help of the Mounted Police. But when a prisoner was to be arrested, the scarlet riders would "sweep into the camp like a prairie fire," seize their man and gallop away in a whirl of dust before any resistance could be offered.

It was well indeed that the Force was so successful in securing the trust of these tribes of the West, for when, in 1882, the Canadian Pacific set out from Winnipeg to drive the track to the mountains, the police had to help them in dealing not only with their hard-bitten and dissatisfied labour gangs, but also with the despairing Indians, who knew, as they watched the steel ribbon driving into the West, that the mountains and the plains would never be theirs again. Yet it was not they, but the shifty-eyed half-breeds, who started in 1885 the running fire of the North-West Rebellion.

Scarcely had the police done their part in its quelling when they were called upon to deal with a new situation—the vivid, violent drama of the gold-rush into the Yukon. From every station in life the actors came—strong men, weak men, old men, young men, and women, good and bad, dragging their children with them. Recklessly they all plunged into the mountains, seeking this new El Dorado. The police had indeed a task on their hands. Not only had they to deal with the gambling, cursing prospectors of Dawson City, with the hard-drinking, hard-shooting crooks who came to rob them by force, and with the wild women who came to rob them by guile; but, harder still, they had somehow to organize and protect this rabble of pilgrims who rushed, every day more of them and more, into the uncharted mountains. Through Dyea and Skagway they came, came night and day, and flung themselves at the snow-clad range which separated them from the Yukon. In the winter of 1898, amid storm and blizzard, Mounted Police posts were established at the heads of the Chilcoot and White Passes, while down below, on the shores of Lake Bennet, a handful of officers and men were fearlessly maintaining order among the ten thousand lawless souls who were camped there to wait for the spring.

All winter the police were occupied in arranging for the orderly passage of the gold-hunters' boats through the lake and down the river, but such was the frenzy of haste when finally the ice went out, and the voyagers charged the first rapids they encountered with such reckless abandon, that the leading boats were wrecked, and those behind piled on top of them. So when the police arrived, it was to find over a thousand craft tangled up in a bewildering jam, from which they rescued, at the risk of their lives, hundreds of men, women and children. Meanwhile Inspector Constantine and his men, awaiting the travellers in

Dawson City, had kept such a firm hand on its saloons and bars that it had earned the distinction of being the best-governed gold-boom town on record.

With the sudden leap to importance of the Yukon, and with the growth of the settlements around Hudson's Bay, the establishment of far northern patrols became necessary. In 1890 Inspector Begin made a patrol to York Factory, and in 1897 Inspector Jarvis led a winter patrol from Fort Saskatchewan to Fort Resolution on Great Slave Lake, thus "carrying the Force in one great stride half-way to the Polar Sea."

Later in the same year Inspector Moodie, in search of an all-Canadian route to the Yukon, set out to lead his epic patrol from Edmonton to Fort Selkirk. Taking with him four constables, two Indians and a small pack-train, he set out from Edmonton on September fourth and plunged into the northern wilderness. Early in the next year it was heard that, after surmounting innumerable difficulties, he had passed through the furthest outpost of civilization and disappeared into the mountains, hoping to find his way through the maze of ranges to the head waters of the Pelly River, on the banks of which Fort Selkirk stood. Spring went by, summer and autumn, and there was no word of Moodie's patrol. Men spoke hopefully, but in their minds they saw the tiny patrol, wandering among the winter mountains, and their hearts misgave them. And then, when hope was almost dead, came the news that Moodie was through. After incredible hardships he had made it. R. C. Fetherstonhaugh in his fine book *Royal Canadian Mounted Police*, gives a dramatic description of the last weeks of the trip:

"On October 1, 1898, thirteen months after leaving Edmonton, the patrol fought its way to the headwaters of the Yukon and, turning over its tired pack-horses to the Indian owner, started down stream in a canvas canoe. Rapids and floating ice wrecked this craft, but in another canoe, bought from a chance-met prospector for $450, and on rafts, for the canoe would not hold them all, the journey was continued. Haste was essential, as supplies were running low, but no fast progress could be made. Time and time again the canoe was punctured by rocks or ice and had to be carefully repaired; hours without end were lost in portaging the canoe and rafts over ice-coated rocks; the men, ice-coated themselves, could at times move only with difficulty; the food was so scarce that starvation weakened them alarmingly. Then, when they were still many miles from Selkirk, the rivers froze up, and the only chance of winning through to safety lay in a perilous overland dash on foot.

Realizing that the dash was hazardous but that no alternative could be found, Moodie ordered the party to cache the canoe and rafts, and to set out on the overland trail without delay. Too experienced in northern travel to panic with the goal in sight, the party avoided the fatal mistake of attempting excessive speed and plodded manfully through the deep snow and biting cold, meanwhile husbanding their strength and the last crumbs of their food supply. They were uncertain of their course and often it seemed that the two days and nights of staggering painfully onward would end only in some deep drift of snow, but their courage met a more fitting reward, and on October 24 they stumbled dazedly into Fort Selkirk."

By 1908, thanks to such heroic patrols as Moodie's, the Force was firmly established in the Mackenzie River District and upon the western shores of Hudson's Bay; and many adventurous patrols made in the early years of the century will go down in the imperishable records of the North-West Mounted Police. But there are records of tragedy as well as of success. Foremost among these is the story of FitzGerald's patrol, who, losing their way in the mountains between McPherson and Dawson, turned at last to go back, but not till their supplies were nearly exhausted. All four men starved to death only thirty miles from their goal.

But the North-West Territories were not the only lands in which the duties of the police were varied and adventurous. Their activities were far from being limited to the maintenance of law and order. If records of all their achievements could have been kept, there might be a longer list of those whose lives the police have saved than of those whom they have brought to justice. The epic struggle of Constable Holmes, who single-handed brought under control a smallpox epidemic among the Indians here in the Qu'Appelle Valley, might well be remembered among the greatest single achievements of the Force. A similar situation was effectively dealt with by Corporal Smith, when scarlet fever and diphtheria broke out among the Indians around Norway House. There are many records of police who rescued Indians from prairie fires, galloping fearlessly into the flames. Perhaps the most appalling of the humanitarian duties which the men were called upon to perform was the rescue of trappers and prospectors who went violently mad in the unbearable loneliness of the mountains.

These nightmare patrols into the forest wilds seem more like fiction than reality. First the journey in—often in winter, by dog team—with the haunting knowledge of what one was to find; then the madman secured—no easy task—and the journey back begun. Sometimes those journeys were over a thousand miles of mountain trail, through all the difficulties and dangers of the winter; and for company the traveller had a maniac, endowed with all a maniac's superhuman power, raving, screaming, tearing at his bonds day and night. No wonder that on one occasion the policeman himself went mad as a result of his ordeal.

While members of the Force worked at their varied tasks in the plains and forests, the early twentieth century sped on towards the first great war. It was not until after the war that the mounted police succumbed to the necessity of using mechanized equipment.

In 1920 their duties were extended to include work in the eastern provinces, and, under the new name Royal Canadian Mounted Police, they took up their headquarters in Ottawa. But in the lonely wastes of the Arctic, their work remains to this day almost unchanged. Still the police drive their dog teams through the frozen forests and up into the naked North. Still

WAR

they labour up rivers and across white lakes. Still they ride out blizzards and fight the famished wolves in the winter mountains. Among their many brilliant and daring comrades they can count one Arctic explorer of real genius. This is Inspector Joy, who died only a few years ago. He it was who was chosen to establish a post on Ellesmere Island, only eight hundred miles from the pole. He seized every opportunity to explore and note down with meticulous accuracy his geographical and archaeological observations. Canada's knowledge of the Arctic is enlarged by his discoveries, and her museums are enriched by his collection of Esquimau remains.

So the Force goes on today, in the old traditions and the new, the Force which since its birth in 1873 the finest men in Canada have been proud to serve, the Force which, in the words of R. C. Fetherstonhaugh:

. . . is grappling in Canada with organized crime, with rum-running, drug-peddling, murder, arson, theft, robbery, counterfeiting and forgery; the Force who are still pushing to far objectives over the frozen routes of the lonely North, whose horsemen are still riding remote prairie and woodland trails, whose canoemen are still travelling distant rivers and streams, whose marine patrols furrow the waters of three oceans. . . .

No wonder we hear, all over the world, the fame of the Royal Canadian Mounted Police.

. . . .

After two days spent in Regina, I went back to where I had left the horses, accompanied by Mr. and Mrs. Allan; and in the morning we set out. The daughter of the family who had looked after the horses, started out with us on a twenty-three-year-old pony. So it was quite a cavalcade which, after much photographing and leave-taking, finally set forth toward Fort Qu'Appelle. When Evelyn's pony grew tired, she rode Timothy. The new horses settled down cheerfully to the road and the farms at which we stopped were in no way put out by our numbers.

I had been long ago invited to stay near Fort Qu'Appelle by a family called Cornish; but it was with some trepidation that we finally presented ourselves at their neat little home—not myself and two horses, but three people and myself and five horses! The Cornishes however, like the good Canadians they were, were not in the least embarrassed by the situation. After Mr. and Mrs. Allan had fed their horses, they went on into Fort Qu'Appelle; while Evelyn and I went into the house and were soon sitting down to a hearty supper, amid the exultations of young Edith Cornish, who was so much delighted to see us that it warmed one like a fire on a wet day. Edith was one of the plumpest, kindest, smiliest people I have ever met; and her ample everyday presence was like a sheet anchor in the days which followed. So I was in the little house by Echo Lake when Europe went to war.

Well, Evelyn went back to her young man, the Allans went back to Regina, and I left the little Fort and went on down the valley alone.

So I reached Crooked Lake and the Catholic Indian School; and the next day, going on, I reached another lake and another Indian school. Here I have been for two days now. The principal and his wife have been delightful to me. I should not have stayed so long, but it is such a happy home, and I have felt ill for some time, and finally today, *am* ill.

Yesterday I went to visit an Indian family, and they invited me to stay the night. They have three little boys at the school and a son and daughter at home; their house is a good two-roomed shack. The living-room is sparely furnished and clean, with a carved oak cupboard, English early Victorian, and one of the few bits of furniture with even a pretence of antiquity which I have seen since I have been in the West. Only Mr. Bear talked much to me. He had been to England in the last war and stated with bland conviction that in the part he had visited the people all lived in castles, and the trees were full of wild monkeys.

The Bears are full-blooded Crees. It was strange and new to watch the four faces, with their dark impassivity, broken only by a rare white smile, and to think that, for all we know, their Indian ancestry goes back pure and direct into ages more remote than any the ancientest of ancient Britons ever knew.

When bedtime came, the women and I went into the bedroom. I supposed that we should shut the door and undress. But the door remained open and the men walked about the living-room, smoking and looking about them without any particular restriction. I fiddled. Suddenly I became aware that the women were all in bed. Upon closer inspection I discovered that they had taken off nothing but their shoes!

. . . .

I have been ill for some time now and am still at Round Lake Indian School. A curious twilight interlude, after all the restless endeavour of the last months. I have been doing nothing for what seems like an age—lying down, reading and writing, and dreamily watching the changing water and the round innocent Manitoba maples which grow brighter yellow every day; sitting on the floor with the principal's little daughter, reading *Winnie the Pooh,* choosing our special friends among the animals— Phyllis' first love is Pooh; mine is Piglet; we both dislike Christopher Robin—exploring together the little English wood, considering which animal had the best house and whether Kanga was too indulgent to Roo; and, when we are tired of this, writing letters from the big grey house-cat to his small tabby friend in Regina.

I have lost all impulse to go on. All the drive which kept me joyfully picturing the next stretch of the trail, hurrying to see what lay round every corner and over every hill, is gone. I can still delight in the moment, thrill at the touch of the horses and gaze in wonder at the autumn valley; but the future has crashed, and tomorrow and the day after and the day after that only lead me nearer to it.

But I must go; I must go tomorrow, for all that Mr. and Mrs. Huston make me welcome as an old friend. I shall go on and finish what I started out to do.

We are on the road again and ride into the magic of the autumn valley. Storm and sunshine are hunting each other through the moving mountains of the sky; the little maples have changed colour in unison and achieved a perfect unsullied yellow, pure as the light of daffodils, more exquisite than gold. The hill-sides are carpeted with burning red against a shadowed background of evergreen oaks. In the flats lie dark sheets of plough-land, and among all this are sprinkled a myriad little trees, yellow brown and gold, scarlet purple and delicate pink—climbing up the slopes, nestling by the water, winding away among the folds in the hills. There are clouds now over our part of the valley, and the lake lies sombre; to the north, rain is slanting down in a purple sheet, but to the west, infinitely mysterious, the little hills are dreaming in dim sunshine. A hundred lights in the sky, a hundred colours in the valley, and hard rain riding down the wind.

Oh, Keats is wrong; autumn is not mellow and pensive; it is racing and tearing with vitality, burning alive with agony and delight.

There have been two pleasant nights with pleasant families. Yesterday the family to whom I had an introduction were not at home when I arrived. So I unpacked the horses, turned them to graze, and sat down on the grass to wait, occupying the time in writing a slightly gloomy poem. Here it is:

War Thoughts

Timothy red as the autumn,
Jonty brown as the plough,

Loved, mysterious horses,
What are you thinking now?

Tim does not pine for the mountains
Nor Jonty for the range,
As I ride them into a country
Infinitely strange.

Oh, horses, share my aloneness,
As the light fades out of the day!
Your thoughts are peaceful and near,
But mine hurt and are far away.

About eight o'clock I heard the rattle of a car and cheerful and riotous yelling. No, it was not the family, but the hired boy come to do the chores, accompanied by his mother and sister and two brothers. So he helped me put the horses in; and afterwards I went into the house with his people, lay down on a sofa, and went to sleep. I woke some time later to find the owners of the farm returned and making supper for me, not the least put out at discovering their unexpected guest. This morning I left them, and go on down the valley, through faerie woodlands burning with autumn.

Last night I reached Lazare (Manitoba, hooray!). I stayed with an Irishman and his French Canadian wife, behind their store. Lazare is almost entirely French, and I aired mine with considerable enjoyment. I shared the bed-sofa in the living-room with a very fat, very French little girl called Fifine. Before bed she sat down at the piano and played—Beethoven, Moussorgsky, then Chopin, the waltz in C minor, and Rachmaninoff—the inevitable prelude:

Bam, BAM, BAM; bim bam, bim Bam, bim BAM, bim BAM.

She was not musical and shamelessly scamped the difficult passages, but the music was live enough to make me home-sick. As I lay and watched Fifine's curls bouncing up and down, I remembered Ruth Spooner—brilliant, humble, exquisitely civilized Ruth; I remembered a happy afternoon at New College Oxford, a large English tea, and afterwards her sitting down to play, superbly, that same Chopin.

Darling Ruth! Grey Oxford wreathed in gardens! I did not know I could long so passionately for a Norman arch, for a little fan-vaulting.

At Lazare we left the Qu'Appelle Valley and are now hitting south-west toward Brandon. I have been lucky and had three companions. The first joined me early yesterday evening. He was a pleasant young man and had a wild little bronc from Alberta. By way of showing me how efficient he was, he got her going full gallop and vaulted into the saddle. But the little mare —by way, no doubt, of showing Timothy and Jonty how she could go one better—put in a dexterous buck and bounced him off again. Then she raced away, kicking up her heels, laughing and squealing. By the time her owner had recovered her, and, considerably chastened, had got on in the ordinary way, the shadows were lengthening over the grass and the trees in the east shone gold in the setting sun. We rode away over the evening fields, thoughtful and slow.

At last, with the sun long gone and only one red streak in the west, we reached a little house on a hill. Here my companion's sister was acting as nurse to an old lady of ninety-six, and here I spent the night. The next day the old lady's young housekeeper took a notion to come with me; so, riding very uncomfortably, bareback on Jonty, she came. After an hour's ride we reached the house of some friends of hers, and the son of these friends mounted his horse and came with me right into the afternoon. I was quite unused to my own society by the end of the day.

The harvest is good in this part of the country and is in full swing everywhere. The fields are patterned with stooks, and at evening the warm farm kitchens are filled with sunburnt men. They are recruited from all over Canada, these thrashing gangs. From Quebec and Ontario and British Columbia they come;

some hitchhike, some ride the freights, and some join together to buy gas and pile into cars. On the largest farms they do the work with combines. These are surprising-looking inventions, reminiscent of pictures by Heath Robinson. They stick out in all directions and go chugging up and down the fields, rattling and roaring and breathing smoke. But they do the work. They cut and thrash all in one operation, shaking down the grain into containers and spewing out the straw behind them as they go. With a combine, a harvest can be cut and thrashed in a fraction of the time taken by the old method, and using far less labour.

We are approaching Brandon, which lies only a hundred and fifty miles from Winnipeg. I ride all day through the gold of harvest, but at evening I ride through fires. They stand around us like beacons, splashed red against the darkening sky, the fires of burning straw-piles. It does not take long for the flames to devour the yellow heap. At morning there will be nothing there but a dark circle on the ground. And before spring, if this is a hard winter, stock will be starving again on the bitter range.

This morning I found a yearling colt lying in the ditch with his leg smashed. A car must have run into him and driven straight on, never stopping. I jumped down and went to him. His coat was matted with sweat and there was foam at his mouth; he curved round his neck and looked at me with broken-hearted eyes. I left my horses on the road, wriggled under the fence, and ran as fast as I could to the nearest farm. The farmer looked over towards the road, where the colt was up now, trying to go to Timothy and Jonty.

"That's ours all right," he remarked.

"Better bring an axe," I warned him.

When the colt saw the farmer he gave a little whinny, slight as a sigh, and began to hobble towards him. The man took one look at the dangling leg.

"Hopeless," he said. He went over to the colt; the axe hung heavy at his side. "We raised him by hand." There was an ache in his voice. "The mare died. Sat up with him nights for more'n a week."

He slid his hand, light and loving, over the matted hair of the little neck. I hurried to Timothy and began to tighten the girth; it was tight enough. I heard thuds behind me, falling, falling, dull and heavy. At last I looked round. The farmer straightened his back; he wiped the axe on his pantleg; a dark heap lay still in the grass.

So perhaps there was no colt any more, or perhaps there was an immortal horse set free. I tried to see him, sound and beautiful, striding up the sky; but I could see only the hurt in the baby eyes.

And may God forgive men for the pain of his animals.

Chapter XIII

INTO WILDERNESS

The last time I sat down to write the journal, we were in the prairies west of Winnipeg. Now we are in Kenora, with the wilderness before us.

Upon the day when we left Brandon, for the first time in nine hundred miles, we followed the highway; and the dead black road with so many cars streaming over it gave me a feeling of desolation which I had never known upon the lonely trails which lay behind. But there was a good wagon-track along the side for the horses, and one beautiful thing came with us all that day—the sturdy briers which tangled in the grass, clustered with round red hips, warm and perky as an English robin.

Next day we were again on the highway, and now without a wagon-trail. It is fortunate that the horses are quiet with traffic, for the traffic is most certainly not quiet with them. Cars come racing past, so close and so fast that the horses' tails are wrenched over their flanks by the rush of air; or another time a great silent limousine will come gliding up behind, and then, just as it is drawing level with the horses' quarters, let loose a piercing hoot; or else a car-load of well-meaning youngsters will come racketing towards us, honking and waving their arms like a distracted windmill. However, the horses accept these manifestations with resignation; Jonty is afraid of nothing, and the only thing Timothy really minds is a train.

On the third day after we left Brandon, the road joined the railway. It was not long before a freight train bore down upon us, hooting its forlorn Canadian whistle, and flapping a blanket of white smoke across the road. Timothy was horrified. He pranced and snorted and tried to swing round, tangling himself tightly in Jonty's lead rope. Now the one thing besides a train which scares Timothy is a rope, so the moment he felt it round his forehand he reared sky-high. The feel of a large powerful horse rearing is superb, and I could not help enjoying it with part of my mind, though with the other I was afraid he was coming over backwards. However, by what was almost a miracle, he subsided upon his four feet again, and I succeeded in persuading him to stand still and watch the monster till it was out of sight. If he had come over backwards on the paved road, we should probably all three have been badly hurt. As far as I know, this is the only time we have been in danger since the beginning of the trip.

About ten minutes after this episode a car stopped in front of us, and out of it jumped a reporter and a camera man; from that time on we were public characters again.

Once more before we reached Winnipeg we were able to leave the highway. As soon as we set our feet on the little farm road, the journey bloomed again. It was in the morning I think, that we met the swallow. Slim and dark it was, and perfectly unafraid of us. It came with us for over a mile, flying round and round— now gliding swiftly in large circles, now fluttering slowly, close to us, low over the horses' backs, under their bellies and past my face so near that I could have touched it. If I had had that kind of mind, I should have felt certain it was trying to tell us something; having the other kind, I wondered whether the smell of the horses could have some association for the little creature. I wonder and wonder ever now. At evening we fell in with a farmer going home on his wagon. So at his invitation I tied the horses behind, jumped up beside him, and went home with him for the night. He had a square house and a round wife and nine children.

Upon the next night we reached Portage la Prairie, so called because here the Indians used to lift their canoes from the Assiniboine for the overland carry to Lake Manitoba. The fort of Portage was built in 1738 by Verendrye, a French Canadian fur trader. I should have liked to stay a day to gain some knowledge of this historic little town, but I was in a hurry to reach Winnipeg, so on we went, and on September the thirtieth we arrived.

My social activities in this city were almost as violent as those in Vancouver, but this time I enjoyed them. To begin with, I had now accomplished at least part of the ride which was being celebrated, and also in Winnipeg I had a home and family with whom to enjoy these things. This again was due to the good offices of the newspapers whose attentions I so little appreciated. For before I left England, Mary Ruttan of Winnipeg had read of my proposed escapade in the Winnipeg *Tribune*, and had written inviting me to stay with her family on the way through the city. Mary was a champion skier, and vitality burnt in her like a flame. With her I enjoyed the parties. I remember best the day when the Tuxedo Riding Club gave us a paper chase. Beautiful the horses looked, streaming over the jumps, swinging and circling through Tuxedo Park among the billows of the yellow trees. At the end of the first week I gave a lecture. My funds are getting rather low, so I shall have to supplement them by earning what I can. It was not at all a professional lecture, I just stood up and told the story of the trip so far, but the audience laughed and enjoyed it.

Between these activities were sandwiched hours of serious preparation. For the Winnipeggers have been describing to me with a wealth of dramatic detail the hardships into which I am riding. We are now heading into five hundred miles of uncompromising wilderness. Forest and muskeg and lake, the few settlements many miles apart. No farms, no grazing for the horses. Only the iron-hard road cutting over the rocks; and, like a wolf, the winter lying in wait for us. They tell me of blizzards in which people have frozen to death a mile from home and of the temperature dropping to "forty below" in the night and waiting to pounce upon you with its icy grip when you go out in the morning. By this time I have heard so much about "forty below" that the words are tied up in my mind like a knot in a shoe-lace, and I shall find no peace till I have at last met the forty-below bogy man face to face. But I am only pleasurably afraid, and, as for hardship, Stevenson as usual sees the real fact about that:

> Men speak of hardships, but the true hardship is to be a dull fool, and permitted to mismanage life in our own dull and foolish manner.

So, having been presented by the Cambridge Riding Club with a fine pair of horse blankets, and by Messrs. Timothy Eaton, Limited, with a pair of ski trousers, two sets of uncompromising underwear and innumerable jerseys, I set out hopefully into the October sunshine. Mary, who, to my joy, had decided to accompany me as far as Kenora, which lies some hundred and fifty miles east of Winnipeg, rode Timothy while I rode Jonty, leaving the pack-saddle, together with most of my bulky and newly-acquired possessions, to follow a week later with Mrs. Ruttan in the car.

Mrs. Ruttan had begged me to stay for the winter, and I should have dearly loved to do so. But there is a fire inside which drives me; I must go on and make it now, *now*, before circumstances take hold of my life and wrench it altogether out of the pattern I have been making.

So Mary and I rode out towards the wilderness. Mary is slim as a deer and muscled like a little bronco, so we made long days, and she suffered not at all. Early on the second day the open farming country began to give place to scrub—first bushes and small birch trees and the beginnings of evergreens. Then, in the afternoon, a heavy island of bush, and all alone one little curly-armed tamarack dancing a sun-gold fandango before the muted gallery of the pines.

At last the road stopped dead at a farm-yard gate; and, asking whether we could go any further east, we were led by a precarious trail over quivering muskeg to a power line, which slashed its way like a knife-cut through the bush. We set out along the path which followed it, and sudden as a cloud-burst we were in the wilderness. No more farms and fields and half-hearted scrub, but swamp and waste and forest dense as a thundercloud. And as we rode in silence, two deer, glowing in the evening light, wandered on to the trail, gazed at us for a moment, then bounded away among the trees.

This is the adventure of Canada—any moment one is liable to be shaken up like dice in a box and flung out into the wild—the wild possessed only by the birds and the animals, ruled only by the sun and wind and snow, untamed, unbroken, the same from the beginning of the world.

At sunset we came to a tiny settlement of loggers. They were all French Canadian and not very anxious to be bothered with us; but one family finally took us in, and their hearts were soon melted by Mary's interest in their separator and my gallant and wildly inaccurate French. In the morning we went on along the power line, first across a very large swamp, where the trail lay over "corduroyed" logs, the water squelched underneath and the horses snorted and picked their way anxiously; then through forest again, then more swamp, more forest, and then, like a snap of the fingers, back into farmland—pasture, plough, houses, barns, and half a mile north of us the town of Whitewood, elevator and all. Slap through the middle ran number 1 Trans-Canada Highway, cold and black and car-polished.

Feeling a little shy, as one always does, we went to a pretty farm-house to ask if we might have some lunch, for there was no hotel. We need not have felt anxious, for before we were in at the gate, a plump, smiling woman came running out, crying:

"Well, we *are* glad to see you! Which is Timothy? Isn't he beautiful? Billy will help you put them in the barn. Sure, we read all about you; come right in!"

So we were warmed and feasted, and at last regretfully tore

ourselves away, and set out on the twenty-mile ride to the next town.

In two miles the highway plunged again into the forest, and soon the real rock country began. Great slabs of rounded stone ran down to the road, with little trees rooting precariously in the crevices. Wind sang in the firs and swished the leaves from the bending birches. We rode on and on till dusk began to fall. A little black furry ball of a bear crossed the road and went bundling away among the rocks. I longed for Daddy. He and I share exactly the same kind of love for evening forests; we imagine witches in the wind and goblins among the trees. Many is the kobold we have seen in German forests, many the leprechaun in fairy-haunted Ireland.

But at this point Mary very justly pointed out that, if we wanted to reach the village of Rennie before nightfall, we had better step along. So we stepped along, but even so it was dark before we reached the town. I left the horses with Mary, and, going into a filling station to ask about accommodation, found a dark Ukrainian girl, handsome as a gipsy, who at once took charge of us. Yes, she knew where we could put the horses. Taking no light, she led us up the hill-side over the bare rocks, and romance took hold of the night again. Before us in the forest a great fire was burning, with sparks swinging up into the velvet sky.

"I love the dark," said the girl, Helen. "It's so warm and friendly; it's the dawn I'm afraid of."

Then there were shadows of men round us, warm stable lanterns, and the horses going into a low barn. Next, Helen set about finding a home for us. "Did yer know," she said to me, "yer've a braad English acksent?" "Did yer know," she added, turning to Mary, "every time yer go over a bump yer groan?" I stumbled over my long mackintosh. "Can yer see?" asked Helen. "It's silly, but I always imagine a person can see better in the dark wearing a white raincoat. Kesan!" she called her curly dog. "He scares me," she said. "Did yer ever have a dog that saw things? He does; he stares into the dark and growls and bristles."

At last we came to a small light. It was in the home of the school teacher, who hospitably received us. We lay in a tent by the house, and rain fell all night, storming and drumming on the roof. I slept to dream of the village, a wash of black pricked by unknown lights, set on rocks which we climbed without seeing them, and girded by the forest. But in the morning we woke to find a plain little settlement, glooming greyly among muddy puddles. . . .

On this day we began to ride into the lake country. We passed lakes large and small, lakes with islands, lakes without, lakes with dark firs fringing the shore, or set in shadowy muskeg, or with silver and gold birches fluffing their slender roundness against the water line.

Every autumn in turn seems to me the loveliest I have ever seen. But I believe this *is* the loveliest. And to be able to ride through it all day, from morning till evening, is a wonder which will colour all the rest of my life. I think I shall remember, wherever I go, the white and yellow of the birches, the deep rose-red of the low-growing moose-berry, and the living glow of the tamaracks, flung up against the sombre firs, like the sun before a storm.

Upon the last night of our ride together, Mary and I stayed with a forest ranger, in a log house under the shoulder of the bush. That was a sleepy, friendly evening, with the stove glowing hot in the living-room, and the round logs in the wall shining solidly in the lamplight. Supper is never so good as when you have ridden all day to get it; and after supper we sat down under the lamp to look at photographs—the forest in summer, the forest in winter, the lake frozen solid and laid out like a blanket, the little house half hidden under a mantle of snow. Soon came photographs of a mother bear and her baby playing round the house, trustfully begging for tit-bits, solemnly investigating the inside of a treacle-tin. Then we turned a page, and there they were lying dead in the snow!

"Oh, yes," remarked the ranger. "I had to shoot them in the end; they kept upsetting the dust-bin."

After that I hardly saw the pictures in the album. At last my eyes began to fall shut of themselves, and, leaving Mary still turning the pages, I went to bed. All that night the picture of the mother bear lying beside her baby was dark in my dreams. The death-sentence seems a high penalty for upsetting a dust-bin!

Upon the evening of the fourth day, we reached Keewatin, a small town just outside Kenora, where we had been invited to stay by a lady called Lucile Witts, whose brother I had met in the West.

What was our amazement upon arrival to find ourselves met by the town band and escorted in glory to the town hall, where a large crowd was awaiting us. The Boy Scouts kept them back with ropes, and a policeman directed them. Never in my life have I experienced such importance! For who should be waiting upon the steps but the Mayor himself with a golden key, to present me with the freedom of Keewatin!

The next day who should make his totally unexpected appearance but Ted, the curly-headed pan-god with whom I had watched the storm on our voyage from England! Here he was living in a log house in the wilderness, working in a gold-mine, and looking exactly the same. So Mary and I went out with him and wandered through the wilderness, scrambling like goats among the rocks, dropping down to the lake shores and at last going back to his cabin, where dinner and a great fire folded down the ends of the day and sealed them with well-being.

There was a curious fairy-tale quality about those happy days in Mrs. Witts' home. In ordinary life the houses in which we live are our geographical centres. We go out of them, but only to return. We are like ships at anchor, riding to the length of the anchor chain, but not leaving the harbour. And so we come to belong to the places in which we live. No matter how much we travel from place to place, we are still only scudding from harbour to harbour, only changing our position from one stationary point to another.

But in these months with the horses, only the journey has been constant. For I no longer travel to arrive. I no longer belong to lights and fires, to pleasant meal times, to books and pictures and windows curtained at night, but to roads and rivers, to fields and forests, to weather and the sky. And so for the first time, as one walking by, I have seen the neat, complete pictures of many hundred homes. I have felt their texture, breathed their atmosphere, and passed.

And our lives are like this if we could stand apart and see them, a stage in a journey—out of the unknown, into the unknown again. As the wise slow-witted Saxons said, twelve hundred years ago: man's soul is like a bird which flies out of the night into a hall in which many are feasting, fleets through the warmth and brightness, then out again into the dark. Never till now have I lived in my own thought Wordsworth's lines:

> Our birth is but a sleep and a forgetting;
> The soul that rises with us, our life's star,
> Hath had elsewhere its setting,
> And cometh from afar:
> Not in entire forgetfulness,
> And not in utter nakedness,
> But trailing clouds of glory do we come
> From God, who is our home.

Chapter XIV

WINTER ON OUR TAIL

On October the eighteenth the horses and I left Keewatin. It was the last day which seemed to have a place in the calendar. On that journey to the Great Lakes, time froze. I knew that we were racing the winter, and I watched the miles anxiously. And yet as we went on through the hypnotic forest, there was no longer reality in the days of the month, in the hours of the day; we journeyed on steadily, suspended in time. The snow came to meet us, and the winter drove it with whips of wind. But we were the days and we were time, and it seemed that only the winter travelled.

All too soon, alas, Mary's family came to fetch her home, and, though I did not know it, the autumn went with her. All through the warm and friendly days in Mrs. Witts' little house, the early winter had been prowling. The evenings outside the storm-windows were frosty and greenish blue, and at night the wind shrieked like a banshee over the Lake of the Woods, wrenching the leaves from the trees and slapping the waves down on the shore. When I rode out it was into a winter forest—the birches naked, a few yellow needles still clinging to the tops of the tamaracks, but with a pale and fleeting look, and only the pine trees dark and unchanged.

Again I was struck by Canada's suddenness. It had lapped me round in a red-gold paradise of an autumn for so long that I had been almost drugged into dreaming that its beauty would never die—and now the same year, only three days older, shook me awake and tumbled me out into this naked and shivering October morning!

Today we had a foretaste of the difficulties which lie ahead of us. We soon left behind the cleared country which surrounds Kenora and plunged into the forest. We have to go ninety miles to Dryden, the next town, and after that there are nothing but scattered settlements all the way to Fort William. "After Dryden . . ." say the head-shaking prophets, and finish with a groan.

In the evening we reached the tiny encampment which I was seeking. We were greeted kindly enough, but with the news that, as far as was known, there was no hay or grain for thirty miles! In despair I unpacked the horses and stood out with them while they rustled a little grass from behind some cabins. The wind moaned in the spruce trees and snow began to fall. It swirled in silent eddies past the lighted windows of the kitchen where my supper was waiting; it laid a pale blanket on the horses' backs and whitened the ground under the night sky. Once I went to the house and asked if there was a car to drive me back to Kenora for some hay, only to hear that my host had driven away in the only motor which the settlement possessed.

"When will he be back?" I asked.

"Oh, maybe any time, maybe not at all," was the vague reply.

Hopelessly I went back to the horses, leant against a cabin, and solaced myself with the sound of their munching. Gradually they would drift away, until their dark forms were almost hidden against the shadows of the bush, so I would sally forth and fetch them back, and then cower against the protecting cabin again. After what seemed like many hours, my mind leapt to attention at the sound of a car. I hastened to meet it. Out climbed my host, and, opening the back door, he began to haul on an unwieldy bundle. I could hardly believe my eyes in the dark, for it was hay, and under it a sack of oats lay hunched upon the floor!

"Oh, yes," replied my host, in answer to my vociferous rejoicings, "I just ran down to an old logging-camp on the lake shore;

thought it was worth seeing if they had some; lucky they had."

Next day, in the midst of the forest loneliness, I came upon a Department of Highways truck and some men mending the road, one of whom, a tall fellow with a kindly face and grey eyes under a thatch of curly hair, asked me to stay the night with his wife. In the evening we reached a settlement beside a small lake, and there sure enough was our friend waiting to greet us, and behind him a pretty girl ran out of the house with a baby in her arms. Room was made for the horses in a small shed; hay and oats were generously contributed by another member of the community, and soon the horses were settled down for the night. So we went in together and were soon deeply engrossed in the joys of venison steak. Ed and Betty sat before me with radiance in their eyes, savouring the experience of having a traveller in their house. It is people like Ed and Betty who give me most of all, for they make me an opportunity to return an infinitely small part of the joy which is so freely given to me. For a traveller is forever receiving—sympathy, help, food, shelter, everything. And there seems to be so little to give in return.

Upon the third day after leaving Kenora we reached Dryden. It was strange to ride out of so much wilderness into this self-contained little town, with stores and a newspaper and business men in business suits walking about the streets. I stayed a day to rest the horses, but was glad to be on the road again, and to reach, on the first night after my departure, the historic Hudson's Bay trading post of Dinorwic.

The romance of the Hudson's Bay Company has always gripped my imagination. Well were the company's pioneers named, "The Company of Adventurers Trading into Hudson's Bay." For a great company they were, and adventurers all. They opened the Northland; they opened the West; they did much to build the groundwork of Canada as she is today. For while Champlain was laying the sturdy foundations of New France in the South, the great company were pioneering on the Bay, trading, exploring, discovering. Before the end of the eighteenth century, they had already penetrated into the north-west wilderness of the Mackenzie country, and their servant Hearne had seen the sun stand in the sky at midnight in the Arctic Circle. For many years, beset by enemies, both in New France and in old England, they nevertheless maintained their posts around the Bay and in the West. It was not until 1869 that their territories were formally ceded to the Canadian Government, and to this day their part is considerable in the life of Canada. All through the West runs the great chain of their modern stores, but they have not changed altogether into a company of storekeepers. For still their servants drive dog teams into the North and hold their lonely posts on the rim of the Arctic Circle; and still they go discovering through Canada's wilderness, "The Company of Adventurers Trading into Hudson's Bay!"

The day we left Dinorwic we came in the afternoon out of the forest on to a sunny sheet of cleared land. Never before have fenced fields looked so good to me. In the midst of them stood a frame house with a red barn behind it. I slid from Timothy's back, and, dropping his lines on the road, I went to knock at the door, for in the wilderness one does not pass a habitation without going in for a few words at least of human speech. This time, before I was half-way across the yard, out ran a beaming, round-faced woman with her skirts flying in the wind and her silver hair blowing round her head in an electric halo of excitement.

"Come right in!" she cried. "We been expecting you for days. Here, Elsie, here, Olaf, here's the girl!"

I followed her in readily enough and found myself in the midst of a family of great golden Norwegians. Wheaten hair they had, red-brown faces and a wide communal smile which filled the room.

"You'll stay over?" they cried in chorus.

Soon the horses were standing in the red barn, with the cows to warm them, sweet straw at their feet, and spicy hay sliding out of the chute upon their expectant heads. I marvelled at them as they stood there shining roundly among the shadows. Fat and bright-eyed they were, with velvet coats and sound legs under them. Even Timothy's nobbly forelegs stood under him squarely, only slightly puffed by the iron-hard road. I pray I may bring him sound as far as Montreal!

So I went into the house and was plunged into a whirlpool of excitement. In addition to the farmer and his wife, there were three husky sons and two daughters, besides the grandmother who sat silently knitting in a corner of the kitchen. Swiftly I was whirled away on a rip-tide of conversation; bright-eyed they asked me about the mountains and the plains and the cities of the West. Their house was full of pictures of far places—the Grand Canyon and the red mountains of Arizona, tropical South American shores and giant trees of the west coast.

"Oh, some day to see such places!" said the father quietly, "but if we never do, is that way good also; at least we think of them."

As he spoke I gazed out almost with enmity at the wilderness which bound these people in, but as my eyes returned again to the shining faces round the lamp, I knew that in truth they were not bound, for in their untrammelled hearts the waves would break forever on unknown shores, and forever brave ships would go sailing into the sunset.

At last, hungry and glowing as though we had battled all day with the winds, we sat down to supper. Afterwards, quiet and dreamy now, the parents spoke of Norway, and of the little fjord where their childhood's home had been. And then the very old lady raised her head and smiled, with a starry distance in her eyes. And I saw for the first time how beautiful she was, beautiful with a serenity already infinitely remote from this elusive world which we strive in vain to conquer. . . .

The next day, they told me, I must ride over forty miles, before I should find the least sign of a habitation. So at dawn I got up to prepare the horses. I went out to find the little homestead pale blue and jewelled with frost. Exquisitely unreal it looked, sparkling like gossamer against the deep background of the firs. The kindly red-gold colours of the lost autumn glowed in the east, where soon the sun would rise.

After a lamplit breakfast I started off. All through the cold bright day I rode in the wilderness, never seeing a soul. At rare intervals a car would whirl past, smooth and strange and perfectly detached from its surroundings. The wastes and the forest were almost silent, only a distant rush of wind in the tree-tops reminded one of the sea.

These are the days when the mind goes wandering. After many hours on the road, I suddenly remembered how my father would say sometimes, "You know it's wonderful how one can put four walls together and make a house."

Then I would laugh and he would say it again to tease me. But he is right. I never learnt to know the wonder of houses until I ceased to spend my life in them. Now I pass through them lightly and soon return to the out-of-doors which is my home, and for the first time I see them separate.

The variety of their characters is infinite. There are little, kind, bustling houses, like round, red-cheeked mothers, who cosset and comfort you, and in whom the kettle is always singing and the fire all winter crackling on the hearth. They purr like cats, these little houses, and the wind howls round them in vain.

Very far removed from them are the houses in which the inhabitants seem only to perch like birds on a branch; where you sit on the edge of your chair, ready at any minute to get up and hurry somewhere; where the very furniture seems to be scattered indiscriminately, so small is its importance in the lives of its owners.

Then there are tense, trembling houses where you stand as in a boxing-ring under the arc lamps, waiting, waiting for something to happen, knowing it has before, knowing it will again; and gloomy secret houses where you are roped around with shadows, where you breathe shallow breaths only down to your shoulders, where you walk dully and do not feel your health, and the windows seem to hide the sky.

But oh, there are houses whose rooms are filled with laughter, where even though there be no children, sliding down the banisters, tumbling in from the garden, flashing and sparkling, bringing the morning with them, yet childhood is there and flies to meet and greet you. These are the houses where the heart laughs for easiness, where the windows wink, where the fire twinkles, where the garden comes in with you as you pass the door.

Then there are houses a little like these, but failing where they succeed; houses which are distrait, houses which are scatter-brained, where the days escape you, where you are active but do nothing, where you talk but say nothing, where you listen but do not remember, where your thoughts wander away into tangled ends and are lost.

And there are houses perfectly appointed but in which you are only part of yourself; where the rooms sink down upon you and the passages regard you in empty silence, where the life goes out of your voice and the light out of your eyes.

But other houses, few and precious, still the soul with their simplicity and fill the mind with energy and peace, so that you may look out of their clear windows, and see beyond the trees to the sky, and beyond the struggle of thought to what lies deeper.

These strong composite characters of houses come not simply from the temperaments of their owners, not simply from the lines of their architecture or the colours of their furniture, nor yet from the ghosts of the past which inhabit them—all these and many other factors combine to create the elusive personality of a house.

Of all the houses which I have known there is one kind above all others which holds and hurts me, which fascinates and torments me, and will not let me go. This is the house of memories, the house of what has been and will never come back, which dreams through the present, inhabiting the past. Ever since I was a child, I have set my face against the past, simply because it *is* the past, because it is the past and can never come again. Its happiness and pain, its love and fear, its fleeting thought and the texture of its days, all slid from under my hand before I could grasp them, before I could do more than touch the fringe of their reality.

But now, as I ride hour by hour through the world without end of the winter forest, memory holds me for the first time without reproach. Living vignettes from the past leap to my mind in vivid completeness. One picture today stands out dazzling clear, the more arresting for its very remoteness from the half-real present. It is the picture of my first dinner-party, far away on the continent of Europe, in Daddy's consular days.

The table is exquisitely laid, and the candles ready to be lighted. Daddy, alert and anxious, is running upstairs to Mummy.

"Dorothy, can you tie my tie again? It's crooked. And look, we must completely reorganize the table-list. Baroness Leibnitz can't possibly sit next to the French Vice-Consul, he's much too junior!"

Mummy's voice, cool and unruffled: "Come here under the light, P. I think that's straight. How about giving her Herr von Hoffmansthal? He's positively hoary. Wooller (meaning me), run down and change the names round."

Then comes the first ring at the bell, and we set sail down the wide staircase. Mummy exquisitely graceful, slim as a willow in her dark brocade dress. Daddy small and springy, with his white eyebrows curling up like horns over his eyes and the wings of his tie tucked resolutely behind the points of his collar. ("It may be old-fashioned, Wooller, but it's the way I've always worn it.") Myself awkwardly important in a rather unbecoming dress, of which, however, I have the highest possible opinion.

There follows shapely conversation in three languages. More and more people arrive. At last we are all assembled and, in punctilious order of precedence, the company files in to dinner. We hunt up our cards and arrange ourselves. The guests of honour are a blind Prince and his Princess. The Princess is pale and perfect, a white greyhound; but the Prince is an odd little man with terrible twisted eyes. "What a pity," I think, "such beauty, and wasted."

Meanwhile, like a stately ship, the dinner gets under way. I juggle happily with French and German, admire Mummy's dress, and wish I could have a second helping of the fish. The Rhein-wine passes. The high dining-room hums with conversation. Only John, our West Highland terrier, loathing the whole thing, but loathing more to be left out, sits morosely in his wicker chair. At last, built up with architectural precision on two great dishes, there enters the dessert. From one of these luxurious structures an apple falls, and is picked up in a napkin and carried into the pantry; I wonder vaguely what will happen to it. Finally the ladies rise. I have taken too many grapes and have to leave some.

Feminine small talk in the drawing-room. *"Qu'elle a grandi, votre petite!"* remarks the French Consul-General's wife. "Petite" indeed! I'd have the lady know that I'm taller than she is! I sit up straight as a poker on my Chippendale chair, displaying my eighteen years for all to see. No one in the whole room is more majestically grown up than I. Soon, mellow in the afterglow of port and cigars, the men join us. We settle. At intervals Mummy juggles us deftly about, but talk flows unabated. At the hour of midnight, still more or less in order of precedence, the company departs.

"Well, I think it went very well, don't you, Vivian?"

"Yes, but I don't think they got a chance of more Hoch up at our end."

"We must remind Maria just before, next time."

"The new American Consul is charming, isn't he?"

"Oh, look at poor little John, he's dying to go to bed."

So the party is over.

So the party is over, and the wilderness comes to life again and glides to meet us down the never-ending road. On and on we go, into the dusk and at last into darkness. After what seems like a perfect eternity of night, we see a light.

I never knew, until these last few weeks, all the warmth and promise that one lonely light can hold. The days are long, but always in the daylight one is aware of progress. The night descends like a blanket upon one's spirit. In the day the wilderness has shape and incident and slides past one obediently as one walks the highway. But in the darkness it hangs suspended, till one seems to be walking in a treadmill, stationary in time and space. The forest waits in a black wash; above it hangs the night sky; and under one's feet, without change, the road goes on.

And then out of the darkness glimmers a light.

The light we saw on this occasion was a strong and encouraging one, and when we approached I found that it came from the windows of a sturdy log house, which had the shadow of a great barn behind it. Already relaxed in the prospect of food and shelter for the horses and myself, I opened the gate and walked into the yard. Out of the darkness leapt four dogs, looking black and enormous and barking furiously. Affecting a nonchalance I did not feel, I walked up to the door and knocked. After some time there were heavy footsteps within, and a minute later a large man, with a stable lantern in one hand and a heavy gun in the other, stood framed in the doorway.

Upon sight of me his shaggy eyebrows drew together into such a frown that they met over the bridge of his nose. He instantly began to shout in an unknown language, hurling what I could only take to be execrations. For a moment I stood paralysed. My horrified eyes dropped from his melodramatic black beard to his great fur-collared jacket, and thence to heavy jack-boots; all of which together gave him so exactly the effect of the Big Bad Russian Bolsheviks occasionally depicted in the older cartoons of *Punch* that I abandoned the attempt to explain myself and fled back to the road, with the relentless dogs in hot pursuit. Dragging the disappointed horses after me, I set off once more.

Again we laboured for an eternity in the treadmill, again we came at last to a light, which this time proved to be shining from the windows of a small house half hidden under the curtain of the forest.

In some trepidation this time, I knocked at the door, which was at once flung open wide, so that light, warmth and a strong smell of fish came flooding out. Dazedly I became aware of welcome. Swarms of shadowy children were admiring the almost indistinguishable outlines of the horses, while older people were begging me to come in, exclaiming that I must have ridden all of fifty miles, and crying in answer to my faint replies:

"Why you *never* stopped at Harkoff's? He's as crazy as a rattlesnake! He didn't shoot you, did he?"

When they found that I could not be induced to come in until the horses were attended to, they set about backing their old car out of the garage, and jolted away through the forest to a deserted logging-camp, which erections, wonderfully provided with no-longer-needed horse-feed, conveniently spangle this part of the bush. Soon we had made the horses as comfortable as we could, and I, my tiredness forgotten, stood in the shed to admire them as they munched. On a journey like this a traveller does not possess his horses; they possess him, body and soul. The warmest house and the most delicious dinner have no charms whatever until one has been released by the sight of the horses contentedly feeding. And even then the restful sight of them holds one and will hardly let one go.

At last, however, the family mildly suggested that I should be wanting some supper, and I was inclined to agree with them. But when we came into the house I was too tired to eat anything; so they showed me a bed in a small alcove of the living-room, behind a rough curtain. I fell into it and was instantly asleep.

It was not until the morning that I began to discover the family with whom I was staying. They were lake-fishers. They had a minimum of possessions, superb generosity and serene contentment. They begged me to stay with them for a few days, so I took the horses through the bush to where the great deserted stable of the logging-company stood on the shores of a lake. Here I settled them, up to their knees in bedding, and with sweet hay piled high before them. Then I went back with the Durphys to their little house. It was a curious house, nestling dusky under the trees. The living-room looked out from under the forest-roof on to the highway; it was piled high with rough, intricate fishing nets and smelt continually, a salty, gluey smell, not unpleasant.

At first I did not notice how beautiful the Durphy children were. They were not talkative, and I thought them pale and dull, so that I did not see at first with what a cool perfection of design the heavy black hair framed their ivory-skinned faces. I did not notice the calm lines of their full pre-Raphaelite mouths, or the statuesque serenity of their growing bodies. But at last I sat down to draw them; one by one they posed for me, sitting stiller than any children I have ever seen, perfectly and peacefully still, with their hands at rest. And gradually, as I fumbled with the pencil, they dawned upon me.

Then the whole pale, dark-eyed family began to take hold of my imagination. Unconsciously they possessed the secret of relaxed effort, of labour without strain. Against the background of their repose shone a good-natured levity, which possessed them alike through hours of drudgery and in moments of crisis. Mr. Durphy and one of the older boys have an aged truck, which they cobble together with haywire, and drive all over the forest. This object caught fire while I was there—quite a serious fire, it seemed to me, with clouds of agitating white smoke circling up into the trees. But its owners, without once losing the grin off their faces, fetched water from a mercifully adjacent creek, put out the conflagration, started up the engine and bumped happily away again, dancing about on the ancient seat like peas in a bucket. Upon the second night of my stay, two of the boys fished all through till the morning, labouring with the heavy nets on the face of the windy lake. But at breakfast-time they came home not noticeably exhausted, with the comfortable grin still ready to lift the corners of their sculptured mouths.

On the last night I went down with Mrs. Durphy and two of the children to pack fish by the shores of the lake. Elfin-cold and heartless the water looked, with the black mass of the logging-company's barn looming beside it, and the sombre bush girding its further shore. The beautiful silver trout lay out on the bank, with a crate of ice beside them. We knelt down and set to work. The smooth elusive bodies of the fish suited the slippery winds of the night, far better than we did, fumbling in our sodden mitts. The full moon sailed arrogant into a cloudless sky; till, gazing upon the lifeless beauty of the moonlit water and the moon-shadowed bush, I was possessed by a consciousness of futility, and in escape from it began to think of the underworld and Pluto's unhappy little bride, till I half-remembered some lines of Oscar Wilde's:

> ... Persephone,
> In the dim meadows, desolate,
> Dost thou remember Sicily?

Yes, the dim meadows desolate. But not desolate for the Durphys, who carry within themselves their warmth and joy.

. . . .

We are on the road again. So far the weather has been perfect, but the local inhabitants continue to assure me with melodramatic solemnity that any morning I may wake to find that the temperature has dropped to "forty below," so I crawl out of bed every day in appropriate trepidation. There is one thing about this snow people make such a fuss about—when it does come, it will make better going for the horses.

Today I saw the fleeting form of a young deer among the trees. The animals here are shy as ghosts, and no wonder, for no one ever thinks of them but as victims for hunting and trapping. If they would keep quiet sometimes and watch some of these animals live, I think they would not be in such a hurry to see them die.

The days flow like slow rivers on and on. When we left the Durphys we travelled between forty and fifty miles and never saw a house. In pitch darkness we reached a small filling station, where they had hay prepared for us and a garage for the horses. Next morning I woke to find that several inches of the much-advertised snow had fallen during the night. I was glad to see the snow at last, after awaiting it so long. Fairy-white the wilderness looked which had been so dark and shadow-haunted the night before. The horses danced out freshly, sniffing the sparkly air, and away we went down the virgin white of the highway.

In all the towns through which we have passed, people asked me, "Haven't you ever been frightened?" The answer to this was "No." But last night for the first time I was frightened, though very likely without much reason.

At midday I had lunch on the highway with a road-gang, big husky jolly fellows who laughed and liked me, and at last asked if I would not have supper with them that evening in the village for which I was headed, and which lay some twenty miles further on. I was delayed on the road after that and did not reach the village till long after dark, when I found my road-gang outside the hotel, all roaring drunk, but by no means having forgotten our date for supper. I was so much horrified at the sight of them that I took refuge in the village store, raced through into the back parlour and burst into tears. The storekeeper's wife came and "Was a Mother to Me," and then, like a *Deus ex Machina*, in came a tall derelict Englishman, quiet as a monk and immaculately sober. Under his protection, having a little recovered my self-possession, I sallied out and had supper with my road-gang as arranged. My knight errant sat over me like the dragon guarding the Nibelungen treasure, and when it was over brought me back to the door of the store, kissed my hand and withdrew. I could almost see the moonlight glinting on his armour and the plume on his helmet fluttering in the wind!

Today, which is October the 29th, I believe, we saw a little silver fox. He crossed the road in front of us, then sat down to watch our approach, his beautiful tail lying along the snow. When we were quite near he got up and loped leisurely away among the trees. I happened to mention him to the people with whom I am spending the night. Their eyes sparkled. "We must set the traps out," they said. God help him now, poor little fox.

We are out of the wilderness and into the farms, and time flows again. Only thirty miles further on, Fort William stands at the head of the lakes. And suddenly here, where the glow of the city toward which we have been labouring can be seen in the night sky, I have abandoned all effort, and in the warm parlour of a spotless farm-house, I lie relaxed, half in Canada, half in England. For in the faces of the white-haired couple who surround me with their kindness shines the spirit of the old country; still in their hearts the grassy lanes of England go winding between the villages, meadow-sweet shines by the hedges, and waves break on the yellow beaches which they will not forget. "Mother and Dad" they already are for me; and, in the wistfulness of this fleeting adoption, I lie and long, as I have never longed before, for the meadows and the beechwoods and the windy downs of home.

Chapter XV

GREAT LAKE

I AM in Fort William, amid a whirl of social activity and complicated travel arrangements. Here I am up against a difficulty of whose existence I had been aware before I left England, to wit, the complete absence of any road round part of the north shore of Lake Superior. I had hoped to take a steamer from here to Sault Sainte Marie, on the eastern side of the lake, but, in addition to the fact that I have hardly enough money to afford it, I find that Canadian boats will not transport stock in the winter.

Some days ago, I believed the problem was solved. For I met a Norwegian sea captain whose freighter was to sail almost at once for Sault Sainte Marie. He was delighted to take us as his guests. Joyfully I began to make preparations. It was not till the day before we were to sail that I ran up against government regulations. Transport of Canadian goods in foreign ships was forbidden. I was distraught. I knew it was vain to reason with the minor officials of a government department, for one might as well make prayers to the wind or endeavour to explain oneself to a tea-pot. Frantically I rushed to enlist the sympathy of Fort William's Member of Parliament. He was convinced that an exception could easily be made and promised to do all he could for me in the time. But alas, the time was too short; and at four o'clock next morning, in a windy dawn, our little ship sailed without us.

Next, with the help of one of Fort William's most enterprising citizens, I pored over maps, telephoned all along the railway and visited innumerable authorities in the hope of discovering some way in which I could ride the two hundred and fifty miles of roadless wilderness. It seemed at first that I might be able to follow the railway line; but then came the insurmountable problem of crossing the rivers, many of which are wide and swift, flowing in rocky canyons, with only the railway bridges over them, whose ties are several feet apart, impossible footing for horses not trained to walk on them. So at last I have abandoned the struggle. Yesterday I gave another lecture, and quite a number of people came. So my finances are pretty good again. Tomorrow I set out to ride the hundred and fifty miles to Schreiber, on the north shore of the lake, where the road ends. Thence we take the train to Sault Sainte Marie.

It was a bitterly cold day when we set out for Schreiber. Wistfully I remembered the warmth of kindness and hospitality which I had left behind me in Fort William; but the horses went swinging resolutely up the highway, shaming me with their undaunted perseverance. Three days now we have been travelling north, with the great lake for our companion. Sometimes we lose sight of it, but never for long; it is there shining between the trees, it is there flashing suddenly as we round a shoulder of rock; when we climb to the height of a mountain it is there, spread out in a silver sheet.

Tonight we have reached Nipigon, where I am staying in a hotel which belongs to a general and his son. There are no tourists so late in the year, so I have my meals with the family, in the warm kitchen.

On the morning when I got ready to leave Nipigon, and asked for my bill, I found that there was none. "It's on the house," said the general's son, shaking hands cordially.

The day from Nipigon was very long indeed. Twelve hours on the road, too cold for rest. I do not know what I should have done if it had not been for the notice. After journeying for some hours through the wilderness, we came round a corner and there it was, neat black letters on a white ground: VISITORS ARE RE-QUESTED TO REGISTER AT THE Y.M.C.A. So, as I rode on, the fairy-tale began to grow in my mind:

At the time when the story begins, the horses and I are plodding along this same stretch of road. But there is snow on the ground, dusk is falling, and the horses and I are wondering where we shall sleep for the night. Behind and before us stretches the road, infinitely lonely. Around us broods the wilderness. Then we turn the corner and see the notice: VISITORS ARE REQUESTED TO REGISTER AT THE Y.M.C.A. I stare at it; we listen. No sound but the occasional swish of snow sliding off the spruce-branches. Then I notice a small trail on the right, winding away into the trees. There are no cart-ruts, but it is crisscrossed with the tracks of many animals. As I look, a squirrel pops up over a fallen log, chatters at me, and begins to skip down the trail, his tail in the air. The horses and I start out to follow him, and he disappears. On we go, brushing our way under the snow-laden branches. The shadows of the wilderness close in behind us.

Soon in the dimness we see before us a high pile of snow. As we draw near, it takes the form of an unusual-looking house; at last when we are quite close, we see over the door, in neat black letters: Y.M.C.A. The word "door" may give a slightly inaccurate impression, for it is a wide opening, covered with spruce-branches. As we wait uncertainly, they part, and a large grizzly stands before us. He is the identical grizzly that Timothy and I met in the mountains.

"Won't you come in?" he asks politely. "I will leave you for the present," he adds; "horses are nervous of me at first."

Snorting a little uncertainly, the horses push their way in, and we stand in a large hall, mysteriously light. Before me stands a desk; on it are placed a sharp stick, some black fungus and some birch-bark. Over the desk hangs a black and white notice: "Visitors Please Register." And underneath: "No hunters, Trappers or Timber-Wolves Allowed." After I have written our three names, our friend the grizzly returns and leads us through an opening into a long low room. On the outer wall is another large opening, covered with spruce-boughs, and the windows are ice.

Down the middle of the room runs a table, around which all kinds of animals are sitting and standing, munching contentedly. At one end the table is shaped like a manger, and here are standing several great solemn moose and deer of every size. I lead the horses up to this end of the room, and myself go down to the other. I sit down with a row of little black bears. Before me sit several porcupines, some long-legged jack-rabbits, and one little silver fox. Further down, a neat row of partridges sit perched on the edge of the table. An army of squirrels and chipmunks scuttle about arranging the food. Some of the guests look up as we come in, then go on munching.

"We don't waste time in talking," says the grizzly as he takes his place at the table, "I make an exception myself when we have human visitors; they are so curiously dependent upon conversation."

"Do you have many human visitors?" I asked.

"No," replies the large bear thoughtfully, "no."

I begin my supper. It is delicious—partridge eggs, and some sweet unknown roots. I am the only guest who has a plate.

"A picnic party left it behind last year in the woods," explains the bear. "I believe humans are used to them."

I wonder what the horses are getting to eat, and how they are behaving. I imagine they will be feeling a little like London children suddenly transported to the country—uncertain whether to be superior or shy. I know they must be thinking that the other animals have a very wild smell, and hope they are not showing it plainly enough to be rude. So I sneak a look down the table and can tell at a glance that Jonty is perfectly at home already. He is standing among some of the smaller deer, with his serious kindly little face half-buried in a large pile of birch-leaves and lichen. Timothy is not so happy. He is standing near the end, tense and jumpy, with his head sky-high, and on his face the expression of anxious disdain which I know so well. But as I watch, a pleasant matronly-looking moose cow pushes up beside him. She sniffs his nose politely and rubs her head against his neck. Timothy thaws perceptibly. He returns the sniff, and his ears go forward. Soon he stands happily munching beside his companion, and I know that he will enjoy his party now.

The grizzly recalls my attention. "I hope you like your supper?" he inquires politely. "We are not very well used to feeding humans. We have some trouble with little Kesan too," he adds, nodding toward the silver fox. "We don't really cater for foxes, but his mother was caught in a trap when he was very young; so we've had to do the best we can for him, poor little Kesan."

Supper is nearly over and there is a movement among the deer.

"The large animals go down to drink at the lake," explains the bear; "it saves hauling." Out they go, and I follow them through the spruce-branch doorway. The snow house stands right on the shores of the great lake. Splashing and crunching, the animals go down to water in the starlight. I turn and find the grizzly standing beside me again.

"The guests usually sleep together for warmth," he explains. "There are some very nice little black bears in one of the larger rooms; would you like to go in with them?" I indicate that that will suit me very well.

"You won't mind," my companion adds, "if one or two field-mice curl up in your hair? They find that such a comfortable bed. Oh, and by the way, I did speak to the porcupines about not eating your saddle, but it might be wise to take it to bed with you; leather is *such* a temptation to them you know." I thank him for his advice and watch the horses come in from the water with the deer. Timothy looks quite happy now and has become inseparable from the motherly moose cow.

So I go into the bears' bedroom and lie down comfortably between the round furry balls already curled up on the floor. Soon

I feel the field-mice warm and tiny against my forehead. We sleep.

I wake to find the little bears rolling over and snuffling. The dawn is pale at the windows; the field-mice scuttle away. I get up and go into the dining-room, where most of the animals are already at breakfast. When the meal is over, I lead the horses into the large entrance hall and pack them. Then we part the spruce-boughs and go out into the morning sunshine. The grizzly comes to bid us good-bye, and I ask how much we owe him.

"That's on the house," he answers kindly. "We hope you'll come back sometime." I thank him and say I hope so too, but I know that we shall never come back. . . .

So ended the story, and soon after, believe it or not, we passed another notice saying: VISITORS ARE REQUESTED TO REGISTER AT THE Y.M.C.A.

In the afternoon the road began to climb among the hills, sometimes coming out of the trees high above the island-studded lake, then plunging into the woods again, to emerge low down by the water, then once more riding high on the crest of a hill.

When we were still about fifteen miles from Cavers, our objective, dark fell. We were still curving in and out by the lake shore, but all we could see now was a pale sheet under the starless sky. I began to wonder what Cavers would be like. My thoughts set themselves to a jingle, and went round and round in time to the horses' feet:

> If only They
> Get lots of hay
> And a good place to stay,
> We'll call it a day.
>
> The thing is They
> Must get their hay.

Over and over the words went; on and on we plodded.

At last, after an eternity of darkness, we came to a small trail leading down to the railway line and lake shore. Straining my eyes I read a notice "To Cavers." Down we went, and in a quarter of a mile came to four little houses at the bottom of a steep bank beside the railway. I left the horses at the top and clambered, as best I could in the dark, to the nearest of the houses. I was greeted by a little woman with a kind, slightly worried smile, and by deafening barking from three large dogs.

"We're delighted to have you stay," shouted the little woman through the tumult; "but what will you do with the horses?"

What indeed? There was no hay or oats, and not a ghost of a barn. Only a rocky hill-side and a railway with trains roaring past all night. The next place was twelve miles further on; it would take us hours to get there, and the horses were tired out. So all I could do was to unsaddle them and turn them to graze on a little meagre grass by the track. At this moment a broad friendly foreigner issued from the house next door, and we were introduced. His name appeared to be "Carsick." He generously volunteered to watch the horses, so I went indoors. About midnight we felt we must go to bed, so I tied the unlucky horses to trees in the forest, rugged them up, fed them some porridge-oats and cornmeal, generously provided by my hostess and Mr. Carsick, and left them to their unpleasant night.

After this came sleep, but not for long. About three o'clock I heard a train clatter past; then furious barking; then the beat of hoofs. Scrambling into some clothes I staggered out into the night. There was Timothy terrified, tearing through the bush and snorting like a wild boar. With some trouble I recovered him and tied him once more beside the patient Jonty. I shall never forget the look of dumb reproach with which the two gazed after me as I returned to the house. It was a tired and listless cavalcade which set out next morning for Schreiber.

But the day was exquisite; and the higher and steeper the hills were, the more lovely would be the view from the top. Suddenly one would come out on to the crest, and there would be the lake below, silver in the sunshine, curving in long bright lines among its dark islands. At Rossport the road dropped down out of the hills and ran for many miles close beside the water. Then it climbed up again into the woods, and the lake was lost.

That evening, which was November the thirteenth, we reached Schreiber. Here I found the famous Y.M.C.A., and one of the kindest welcomes I have met anywhere. I stayed with the president of the Board of Trade and his wife; but this stately description gives a slightly mistaken impression of big schoolboyish Dave, whose chief amusement while I was there was to grumble about what a fearful nuisance it was to have me, beaming all the while like Santa Claus.

I made a great many friends in the little railroad-town. First there were Dave and Ethel, my host and hostess; then there was their little niece, Jeanne, and the tall, serious principal of her high school. Then there were the Scotts, some of the greatest horse-lovers I have met. Young Short Scott worked for the horses like a hero. He groomed them till they fairly sparkled; he decorated Timothy's bridle with brass studs, and spent a whole day driving his father's cart round town collecting lumber, after which the two of them built a magnificent pair of stalls in the large forbidding box-car which was to house the unlucky horses for two nights and a day. Then there was a plump, humorous, middle-aged lady, one of whose charms lay in the unique aptness of her name—"Auntie Bun." Last but not least there was Duke. Duke is large, broad in the beam and important in manner. Well he may be, for he is a Hero Dog. He saved the life of a transient, who fainted on the railway track, by meeting the on-coming train, running beside the cab, and barking until the driver stopped. Now he lives in modest state at the Y.M.C.A., and visitors are privileged to meet him and admire his medal and framed certificate of valour.

In Schreiber I gave a lecture to about five hundred people. This is the third I have given, and much the largest. Women and children sat in front; men stood in solid formation at the back

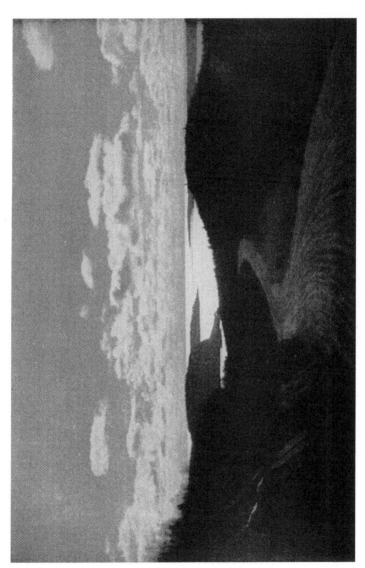

"CURVING IN LONG BRIGHT LINES AMONG ITS DARK ISLANDS"

of the hall, and little boys festooned themselves along the window-ledges. I was rather glad when it was over.

At last, with the help of my friends, I packed the horses into their box-car, said an anxious farewell to them, and next morning went down to the big trans-Canada train which was to take me as far as Franz. A large party saw me off—Dave and Ethel, Short Scott, and several of my railway friends, looking very different in their working clothes. At the last minute, along bounded Auntie Bun, occupied as ever, seeing off half a dozen people at once. Punctual to the minute, the big trans-continental train came clanking in. Dave found me a place; sadly I said good-bye. These partings are the worst part of the trip. Some one in railway overalls took a Johnny Walker charm off his watch-chain and hung it on my shirt-button. Auntie Bun, not to be outdone, took a green handkerchief out of her pocket and crumpled it into my hand. The great train belched steam. I bolted up the carriage steps, and slowly, ponderously, we got under way.

At Franz the horses and I changed onto a freight train of the Algoma Central Railway. They must have had an awful time, bumping in their box-car over the rocky track, but I went in the caboose and enjoyed myself greatly. The caboose is a regular little house, with a writing-table, kitchen-table, cooking-stove and four bunks. Two little ladders lead up to the glassed-in look-out.

I sat up there for hours and watched the long train winding its way before us, in and out of rock cuts and spruce trees, across wide rivers and along the shores of icy lakes. Curious it was to sit high up above the curving train and watch the sun setting in winter gold above the rock-bound hills. Night fell wild and windy, with clouds racing across the moon, and the lights of the engine driving their way through a tunnel of blackness. As I watched the smoke billowing red in the light of the furnace, I thought that poor Timothy had had every reason to be afraid of the dragons that came hooting and breathing fire out of the darkness, the night the horses were tied by the railway line at Cavers.

At nine o'clock I climbed down from my look-out and shared supper with the brakemen, to which they contributed hamburger steak, and I contributed hard-boiled eggs and apples and jam sandwiches, given me by Ethel. After that they let me lie down in one of the bunks, and I knew no more, except occasionally when a train reached a station and stopped, with the devastating crash apparently inevitable on the Algoma Central Railway. At three o'clock in the morning we reached Sault Sainte Marie, and I was shaken awake and taken home by the head brakeman, whose wife came down stairs, broad awake and perfectly charming, and cooked us bacon and eggs.

So here we were in Sault Sainte Marie, and here, with an inconsequent bump, the journal stops.

For it was after we left Sault Sainte Marie, that the adventure, which hitherto had obediently followed the pattern which I had designed for it, got out of hand, and began to push me into a pattern of its own. For on leaving Sault Sainte Marie, Timothy went lame; nothing spectacular, nothing dramatic, just slightly lame. And a few days later, we reached Dayton.

Looking back now upon the little community to which for eight months my life belonged, it is hard to remember how it appeared on that first day. I know that the wind was cutting like a knife across the highway, and I was glad to leave it and climb up a sandy road into the bush. For about an hour I rode through the trees; then the trail led out into the open, and on either hand stood farms in the midst of their land, with the bush beyond. For two miles we followed the road between these farms; I little knew how familiar their occupants were to become. All I knew at this time was that somewhere south of the road stood a house with a windmill on its roof, whose owner, Mrs. David Gordon, was expecting me to lunch.

At last the little house hove in sight. It was brown and unadorned, standing high, and below it stood a great barn. I rode up the lane and was preparing to knock at the door, when a perfect whirlwind of energy came flying out to greet me. Mrs. Gordon it was, with her grey hair swirling and a smile of welcome wreathing her vivid face. We put the horses in the barn, went into the house and were instantly happy. Our racy, intuitive minds went home to each other in enchanted discovery. Mrs. Gordon watched me as I galloped through my dinner, and I watched her, as her elfin eyes cracked sparks from her mischievous, generous face. We decided that I would stay over the next day to rest Timothy. In the evening the boys came home: fair-haired Harold, broad and strong, back from hunting, and big boisterous Bob, down from the lumber camps. On Sunday morning I left, not knowing that I should ever see them again.

I was to spend that day with some English people called Skerten, who lived six miles further in, at the eastern end of the little community. At midday I reached a neat red house on the shores of a lake and found a delightful family, with a welcome for me which warmed my heart. Soon we were sitting down to dinner in a sun-parlour looking out upon the lake. Some neighbours were there, Shetlanders called Tait. So we sat and talked of England and the salt sea-breezy Shetlands, till our thoughts sped home together over the sea. Then the Skertens invited me to stay for the winter, and I was sorely tempted, but I still believed then that we should reach Montreal, so regretfully I tore myself away, and we started out once more.

On we went, up the lonely highway. The weather was not cold, but grey and lifeless, the fields and the bush stood stark and brown, and Timothy continued to be lame.

One night I stayed with a family of Icelanders, and ever since that evening this vital and tragic nation has lived in my mind. Driven from their own country by catastrophe and failure, many Icelanders have come out to Canada to settle in Manitoba on the shores of Lake Winnipeg. But the power and poetry of their national character has come with them; so that the mothers still teach their children to do right from pride of race, still gather them on windy nights to sing them the sagas of their ancient nation, and warn them of the "hidden people" who inhabit the storm. Among these virile Northerners a literature has grown up which has made a valuable contribution to Canadian life.

After we left the Icelanders the road was lonely again. Timothy, for all my cosseting, grew no better, and I began to realize that he would not get to Montreal. Then rain began to fall, bitter steely rain, beating into our eyes and soaking the pack, running in muddy drops off the horses' shoulders. That evening I reached a French Canadian settlement and went to a large farm to ask for shelter. The farmer's wife indicated that she knew no English, and I repeated my request in halting French. Madame looked at my dishevelled hair and sodden clothes with justifiable distaste. No, it seemed she could not support the idea of my staying for the night. But as I was about to set out again, her husband arrived and, after an altercation, he led the horses and me away to the barn, after which I returned with him to the house and asked diffidently whether I might dry the pack. But at this Madame was thrown into fresh transports of disgust. Not only was I to leave my pack in the woodshed, she said, but I should oblige her by leaving my boots as well. I complied with her request and crawled into the kitchen with the humiliation of a tramp. Madame grumped over the store, in no way reconciled to my presence.

Next morning rain was still falling in a forbidding sheet. My boots and pack were sodden, but I hurried through my breakfast and thankfully set out again. Madame charged me two fifty for my night's lodging, more than I have ever paid before or since. All day we travelled and dripped and the mud splashed round our legs.

At last, as dark was falling, I saw a large farm-house on a hill at our left. Acutely conscious of the increased repulsiveness of my appearance, I trailed up the wagon-road towards its square outline and knocked faintly on the door. It was thrown open, and a sea of heat and laughter came billowing out. Blinking in the light my eyes discerned several big blond men, blond children rolling on the floor and a fat blonde woman among them.

"What you standing out there for? Come right in!" she commanded.

I murmured inarticulately about my muddiness.

"Lord, that don't matter; we got lots of mud," replied the fair-haired amazon, sweeping the boys aside and drawing me in by the arms.

"Who you got with you?" she asked. "What, nobody, only horses? Well, for goodness' sake! Put them in the new barn, Emil. You come along in now, and get dried off."

But I slipped from under her hand and went out to the barn with Emil, rubbed down the horses and dried their heels, while he fed them, gazing at them and gazing at me, and turning us all over in his big blond mind.

Back in the warm kitchen, I found that my friends were a family of Finns, a noisy, kindly, light-hearted family, for whom the arrival of a visitor with two horses was a great bit of fun. They put me to sleep on the living-room sofa, where their father, coming home at midnight from the Sudbury mines, shone the lantern in my face in very natural surprise. This woke me, and I settled down to some thinking. By the morning my mind was made up.

Timothy was not going to recover his soundness without a rest. Winter was nearly upon us, and we still had five hundred miles to go to Montreal. Timothy would not make it. So I telegraphed to the Skertens to ask if we might come back, received a delighted reply, put the horses on a truck which was returning empty in the direction of Sault Sainte Marie, and cheerfully exchanged the prospect of reaching Montreal for the prospect of a winter snowed up in Dayton.

It was a windy evening when we turned in at the gate of the

Skerten farm. The children ran to meet us. Cyril Skerten helped me put the horses in the barn; Elsie, her rosy English face shining with welcome, was waiting for me in the fire-lit house. And so, easily and without disappointment, I abandoned myself to the luxury of a home.

Chapter XVI

WE DROP ANCHOR

LUXURY it certainly was, such as I could never have imagined; the perfection of which was the product of our journeying months. To unpack my few possessions and put away the saddlebags; to belong day after day to the same warm house, to the same circle of friendly faces; to cease from the continued effort of progress into the unknown, yet not to have failed and abandoned it forever. So must Caesar and his armies have felt when they "went into winter quarters," and discovering ships when they anchored in quiet bays to wait for the spring.

There were four in my new home—Cyril and Elsie, Sheila, their quiet twelve-year-old daughter, and little round rosy-faced four-year-old Lee. I was soon established in the routine of the new life and began to learn the work of the farm.

Before dawn, Cyril and I would take the lanterns and make our way to the stable, where he would milk, while I fed the stock. Every day I was bound afresh by the wonder of the early morning barn. We would hang the lanterns in the rafters, misty among the creatures' breath. The shadows would huddle into the corners in hollowed bodies of darkness. The faces of the animals, headed into the light, glowed warmly, while beneath and behind them clustered the shadows, rounded, rich as the night. I would go to the pile of hay under the chute, twirl a coil of it on to my fork, and begin to feed the horses. Then they would cease to be mere shapes and light-effects and would become characters again. The nervous black-faced mare would snort and start back, never released from her fear-obsession. Her white-faced work-mate would drop her nose into her feed without a look, while Timothy, his regal head sky-high, stamped and nickered to me imperiously to hurry, and little Jonty, last of the line, waited patiently with his ears cocked, making no demonstration, knowing his turn would come. In the sound-background, as I fed the calves, would be stamping and munching, the swish of hay and the rhythmic chime of the milk ringing changes into the pails, first lean and cutting against the side, then plump and generous into the white bed which soon frothed up to meet it.

So we would return laden towards the house, and see where the promise of light was glimmering pale above the bush. In the warm kitchen breakfast would be ready, and as we made away with porridge and coffee and good brown bread, we would look out through our eastern window to watch the dawn leading the sunrise up the sky.

Breakfast over, Sheila would start out for school, and we would stuff Lee into his snow suit and watch the red roly-poly figure issuing out into his new morning. Then there would be the horses to water, separator and dishes to wash, and afterwards churning, sweeping, dusting, washing, whatever was the order of the day—and in no time dinner to prepare.

After dinner, when the animals were fed, Cyril, one of the most systematic and unremitting workers I have ever seen, would soon be deeply occupied again; young Lee would set out once more upon his absorbing avocations; Elsie might sit down for a little while to read; and I would either write an article for the Sault Sainte Marie *Star*, for which I soon became a regular columnist, or else saddle Jonty and ride into the bush.

I would turn back with the dusk, and perhaps meet Sheila on the road from school, and put her up to ride, running beside her. So we would come in to help with supper, and after supper there would be the milking and feeding again, and the barn, with the animals standing in the shadows. When all was done, we would go in again and find Elsie waiting for us by the kindly wood fire. So we would sit down together and read and talk and dream, sharing our quiet English origins, so remote from the

"AT NIGHTFALL THEY WOULD COME BACK, SECRET AND SATISFIED"

majesty of Ontario's half-tamed winter forests. . . .

Slowly as the days went by, I began to know some of our nearer neighbours. On a fine farm across the lake lived Magnus Tait and his family. Magnus was from the Shetlands; it was fifty years since he had left the windy islands of his home, but the sea was still in his heart. He could talk for hours of his youth, when he went with the other boys fishing. "I'd like to be off the coast now," he would say, "with my hand on the tiller, a heavy sea on our weather bow, and the waves leaping up thirty feet into the air." Then his weathered blue eyes would look beyond the bush, and the far-away days would be in them, and wet sails and salt nets and great seas and little ships, and young men battling lean and strong, and one of them he.

Magnus had three children: Bruce, who had a fine head and a remarkable mind and insatiable energy; Alfred, shy and quiet, and possessed of a delightful wit not easily discovered; and Anna, whose fine spirit struggled with ill health, a weary unremitting warfare.

Two miles to the south of Magnus, the farm of his forty-year-old nephew nestled in the bush. Johnny Tait was a wholly delightful person. He was broad and fair, with the round radiant face of the perennial schoolboy. He was a bachelor and lived in his pretty white farm-house alone with a young hired man. Johnny liked me because I had energy and a sense of humour and curly hair. "If you had blue eyes, Mary, you'd be a stunner," he used to say. I liked him for his goodwill and his generous laughter and the way the wide smile would spread over his little-boy face. He is married now, to a fine strong young woman, with a voice like a lark and laughter to match his own, and I can picture how the little farm rings with their happiness. She has blue eyes too!

Well, these were our neighbours south of the lake. Beside us, on the north shore, lived an ever-lengthening family with a happy-go-lucky nature and most beautiful hair. Every child as it came inherited this lovely hair—tight curls of it or loose waves, red or nut-brown or fair, each different and each a glory.

A little way beyond them lived a quiet, pleasant family of four: mother and father and two daughters, a golden one and a brown one; and west of them again lived Mrs. Henry Kirby, whose husband, with their best team, was "up in the bush."

Many of the Dayton men spend the winter working at the logging-camps. Sometimes this is called "up in the bush," sometimes "in the camps," and sometimes "up north." The words made a legend in my mind, and at night the north would build winter fortresses into my dreams, fortresses of ice-bound wilderness with snow-white trails under arches of black forest, men labouring and great horses straining into the collar, with sweat-frost on their shoulders; then evening, and men clustering round the lamplight in the warm cabins; then frosty dawn behind the trees and teamsters tumbling out to feed the horses, to harness them and drive out again into another morning. Anyway, Mrs. Kirby's husband was "up in the bush," and meanwhile she managed the farm very competently on her own.

West of Mrs. Kirby, on the other side of the road, lived an old lady and her son; then came the church. Every second Sunday, in winter, a young minister came out from Iron Bridge to give us a service. After the first heavy fall of snow, our roads were impassable for a car. The inhabitants of Dayton were very thoroughly "snowed in." So young Mr. Mackay would drive out in a cutter or walk out on skis, and a long day Sunday was for him. But he was always there, cheerful and energetic, with a story in his head for the children and a vivid address for us. Afterwards he had news of the doings at Iron Bridge or plans for a skating-party or a good joke to tell us. Pleasantly we all looked forward to the afternoon hour in the little church.

A mile west of the church lived a large family of the name of King. At their house the road turned at right angles and ran south for half a mile. Where it turned west again stood the school-house, and opposite the school-house lived some more Taits, Katie and Billy, who soon came to be particular friends of mine. They lived in a very small, very neat house, and they had one child, a quiet, affectionate little girl who conceived a great love for the horses and me. Katie was the most methodical person in Dayton. I have never known any one so serenely immune from the disease of clutter. As soon as I settle anywhere for more than a few weeks, clutter accumulates. I do not go to get it; it comes to me. Books, papers, handkerchiefs, mending, knitting, letters—all kinds of things which I can neither find when I want them nor throw away when I do not want them—clutter. But Katie's house and Katie's life had in them exactly what was needed, and not one atom of rubbish over and above to cumber the ground. What we found in each other was the charm of the opposite; Katie loved me for my scatter-brained sea-breeziness, and I loved her for the swept and garnished serenity of her ordered life.

Beyond Katie and Billy lived the Smiths, another Shetland family. This sturdy sea-faring stock from our most northern islands form the very root and branch of the East Dayton community. Opposite to the Smiths lived a Scotsman who rejoiced in the romantic border-ballad name of Lauchie McKinnon; and on the hill above Lauchie McKinnon lived the Charlie Kirbys, a quiet, gracious family, possessed of an exquisite unconscious distinction. The children were beautiful with a beauty not striking but penetrating; slender they were and strong, with light-boned, delicate faces and long light hands. I never watched these children but my mind saw thoroughbreds, long-legged and perfect, moving over English meadows.

So these were our neighbours in East Dayton; and, busy with the adventure of so many new people to discover, busy in my new life and my new home, I settled down to meet the Canadian winter. Soon the weeks drew on towards Christmas. At this time I was writing articles with great energy for the Sault Sainte Marie *Star;* here is one which describes the last week of the year:

Christmas starts early in Algoma. For us it starts with the school concert.

There is snow on the ground and sleet in the wind, as the car bumps its way along the road. The night is black and the storm wails through the bush. We shiver and pull the rugs closer round us. At last we reach the little school-house and stumble through the snow into a warm, lamplit world. By the platform stands a magnificent Christmas tree with presents piled high beside it. The walls are garlanded with pine branches and bright with Christmas decorations. We squeeze ourselves into the waiting desks. In the front two rows the seventeen prospective performers bounce and wriggle in anxious expectancy.

We wait. Bumps behind the curtain. Repeated calls on Miss Mitchell, the teacher. We re-arrange ourselves in our desks. We wait. At last, three quarters of an hour late, but debonair and unashamed, the chairman arrives.

Then we go to it. It is an incredibly generous program. First an opening chorus, then an opening speech by a small boy, finally an opening speech by the chairman; and after this a perfect galaxy of carols, recitations, dances and plays. The children enjoy themselves immensely and so do the audience. I am sorry when we come to the last item, or rather the last but one. For the high light of the evening is yet to come. At last there is a stir at the back of the room. Children crane their necks; babies in the audience wake up, and their eyes grow rounder and rounder. For here, beard and corporation complete, red-coated, red-faced and as friendly as you please, comes Santa Claus himself! Up he goes on to the platform and begins to undress the tree and hand out the presents. There is one for every child in the community, one for the teacher, one for the pianist and one I think for the belated chairman. So ends the evening.

After this party there is a few days' lull, and then comes the big business of fetching the tree. On Friday morning we set out. It is a lovely blue and white day, with the sunlight sparkling on the snow, and the naked trees standing graceful against the winter sky. Soon we are deep in the bush. We choose a sturdy little spruce; it looks strong and fearfully alive, standing up in the forest, and I am sorry to see it fall.

We come panting home, laden with our spoils; then the decorating begins. With the cold fragrant little tree, the spirit of Christmas comes into the house. We sing and laugh and race up and down the stairs, going everywhere in a hurry. Young Lee is the busiest of us all. He stomps about after us, repeating solemnly to himself, "Dingull Bells, Dingull Bells, all a way."

And then over the radio comes Mummy's favourite carol, "As with gladness men of old." Suddenly I can see her, slim, dark-eyed Mummy, and hear her voice singing it, trying to teach it to me long ago, when I was a very little girl. But I have not long to be home-sick, for we are much too busy twining pine branches up the stairs, blowing up balloons, sticking paper chains and stretching them across the ceiling. At last we are finished, and lovely it all looks, more like a fairy-tale forest than the inside of a house.

And so comes Christmas day!

By a quarter past six, the children have us all awake, examining the contents of our three stockings, for there is one for me too. "Did you see Santa Claus last night?" Lee asks me. "Did you see his deers?" When everything has been admired, Cyril and I go out to do the chores. Dim and lovely the barn looks in the light of the lanterns. The animals stand shadowy in the mists of their breath. And I think of a stable not so very different, and of another Christmas morning, and remember a verse of Christina Rossetti's carol:

> Enough for him whom cherubim
> Worship night and day,
> A breastful of milk and a mangerful of hay;
> Enough for him whom angels
> Fall down before,
> The ox and ass and camel
> Who adore.

With a bump I come back to December twenty-fifth, 1939, finish feeding and run back to the house. Nobody eats much breakfast. For the children the idea of eating is pure nonsense, and the rest of us providently leave room for our Christmas dinner. Soon the dishes are cleared away, and the children drag us by main force into the living-room. There stands the tree with bright lights on its branches and another behind, throwing the shadows of the boughs against the wall. But the children do not waste much time in admiring dramatic effects; in no time the curtains are thrown back from the windows, and out come the presents. There are all kinds of toys for Lee, skis for Sheila, and for me the loveliest pair of skates. Cyril, registering appropriate surprise, receives the jack-knife which Lee has been more than hinting at for the last week. Then we go out on the lake. I put on the beautiful new skates and happily make a fool of myself for the rest of the morning.

When Christmas dinner is over, we are soon out again. In the middle of the afternoon Johnny Tait comes over the lake on a highly ingenious contraption which he has just built. He assures us that he has never seen any of Heath Robinson's pictures, but I find it hard to believe that he was not inspired by that artist. The front of the conveyance is formed by a toboggan, on the tail of which sits a McCormick Deering engine. Behind this is a kind of wheelbarrow, on two motor car wheels, connected to the engine by a slightly precarious belt. The vehicle seats four and races about the lake at a prodigious speed. In its early stages it was called "the boomerang," from an original tendency to run in circles, but I understand that the steering has since been adjusted to a nicety.

On Christmas evening the neighbours come in. We talk and sing carols. But Johnny Tait is back again with his boomerang, and soon a number of us leave the fireside and run down to the moonlit lake. Johnny has his car out as well, and we jump in and he drives us across to the other side. There is a strange thrill in driving a car over a lake, with the ice cracking and booming under you, and the shores so far away. On the other side there is a great fire burning, and a circle of skaters around it, their faces glowing in the light of the flames. We sit down and warm ourselves, and then away we go on the boomerang. Back to Brighton Beach again and into the house, where we persuade and cajole, until we finally haul the whole party out on to the ice. Midnight draws on; and then some one looks up at the moon. Have you ever seen a moon-rainbow? I have heard of them without its making much impression. But now that I have seen one I shall never forget it. The moon is full, sailing in amber light; and around it are two perfect circles of the prismatic colours.

So with moonlight and a rainbow, Christmas ends.

. . . .

It was not until the new year that the winter really closed in upon us. The lake had frozen over, quickly and completely, in the middle of December. The dark waters which splashed up under our windows lay suddenly white and still. Soon we were walking tentatively across; then driving, and finally faring backward and forward as though on the solid land. But the snow tarried. Only half-hearted flurries had decorated the trees and laid a thin carpet upon the ground. It was not till New Year's morning that Cyril and I, starting out to do the chores, stumbled almost on to our knees in a nest of snow. As we left the shelter of the house, the storm swept blinding into our eyes; between its whirling skirts we caught glimpses of a white-blanketed world. The dogs' kennel, half-hidden under a drift, laden trees bending down, and only the wall of the barn standing up, dark and naked, with the white veil of the storm swirling across its face.

So here was the winter at last! Here was the demon who had hunted us through the wilderness. Wild horse Winter with his white mane streaming, galloping down the wind—here he was!

As we went on into January the work of the year began. First ice-cutting. It was a brilliantly sunny day when I looked out of the kitchen window to see Cyril at work on the lake, with the fortress-wall of sky-blue ice-blocks rising around him and the small scarlet figure of Lee solemnly watching. The little fir trees put to mark the hole were dark against the snow; so were the figures of the two dogs, trotting away across the lake, leaving a zigzag track behind them.

Some days later I walked over the lake to watch ice-cutting on a large scale by the Taits. Johnny Tait had invented a highly efficient machine for cutting and loading the blocks, worked by the same faithful donkey-engine which had propelled the boomerang.

By this time Timothy was sound again, so I would ride him through the bush with Jonty running beside us. At first I would ride slowly, watching the intricate pattern of the shadows under the trees, and the red-gold fire of Timothy's coat against the blue and white of the snow. But then the winter would take hold of us, and away we would go, swishing under the branches of the pines, swinging round the curves of the trail, Timothy bounding under me, steady and strong, and Jonty, a little dark spirit, flying beside us.

Sometimes, on days when I did not ride the horses, we would turn them loose, and they would gallop away into the bush, kicking up their heels and calling to each other. At nightfall they would come back, secret and satisfied, and I would wonder what adventures they had had and what they had seen in the forest. Wherever I went the horses took me. I remember one evening when I rode Jonty over to a party at the Smiths'. When at last we set out for home, there was snow in the wind and the night was black. But Jonty, undaunted, galloped up the centre of the road, swinging round the corners with never a false step. So I let him out and raced into the dark, with the wind in my hair and snow in my eyes and the pony's fine muscles rippling under the saddle. As long as I remember Jonty, I shall remember that night.

The horses had the depths of my love in those winter days. They have it now, though I may never seen them again. Timothy is magnificent. His coat is red as the sunrise and smooth as satin all through the winter; the cascade of his splendid tail is silver and gold; he carries his head like a king and disdains humanity; he is power and beauty and pride. He is a horse to admire for hours, leaning against the barn-door; a horse to groom and groom, slowly and lovingly; a horse to sit straight in the saddle of; a horse with a dignity to be respected, with a solemnity not to be shaken; a horse to ride upon like a princess, for he walks like a prince. Just a horse though, and no more.

But Jonty is different. He has no particular splendour. He is little and dark, and his coat in the winter would do credit to a bear. There is no pride in his small face; it is simple and innocent and vivid. But Jonty is spirit for me. He is all I love and long for and have and have not. He is fire and flood and storm and laughter and loneliness. He is freedom and fearlessness and the will to do and the will to give, and passion and poetry and search. He is the secret of the wilderness and the sunlight of the plain; he is mountains and rivers and the moon in cloud-rack and the sun riding into a storm; and all that is lost to cities, and all that is hid from the wise; all I have found, all I am seeking, all I shall never find—little Jonathan, little dark Jonathan, with all of Life in his eyes.

Chapter XVII

ACCIDENT

THEY were so beautiful that they were only half real, those weeks of the Canadian new year. For always the mind laboured in Europe, taut with the suspense of this first strange winter of the war. In varying degrees of anxiety, we, remote in Dayton, waited with the participants in the central struggle for the explosion which we knew must come. Meanwhile little Finland fought for her life. Always as I watched the snow deepening round the barns, mantling the bush thicker and thicker, my mind saw the Finns and the Russians fighting in the ghostly winter forests beside Lake Ladoga. Always in the background of those nights and days the conflict was joined.

It was at the end of January that a mishap occurred which altered the pattern of my life at Dayton. At the time I was paying a few days' visit to the Smiths. One morning I was riding Jonty bareback along the road from the school-house; and Timothy, with another rider in the saddle, was cantering decorously ahead. We were making for the farm, and Jonty was frantic to go; he was pitching and throwing his head and bouncing me all over his smooth, naked back. At last, dexterously combining body and head action, he flipped me up on to his neck; then he seized the bit and away he went like the tail of a wind. There was no hope of stopping him, so I slid back into position and sat confidently enough, knowing that he would gallop up to the barn and stop. But I had not considered the speed at which he was going. He swung into the farm gate but could not make the right-angled turn; instead he shot off the road and headed straight for a tree. When he was almost breathing on the bark, he swerved to the right, while I went straight on and hit the tree with the full force of our meteoric approach.

At first lying in the snow I could not breathe or move, but I found that my mind worked exactly as usual; I remember thinking:

"Of course—this is what an accident feels like."

"Thank Goodness Jonty is all right."

"I hope I haven't hurt my inside."

"I hope they won't come for me at once, because until I can breathe again I shan't be able to speak."

Well, they did not come at once, because, as they afterward told me, they were afraid I was dead. So when some one did come, I was able to speak quite well and walk into the living-room, where I lay down on the sofa and became quite busy controlling all the pains which began to wake up down my left side. For some days I could walk very little, as I had apparently struck the tree with my left hip. So I lay and thought of Finland, dreamily watching the sunshine climb up the kitchen door, absently following the oiled lines of the aspidistra which inhabited a green pot on a small table at the foot of the sofa.

I soon began to recover, and in order to show the sympathetic neighbours how little I was hurt, I went to church on Sunday, and illustrated my meaning exactly by fainting like a stone in the middle of the first hymn. I returned to somewhat vague consciousness to discover that the service had stopped and that the congregation in the front pews had turned round in a body and were regarding my exhibition with horror, while the minister had come down from his accustomed eminence and was plying me with aspirin. When somewhat recovered, I was removed to the porch, where I sat on a woodpile shivering and mortified, while a young man ran to fetch me some water. He revived my drooping spirits considerably by returning five minutes later, panting and purple in the face, with an entire pailful. Whether he was under the impression that it was to be poured over me, or whether he expected me to drink it all, I never discovered.

Soon after this ignominious episode I went home to the Skertens, and finally set out on a lengthy pilgrimage to the doctor. First a four-mile sleigh-ride to Iron Bridge, Elsie driving, with Lee sitting beside her and me behind on the floor of the sleigh. At Iron Bridge, lunch with the minister and his family, finally the arrival of the doctor on his return from the bush, where he had been visiting the camps, and the drive in his car to Blind River. Examination showed that I had done no serious damage except to my arm, which was broken, and proved very hard to set. I shall never forget the kindness of the doctor and his wife, who kept me with them for days, nursing me as though I belonged to them.

When I returned to the Skertens, their kindness was as great. I think one of the most wonderful things about an accident is the sympathy and kindness which it awakes both in friends and strangers. Another discovery which I made is that, when the body is rendered to some extent inactive, the mind goes adventuring with all the more freedom.

For some time I could use my arm very little, and I was sternly forbidden by the doctor to ride, skate or otherwise disport myself; so I would walk for long hours in the bush, gazing at the winter, and struggling with my own incapacity to receive such glory.

I never knew before (I wrote at that time with hopeless inadequacy) what it could be like. I have never known this brilliant snow and the blue shadows bending under the trees with such a startling grace that it sets the mind racing through labyrinths of remembered language, searching in vain for words alive and vivid enough to hold them. And the sleigh-trails—I do not believe anything in the summer can be lovelier than these winter trails, winding through the bush, dappled blue and white with sunshine and shadow; then suddenly sweeping out on to a wide white field, which goes curving up on every side to its dark border of pine.

These winter pine trees are not green. When you watch them massed between the snow and the sky, they are not green or blue or brown or purple or red; they are all these, blended into a shadow-colour, deep as the night, but with life which the night shadows have not. And before this dark vivid background the dazzling stems of the silver birches spring up like shafts of light. On days like this, when I have gazed till I am half drowned in the sunshine and the shadow, I long suddenly for a cutter with a thoroughbred in the shafts, and to go flying home over the snow like a woodcock down the wind. It seems waste of such a world to stump about on one's slow feet or bump along with a team and sleigh.

I often think of my mother. She has no love for the snow. She has seen it in Sweden and Switzerland, in Finland and Germany and Russia, but still she would wait all winter for the spring. I wish I might have her here—on a morning when the hoar-frost decks the naked trees with silver and jewels, or an evening when the shadows lengthen and the light of sunset is warm over the snow.

Certainly I did think often of my mother, and not only of her, but of the whole quality of our family life; and in those days, far away in the Canadian bush, the intimate reality of all that we share came vividly alive in my mind. In the quarter of a century which we have known together, we have had as a family two distinct lives—first the official, dignified life in Daddy's consulates on the Continent; after that the walking, working, gardening, pony-riding life in the thatched manor house of Beechingstoke. But somehow we are too compact, too well-centred a family to vary very much in varying surroundings.

There are only four of us—my father and mother, my brother and I. We are all quite dramatically different one from another, and we fit together like pieces in a puzzle. Peter is tall and quiet and humorous and efficient; my father is small and square with a dazzling sincerity which is instantly captivating; and my mother is dark and beautiful and perfectly unaware of herself; and her life belongs to every one she meets and never to her. I am the bronc in the bunch never quite corralled; belonging and yet not quite.

We have, like many families I suppose, a private vocabulary. Ours is composed of three languages, with all kinds of modifications and variants on familiar words, and many words entirely its own. "Whuskers!" is one, an untranslatable ejaculation having many distinct variations in meaning. "Pinking" (adjective) is another. It means appealing, but much more than that. It means so wistfully appealing that the heart melts away like snow, and the pinked victim is conquered utterly by the pinker, be he man, child or animal.

In addition to the language we have an entirely fictitious family cat named Juggins, to whose graceful and serene activities my mother in particular makes recurrent reference. In the presence of visitors the family language is necessarily abandoned, and Juggins undoubtedly should be. An aged governess of Daddy's, who once paid us a lengthy visit, was seriously exercised by the occasional inadvertent entry of Juggins into the conversation. At last we carefully explained to her his wholly imaginary character and believed that her mind was at rest. But on the day of her departure she drew my mother aside, and gazing at her with anxious eyes she inquired, "But I thought you never really had a cat at all?" Since then we have made renewed efforts to keep Juggins from disconcerting visitors!

Besides Juggins we had for twelve years a perfectly solid flesh-and-blood dog, a West Highland terrier called John. He was not spoilt; he had one meal a day and nothing between; he was not allowed on all the chairs, and he was generally made to come when he was called; but he was our household god, nevertheless. He was a small dog, but with a great and stately presence, and with a voice as deep as a bloodhound's. He lived with us in our

ACCIDENT

years at the consulate and afterward at Beechingstoke. Always he occupied a central position in family importance, which was never in any degree accorded to any other animal—not even to my succession of horses, my consuming passion for whom was never shared by the others to any appreciable extent. When I ran from room to room of the upstairs, to watch them racing up the long field and swinging left-handed into the paddock, it was never a family-running. If any went with me, it was because I seized the victims and dragged them by main force, beseeching them to admire the clean, flowing lines of the filly and the stocky beauty of the cob. Their agreement when secured was purely academic. Very different was the reaction in the case of John. Some one had only to murmur, "Just look at HIM burying his bone!" for the family instantly to rush in one piece to the window, and stand rapt in ecstatic contemplation till the small figure completed its excavation of the rose bed.

I believe now that the importance of John rested in the fact that he had gradually become the embodiment of the airy, undecorated simplicity which is the basis of our life. For John was not confined to being an animal. He was intimacy and mystery and all imaginings. For my father and me, walking in evening forests, the little white dog would turn into a kobold, inhabiting a world where Erlking rode in the wind and his daughters wept in the willows, where Undine slid through the shadows and was gone, and Kühleborn shook his tangled beard among the waterfalls. He was a spirit for us, little serious John.

Whatever we did together, John and Juggins were with us. They were with us when we read in the evenings, when we weeded the garden, when we walked for long days over hills and up river-valleys and along the roof of the downs; or when we set out for an expedition in one or other of the dilapidated open cars which tenant the coach-house in a changing yet remarkably similar succession.

"J is a D, and J is a C," Mummy will remark pleasantly in the midst of other conversation. This means, "John is a dog, and

Juggins is a cat." Which observation, like many others, was first made by Daddy, and incorporated into the family life by Mummy.

Daddy has a round face and a slightly Alice-in-Wonderland look. He will occasionally shake Mummy's serenity by saying:

"One morning you'll wake up and I shan't be here. You'll find nothing but a large white cat on the pillow!"

Then Mummy will look at him with forboding and say:

"Don't put it into the air, P dear."

Looking for the first time consciously at our life, it seemed to me that we must be a little bewildering—out-of-door creatures, quick, untidy, vivid, blowing about the house like winds, calling up and down the stairs in the half-unconscious family language.

Then suddenly I saw a picture of our life at Frankfurt; the lofty silk-hung drawing-room of the consulate, and my mother and father, stately and gracious, receiving guests, standing before the marble fireplace, still, serious, carefully dressed—what a contrast to the natural us!

But watching them again in my mind, I realized that there was no contrast; and I knew why the polished society of that continental city had loved my mother and father with a rare sincerity. For they were the same people, perfectly unalterable, forever clothed in the vivid simplicity which was their being. Forever in their hearts there were birdsong and spring budding and autumn winds and great green distances; and even as Mummy stood tall in her silken drawing-room, her airy fairy Juggins stroked his invisible form about her legs. . . .

Not long after Jonty's escapade, I went up to spend a week or two with Katie and Billy Tait. By this time the ice-loading was over, and the men were cutting pulp-wood and hauling it out of the bush to the shores of Lake Huron, there to wait to be floated down to the mills after the break-up. Billy was working all day in the bush with a young hired man. I would watch them for hours, swiftly felling the straight live trees, shaping them into logs and drawing them away to the lake shore behind labouring teams, over the sun-splashed trails. Or I would sit in Katie's neat kitchen and watch her knitting the soft wool her mother sent her from the Shetlands. When my arm was better she taught me to make all kinds of different cookies and to fry a concoction called "skirley," in which I greatly delighted. This is a highly economical dish, the ingredients being a few table-spoonfuls of oatmeal, an onion and some butter; the result is delicious. So we lived along in those February days, laughing and working and waiting for the men to come home to supper. Katie tried so hard in those days to give me her own tidy mind! How she wanted me to have a peaceful practical life with no tag ends; how she believed in me, scatter-brain and all!

From Katie's house I walked every day for many hours in the bush, and my thoughts would go ranging through many worlds, into the past, into the future, and through the uncharted regions of all that is perceived but not known, sensed but not spoken.

It is curious how some fragment of a tune, some long-remembered smell, some word or name or line of poetry can suddenly enable one to experience again a snatch of one's life in some past time. Now there is a particular smell of horses out-of-doors and sweating, which transplants me again to the West. I can see high corrals trampled by milling hoofs, tooled saddles hanging up by their stirrups, tall cowboys mincing in high-heeled boots and little lean horses snorting nervously. I can feel again the sun-baked stillness of the range at noonday and the vaulted cool of Western barns, where the wary eyes of broncos pierce the shadows. And I know again how it felt to be me in the West, in old slacks and a blue cotton blouse, riding Jonty into the sunrise.

And in this same complete but passing way, by singing in my mind two lines of a mediaeval carol:

> "The boar's head in hand bear I
> Bedecked with bays and rosemary . . ."

I can be again in thought exactly the person that I was one Christmas many years ago, at a time of youthful upheaval.

And like this, one day at Katie's, there came over the radio a melody which for a moment made me again the cool, convinced creature which was me at nineteen; when I wrote, in a luxurious abandonment to disillusion:

> Lovely unhappy pagan paths, and the end black,
> Beautiful and unmistaken,
> These are the ways which I have taken
> With no way back.
>
> Dim sacred paths my childhood trod,
> In the warm wonderland of God,
> Are lost.
> These roads are cold
> Shining and old
> As frost.
>
> What though the feet
> May long to meet
> The land that's gone?
> There is no track
> To lead them back,
> And so
> Through the bright snow
> Laugh, and go on.

How certain I was, in those arrogant adolescent days, that I had discovered, beyond a possibility of doubt, life's ultimate futility! For a few moments, walking in the bush, humming the little reminiscent tune, I was I again at nineteen; then slowly, watching the "bright snow" as I walked, I began to go back over the years since the poem was written, and I considered whether now I were not learning at last something of the nature of the wonderland which long ago I believed I had abandoned with such melodramatic finality.

For the existence of God cannot be proved, but it can be

demonstrated. The experience of life comparatively soon transcends the limits of that which can be proved. The experience of God is an experience of the spirit; for the reality of God is not waiting compact and producible, at the end of human argument. It is in a realm beyond the limits of language, beyond the laborious building of fact on fact, that we touch the Infinite.

Chapter XVIII

WINTER DAYS

At the end of February I went to West Dayton to pay a long-deferred visit to Mrs. Gordon. Jonty went with me, though I was still forbidden to ride him. Timothy had been lent to Mr. Mackay, who rode him over when he came to hold services at East Dayton, and handsome they used to look, Mr. Mackay dark in his black coat, Timothy red as amber cantering up to the church door. But I was afraid to lend my wild, wilful Jonty, so he went with me. I expected to stay with Mrs. Gordon only until the break-up, then start out again and finish the ride. By this time I was able to work again, and there was plenty to do, though I often felt that my share was too small. But Mrs. Gordon would assure me that she needed me as much as she wanted me, and so, partly because her persuasions were irresistible, partly because of events in Europe, which put thoughts of the ride out of my head, the Gordon farm remained my home till late in the summer.

I remember once writing of Henry of Navarre that he loved life and laughed at it, and changed the whole destiny of France while he laughed. I used sometimes to fancy that in another life Mrs. Gordon could have changed the destiny of a nation with hands as fearless and intuitive as his. She was a person of that light, daring calibre. She had that degree of vitality, audacity, and unrestriction.

She had five children, two married daughters and three sons, of whom the eldest ran the farm, the second worked in the lumber camps, and the third worked in the Sudbury mines. Her husband was dead. I do not think she often boasted of her children; it was not her habit to boast, but she was a person whose sincerity was so vivid and complete that her thoughts shone out of her in any case, and it made little difference whether they were expressed or not. What she thought of her children was certainly apparent in five minutes, and I used to tease her by calling them "the five paragons." She soon disarmed me, however, by adopting me unconditionally as the sixth, and giving me a daughter's place in the warm depths of her heart.

As for me, I belonged every day more completely to my Irish-Canadian "Mum." We shared our love for risk and freedom; we shared our love for the out-of-door world. Mum is one of the few women I know who understand and share my affection for the barn, my comparative indifference to houses. I did not have to waste a word explaining to her why I had wanted to ride across Canada, why I was not afraid, why with the company of two horses I was not lonely. She knew as though it were she herself. She knew with the humour and depth of understanding which was her being. The enchantment of Mum lay in this gossamer-light seriousness of hers. Like the spirit of Ireland which she was, she could pass in the flick of an eye from amusement to tears; and from the solemn confines of rational discussion she could spring up like a skylark into limpid sunlights of laughter.

As for the family into which I was adopted, they were handsome and healthy, vivid and generous, with a genius for repartee and practical jokes which threw the little house into an uproar whenever they were assembled. Nothing made Mum happier than to collect the whole family around her, but this she was seldom able to do. Only Harold, who ran the farm, was permanently at home, and Bob came down at the end of the winter from the lumber camps. When I first went up to the Gordon farm, however, I found the household augmented by the presence of two elderly bachelors.

Jim and Sam were in perfect contrast one to the other. Jim was long and lean, and he cocked a cynical eye at the world. It was evident that the entire human population of the planet might go hang as far as Jim was concerned. He quite manifestly thought more highly of the animals. Jim seldom said anything funny; he seldom said anything whatever, yet we were all unquestioningly certain that he was a great wit. He successfully conveyed this impression by an occasional perfectly timed quirk of the eyebrow, and by maintaining observant silences, pregnant, one felt, with unspoken comment. Personally one was aware of being an open book to Jim—an open and exceedingly funny book.

Sam was also long and lean, but here the resemblance ended. Sam had little sense of humour and the most original mind in Dayton. He was a prophet without honour. For by reading and pondering, he had made contact with the thought of the twentieth century. To the mind of Dayton, which is rooted and grounded in the serene permanence of the land, he was incomprehensible. What Sam believed he believed passionately and in complete isolation. He was so deeply absorbed in problems of social reform that his striving spirit seemed only lightly to inhabit the lean body to whose comfort and appearance he was so superbly indifferent.

With regard to diet, Sam was in the van of modern opinion. Wholemeal bread, raw vegetables and cereals with every imaginable vitamin meticulously preserved, took unquestioning precedence for him over the white bread, meat, cookies and well-boiled vegetables which formed the staple food of Dayton society. In Mrs. Gordon's household Sam compromised by partaking selectively of the evening meal, and afterward seizing several raw turnips, potatoes and carrots, when available, and departing to his bedroom, whence there soon issued sounds of laborious grating, followed by a silence during which the resultant product was presumably consumed.

Most interesting of all, however, were Sam's theories on education. In a community of hard-working, hard-spanking mothers, for the most part unaware of the very existence of the bugbear "child-psychology," of fathers who made their small sons "mind" with the use of the stick if necessary, Sam, completely isolated, had arrived at the best in the twentieth century theory of child-management. The necessity for developing initiative in the young mind, the un-necessity of punishment, the importance of rational explanation and avoidance of don'ts—how often have I heard him propounding these theories to a Dayton mother embattled in scepticism!

In only one particular did he depart from the modern attitude with regard to children—this was in the matter of religious education. Christianity was the mainspring of Sam's life, and he felt that the child must grow into a Christian at all costs. It must be instructed, it must be read to, it must be prayed for, it must be reasoned with; for if the child were not a Christian, all else was vain.

Once in his earlier days, Sam had had an opportunity of applying his principles. His mother adopted a small granddaughter, and, as she grew older, left the child more and more in Sam's care. Little Grace is married now and living in Ottawa, and is a wholly delightful person; nor has her early religious education occasioned the antagonistic reaction which psychologists would doubtless have predicted. With an affectionate twinkle she told me about her uncle's family prayers—how long they were, and how once, to avoid them, she ran out and climbed into an apple tree. Prayers over, Sam searched for her anxiously, and at last, finding her, fetched the Bible and read her the morning's lesson, as she sat self-imprisoned in the tree. I think if one were searching for a moment in Sam's life to epitomize the whole of it, this would be the one. I can see him standing in the sun, so serenely assured as to be perfectly immune from the ridiculous, standing in the sun and reading, reading very well indeed, while the small face regarded him rebelliously from among the apple blossoms.

Grace's eyes twinkle when she speaks of her uncle, and her cheeks dimple, but there is perfect seriousness behind her smile. I believe she is the only person who has ever really known Sam, and her summing up of his character is simple, and I believe it is true.

"Uncle Sam is a saint," says Grace.

I have been trying to remember the routine of the farm, but routine is not the right word, for, beyond the fact that every morning started with the milking, no two days were ever alike. Before I went to the Gordons, I had tried many times to milk without success. But with them I learnt quickly, for it was so unhurried and unworried a business that all anxiety was removed from the operation and, being relaxed and at ease, I soon found that I could milk with the best.

There was only one stable element in the morning; that was the half hour spent in listening to the eleven o'clock radio drama. It was one of those called *One Man's Wife,* or *Two Men's Children,* or *Dr. Steadfast,* or *Your Friends the Finnigans,* but its exact title was inextricably confused in my mind among the titles of all the other dramas which it was not.

In common with the rest of its kind, it succeeded in subtly suggesting that here was a story of Life as It Is Lived, and that we gathered round the radio to hear of lives not less average than our own. With a shivering conviction that It Might Perfectly Well Be Us, we listened in agony while the unlucky participants were catapulted without a single half hour's respite from one soul-shattering catastrophe into the next. Though every disaster was at the last moment averted, we experienced no relief, for already we were waiting, tense with anxiety, for the next staggering blow.

On my arrival at the farm, I was plunged into the midst of *One Man's Wife* (or was it *Two Men's Children?*) to find that the heroine, distracted by her husband's imagined infidelity, had rushed blindly from the house on a dark night and fallen into a deep and conveniently situated pit. This solved the infidelity problem, for the husband, upon recovering her, registered such overpowering anguish over her sufferings as to convince even

"MY IRISH CANADIAN 'MUM'"

the heroine of his devotion. But tragic possibility number two now reared its ugly head. Peggy was of course disastrously hurt, and the question immediately began to loom: Would She Ever Walk Again? For two weeks of tortured half hours we agonized on her behalf, while specialists of world-wide renown made the pronouncement that Maybe She Would, and Maybe She Wouldn't. We were anxiously present in all but the flesh, while she tried to walk and failed. We witnessed her exhibitions of inspiring fortitude, succeeded by heart-breaking collapse.

Her final recovery was sudden and complete, but we were allowed only one short half hour in which to rejoice over it, for already her husband Tom, who had been having altogether too normal a time lately, was becoming involved with a hive of blackmailers. In spite of his complete innocence, he was soon entangled in a perfect wilderness of intrigue. We listened for weeks while he first Kept It from Peggy, then Failed to Keep It from Peggy, and finally was extricated by a Deus ex Machina in the shape of an old school friend now known as Dr. Bob, who, in addition to a booming voice and a splendid nature, had a perfect genius for handling intrigue and had Tom perfectly reinstated within the space of two half hours.

But we knew very well that Dr. Bob must have something disastrous up his sleeve; and so he had, in the shape of an hysterical wife, who decided, on no grounds whatever, that Dr. Bob and Peggy, now fit as a fiddle again, were engaged in an affair of the blackest order. The only course open to her in radio drama was to pour out her convictions to Tom, who instantly subscribed to them, and so knew without a shadow of doubt that Peggy No Longer Loved Him. So the wheel came full circle and returned us to position one, with the characters reversed. Peggy having been the first to think of the expedient of falling down the pit, there was nothing for Tom to do but take the mundane alternative of Going to Sleep at the Club, where I inconsequently left him.

Having enjoyed half an hour of vicarious anguish, Mum and I

would snap back to normal and look round to see what we could cook for dinner. Dinner over, the afternoon would stretch before us, pregnant with possibility. One favourite afternoon occupation was visiting. It was not often that we "got around to it," but if Harold had to take out the sleigh to haul ice or deliver cordwood, we would make it an occasion for a visit to some neighbour who lived in the appropriate direction. To my regret I never succeeded in acquiring the taste for visiting. Often our hosts would be people of whom I was very fond, and to go over and help them paint window-frames or hang paper or stain the floor was a really delightful event; but to sit down solemnly for three hours and "visit" continued to be a penance; and the only oasis in the desert was provided by the appearance of "the lunch," before the consumption of which, no visitor was allowed to depart. To the lunch I looked forward with fervour, but the pleasure was of short duration, and on either side of it stretched interminable wastes of unrelieved visiting.

No, not entirely unrelieved. Sometimes there would be expeditions upstairs to admire quilts. The making of patchwork quilts is positively a national industry in rural Canada, and very beautiful the results often are. There are a great number of classical patterns with names full of poetic suggestion: "snowflakes," "bears' paws," "Dresden plate," "great star," "Grandmother's flower garden" with many others, and "King Solomon's temple," most romantic of all.

On our return to the living-room we would cluster round the table to admire photographs.

"This is George with his girl-friend and two people from the Soo"—"This is the two people from the Soo standing up against the barn"—"This is George—pity his head is out of the picture" —"This is Slate Falls; you *must* go there"—"This is another of Slate Falls— Oh, no, this must be the time the creek flooded and the water poured down into the vegetable garden"—"This is another of the creek flooding; no, it's the other way up; oh, no, I'm sorry, it was the right way up before"—"This is a picture of the team, only the light got in; you can see the hind legs of the mare on the right"—"This is Harold and one of the pet bears we had once; the one in the hat is Harold; good of the bear, isn't it?"—"This is the back of the barn; yes, just the back of the barn; George took it because there was a hawk perched on· the roof and he thought it would come out, only it didn't"— "Oh, and this is George with his girl-friend again."

For a long time I would sit politely saying, "Oh, that's beautiful; which way up is it?"—"That's awfully good of George— Oh, it's David? Oh, I thought it was George"—and—"Oh, *that's* a good photograph—oh, it's a post-card you bought in Thessalon?"

But at last I would make an excuse to see how the two-year-old was making up or look at the new calf, and so I would run out to the barn. Here the day would come alive again. Standing in the midst of the cows' breath, I would watch the horses stamping in the shadows. I would hang over the pig-pen and watch the old sow, with her litter of thirteen, and one spotted. Then I would walk over to the new calf, lonely in his stall. I would give him my hand to suck, watching his great purple eyes and his angular baby body, and thinking how only two days ago he had been curled up in the dark, so safe and warm; and I wondered how this great world of the barn looked to him, so lately arrived in it.

At last the visit would be over, and we would bump home on the sleigh, have supper and go over to the barn to do the chores. Jim always maintained that he could not milk. We had a suspicion that he could, but no one had ever been able to surprise the truth out of him. My particular favourites among the milkers were an old roan cow, Sally, a small red one and a large bony white one. From these I patiently extracted their contribution in the time it took Harold to milk five others. Occasionally Mrs. Gordon would come blowing down and beat us both with ease.

By this time affectionate thoughts of bed would be drifting into my mind. But it was not very often that my whim for a good night's sleep was gratified, for the Gordons were leading spirits in the local night life, and there was not a skating-party, toboggan-party or box social which we did not somehow manage to attend. Sometimes I would murmur a little wistfully about the need for my beauty-sleep.

"*Beauty-sleep?*" Mrs. Gordon would repeat, bustling round to get ready. "Well, some people are optimistic!"

One of the pleasantest amusements in which the boys and I indulged was the attendance of the Friday night dances in a not too distant school-house.

Tucked warmly on to a hay-piled sleigh, we would drive an hour through the bush, till, coming out into the open at last, we saw the dark outline of the school, with its windows dimly glowing across the snow. Inside, the desks had been cleared away and ranged along the wall. On a stove at one end, water was already heating to make the tea for our midnight "lunch." Two lamps, hanging one at each end of the little hall, gave a pale yellow light. Already the band—two fiddles and a piano-accordion —were tuning up.

"Take your partners for the first square," came the order. Immediately the men dived in among the girls, who were sitting ranged along the wall in a decorous row, seized their partners and hurried into the middle; for already the caller was chanting his directions in a sing-song voice:

"Honour your partners,
Corners address,
Join your hands,
Go way to the west.

"Break the ring
And all swing,
And promenade back. . . ."

So we would dance and dance, square after square. After a time the band was sometimes augmented by the inclusion of a young man who drummed upon an upturned wash-basin, and then our energy would be redoubled. On and on the music danced, in a steady, swift, unsubtle rhythm. Like the beat of

"I SOON FOUND THAT I COULD MILK WITH THE BEST"

"THE GORDONS BOIL DOWN RIGHT OUT IN THE BUSH"

blood in the arteries of life was the beat of our tireless feet. The notes of the simple undying melodies ran up and down in an automatic pattern of repetition, weaving into the pattern of the dance, while we went on—backing and advancing, setting and turning, swinging and circling and threading the chain, till at midnight we broke apart and set down panting, to enjoy the well-earned lunch. But soon we were on the floor again, and now there would be no rest until, at two o'clock, mindful of the milking, we broke up and drove home, singing and laughing, under the silent stars.

The West Dayton nights were a high adventure, whether one spent them in bed or not. But best of all they were on the windy nights when I lay and listened to the storm riding through the dark, until the whirring of the windmill on the roof got tangled into my dreams. For at night it was no longer the sound of the windmill; it was the wind in the rigging of a gallant ship, and waves breaking on secret shores, and the roar of an ocean that rolled illimitable, beyond the bounds of the world. Close by my head the walls of the house would creak and groan, like the spars of a labouring vessel, and so, free from the moorings of the day, we would voyage all night into the storm.

On other nights, still and heartless with moonlight, the wolves would come down to the edge of the bush and howl across the snow. They howled till my heart broke for them, till I cried for their loneliness, till I yearned to go out and comfort them and give them their wild hearts' desire.

On such a night I lay anchored in bed, but my spirit went out shivering to the edge of the bush and was gripped by the power of the Wild. For still the Wild holds the soul of Canada. It lies in wait by the highway; it waits at the gates of the cities; airplanes fly over it; railways cut through it; cars rush by its borders but leave it unaltered. Canadians may barricade themselves as they will in their steam-heated apartments; they may gird themselves around with refrigerators, electric washing-machines and the latest thing in radio sets; but still the Wild is behind them, before them, at their very doors. This is their opportunity, their adventure, their strength. Europe belongs to its peoples, but Canada belongs to the Wild.

As the days drew on towards spring, the nights began to overpower me with their heat. The house was warmed by a furnace of surprising vitality; which, not content with its good offices during the day, would continue its ministrations till far into the night. I, accustomed to windy, rain-spattered English bedrooms, would writhe under its torrid breath. Finally, some time around the end of March, I decided that I would sleep in the hay-mow. The boys were horrified at such asceticism, but Mum took it without surprise. She is one of the few people who have been able to accept my rather unusual scale of importances without the necessity of a mental effort.

Accordingly, every evening at bedtime, Harold would take the stable lantern and light me through the snow to the door of the hay-mow. Inside, my sleeping-bag and a pile of blankets would be waiting. I would be dressed in all my clothes—slacks, ski-pants and several jerseys, and, without taking anything off, the temperature being in the neighbourhood of zero, I would gratefully burrow into the sleeping-bag, swathe myself in the blankets, pile a mountain of hay above me and snuggle deep into the sweet-scented nest. Over my head the great roof would go vaulting up into darkness, and the wind would go singing through it. Muffled through the hay would come sounds of the horses stamping on the barn-floor and sleepy twittering from the sparrows among the rafters. So, with the animals below and above me, I would sleep, and wake in the morning with a nest of icicles round my face.

After I had enjoyed several nights in the hay, the family decided that I was right; the furnace really was working overtime. So they suppressed its ardours; the bedrooms became pleasantly cool again, and I went back to sleep in the house.

But sometimes I would remember a little wistfully my nights under the sparrows.

At last, after many weeks, my arm was taken out of the cast and I was allowed to ride again. I shall always remember that first ride. Away went Jonty up the road, with his legs flashing and his tail streaming behind him. We galloped until we came suddenly on to the top of a hill and out into the sunset. On our north side stood the sombre bush, before us one birch tree in slim silhouette, and behind it the sunset sweeping in a red curve up the windy sky. I wish I could have seen Jonty too, standing on the hill. . . .

Soon after this Mr. Mackay no longer needed Timothy, so I fetched him over to the farm, and after this the boys and I would ride together in the bush. We had one favourite trail—up the great fields behind the house, then through the trees to a clearing, on from the clearing to an Indian village and out of the forest at last on to the farm road that I had followed when first I came to Dayton, and so home again past the bordering farms that now I knew so well.

So we worked and played and rode the horses, and the year went on towards the spring.

Chapter XIX

SPRING AND SPY MANIA

In April the brown fields began to come out from under their blanket of snow, the frogs in the swampy ground began beating their hearty percussion band, water ran off down the roads, and I felt that the time was coming for me to leave. Mum said, "Nonsense!" And, though I knew it was not nonsense, I realized with a wave of loneliness how deeply I loved the Gordons and how hard it would be to go; for I knew that I could never come back to this life; I knew that when I went I should pass over again into my own world, and the door would be shut.

"Anyway you must stay for the syrup-boiling," said Mrs. Gordon, so I stayed.

Then, on April the tenth, with the fall of Norway, Europe's disastrous spring began; and as we listened and read and waited, finishing the ride seemed a very little, a very unimportant thing. It only mattered to know what would happen tomorrow, what would happen the next day and the next.

So as we waited the sap began to run, and I was initiated into the mysteries of syrup-boiling.

"Write about it," said Mum, so I wrote:

The Gordons boil down right out in the bush among the maples. Under the trees, a fire glows and crackles; all around, the wood is piled high. From tripods and a cross-bar, bound with heavy black chains, hang two great cauldrons, and in their depths the dark fluid is seething and foaming. It is warm and still by the fire. Overhead the maple buds swell with the stirring of baby leaves, and above the swaying branches, the sun goes riding up the sky. There are many sounds in the day—wind rustling through the edges of the bush, with a noise like waves on a distant shore, near us twigs moving in the breeze, the fire crackling, and somewhere the voice of a bird, far away a dog barking—sounds everywhere. But behind it all there is a great silence; and, as the mind sinks into it, the bands which hold consciousness are slackened and thought is caught in the circle of the year, forever the same and forever different, the circle of the year.

Watching the syrup, watching the spring, I am slowly lost in the mystery of time; and, trying to think of a year, of a life, of an age, I find that I cannot; for in the silence of the bush I know that there is no moment of which one can say, "This is a beginning" or "This is an end"; for every moment is an end and a beginning, and the ripples of every moment spread circling into eternity. . . .

Meanwhile the brew in the cauldron boils over, and quickly I must pour in a bucketful of raw sap to settle it again. The sweet, woody smell of the syrup is round and living; breathing it you think of the quarters of horses fat from the fields; you think of cats bunched neatly before farm-house fires; and of cherry-wood sticks and chubby children and plump chestnut buds—then the wind whirls the wood-smoke into your eyes and stings you awake again; time to pour in more sap. So you watch the syrup and the hours lose themselves in watching.

I have watched it boiling in the sunshine and in the grey of rain, and swirling darkly in the dusk under its ghostly mist of wood-smoke. The hours go on and on till the mind is lost in this ritual of the boiling down.

With the syrup-making, spring came to Dayton. It was true that the snow still piled obstinately in the ditches, still humped itself in uncompromising coils under the shoulders of the bush. It was true that the roads were still a morass, true that for many weeks the maple leaves would still be tightly coiled inside their buds. But spring was with us, nevertheless; and there was much ordering of cotton dresses through Eaton's catalogue, much visiting around and tasting of syrup, much discussion of what crops to put in at the seeding. Family motor cars were roused from their winter's hibernation and eased gingerly on to the streaming roads. Many a cheerful hour was spent in digging them out of snowdrifts, hauling them out of bogs of mud and tinkering among their winter-stiffened bowels. Great was the triumph of our first arrival in Thessalon, the small town on the highway from which we had been so long marooned. With a gay laugh we dismissed the difficulties and dangers of the road, but great was our triumph, nevertheless. Wherever we went we carried gifts of maple syrup, and we received a welcome proportionately rapturous.

But the glories of the maple syrup season reached their consummation at Johnny Tait's taffy-pull. Johnny made syrup on a lordly scale. He had a shanty in the bush which contained an evaporator, a device which passes large quantities of the sap through a series of shallow baths, gradually bringing it to the required consistency. On the evening appointed for the taffy-pull, the neighbours assembled at the white farm-house. First we made our way to the shanty and, when we had stewed in its generous heat, watched the evaporator working and drank sweet cupfuls of the warm syrup, we returned and crushed ourselves expectantly into the kitchen, where the taffy was in process of manufacture.

Great pans of syrup were boiling at speed over a raging fire. When the right moment was reached, they were taken from the range and their contents flung into the snow, where they spread sizzling, like volcanic lava, and then set in their form, taking on a delectable consistency which is the whole point of taffy, the central feature of taffy-pulls. For the only means of detaching a small portion of taffy from the original mass is to pull. No other means of cutting up or dividing it has ever been devised. Quickly the dark substance was returned to the pans and carried into

SPRING AND SPY MANIA

the house. Then the pull began.

A fearless pioneer seized a handful and retreated across the room. A thinning rope of taffy accompanied him. Reaching the kitchen door, he found himself still attached to the original taffy by a slim golden thread. Then it broke, and with it the spell that bound us. Running forward we plunged our hands into the waiting pans. Gnashing, clawing, hauling upon ropes of sweetness, we laboured and luxuriated, like wasps in treacle. I have heard since that at serious taffy-pulls the taffy is pulled and pulled until it turns white. Long before this, however, our particular taffy had reached its final destination! It was an utterly gorged and glutinous party who finally set out into the night.

So the weeks went on. And one half of me said to the other half:

"Well, what are we waiting for?"

And the other half said:

"Nothing. But I love the Gordons and I love Dayton, and when we go we shall go forever."

Meanwhile Germany, passionately proclaiming her respect for neutrality, massed her troops along the Belgian border. So we waited, and I said to my fretful half that, as soon as we knew what was to happen in the Netherlands, I would saddle the horses and go.

Then Bob Gordon made his suggestion: any time now the drive would be starting from the lumber camp at which he had worked in the winter. He was to come down with it; how would I like to go up into the bush and see the drive? I leapt with delight. For weeks "the drive" had been a constant topic of conversation. A dozen times I had made Bob describe a river drive for me. But that I might actually see one for myself had never entered my head. The Faust in me was routed neck and crop. Joyfully I decided to stay.

Every Saturday night, as the spring went on, we would pile into the car and set out for Thessalon. Saturday night in the little town was a great occasion. The street would be so full of people that the cars had a hard time indeed to pass up and down. As for us, who came in from the country, for this one evening of the week the town was ours. We streamed in and out of the shops, we went to the show, we "visited" on the sidewalk, we called to each other across the road, we drank coca-colas and ate ice-cream cones, we drove and we walked and we stood on the corners. And in every small town in the length and breadth of Canada others like us were walking and standing and laughing. For, on this one night of the week, the little towns belong to the country, just as on Sunday the country belongs to the town.

It was about this time that I heard of the spy rumours. They had been current for over a month, but the Gordons had tactfully kept them from me. At last it was one of my small friends at the village school who innocently let the cat out of the bag. "How do you like being a spy?" she asked laughing. So they had to tell me: It was generally suspected in the surrounding district that I was spying for the Nazis. Even some members of our own little community felt uncertain.

Evidence was strong against me—I walked and rode all over the bush; I took photographs; I could speak German. There was a section of opinion which believed me to be a man in disguise. This sinister suggestion was presumably based upon the fact that, having only one skirt, I generally wore slacks; the fact that to dress a man in slacks would be the worst possible way of disguising him had evidently escaped their consideration.

The fact that I find myself incapable of hating the Germans was also counted to me for unrighteousness. When you have been a child in a country, lived with that country's children, played and learnt and talked nonsense in their language, gone into mischief with them and laughed, and been scolded and cried; when you have climbed in their mountains, swum in their rivers, been lost in their forests and found again, been frightened and excited, been miserable and happy with them—then hate is not in you. I know now that it is not often possible to explain this to people, but I used to try.

Well, I was branded. At first I laughed and published facetious remarks in my newspaper articles. The loyalty of my friends surrounded me like a fortress. They shielded me; they fought my battles; they were enraged on my behalf. I myself was too much amazed for anger. I drove the team, walked in the bush, rode with the boys and forgot the rumour. But rumour did not forget me. One day I went to a quilting party in Thessalon. A small woman rose, remarked that she did not like the company and walked out. A month later I went swimming in the Y.W.C.A. at Sault Sainte Marie. A few girls talked to me pleasantly enough; the rest went into small huddles, giggling. Excited whispers came sizzling across the water: "She is"—"She isn't"—"She is"—"She isn't," hissed the girls.

Soon sensational stories began to drift home to me from the West. Friends in Kenora had heard from the police that I was in prison; in Alberta it was stated on circumstantial evidence that I had been shot; over the radio in the Prairie Provinces went the news that I had confessed my guilt; in British Columbia my very confession was quoted: "You can do what you like with me now," it ended dramatically, "for I have finished my work."

Agitated letters reached me from my friends of the road. I answered, setting their minds at rest, but my own was in bewilderment. Funnily, the part of all this which hurt the most was the fact that the Friday evening dances were spoilt. When the milking was over, I would dress as usual in my blue coat and skirt and brush my hair till it shone. Big handsome Bob would flick a look at me as I came downstairs and say, "You're not such a bad-looking cuss, Screwball!" Harold would smile a little and say nothing, and the three of us would pile happily into the old car. But as we drew nearer and nearer to the old school-house, my heart would sink, for I knew what was to come.

In the old days the men had wanted to dance with me—I was

an intriguing stranger, surrounded by the glamour of the half-accomplished ride, and I looked well enough in my blue suit. Some of my friends held a theory that the spy rumours were started by a few of the girls at these dances, who were angry because sometimes their boy-friends left them for a little while in order to dance with me. Whether this was true or not, the tales certainly had the desired effect, for now not many people took much notice of me, and if it had not been for the Gordon boys, I should have sat out a good deal of the evening. I have never thought that jokes about "wallflowers" were funny; now I know that they are cruel.

When I could not bear any longer to watch the figures of the square dance whirling without me, I would say to Harold that I was too hot, and we would leave the little hall and walk up the dark road towards the bush, watching the lines of the trees against the sky and listening for whippoorwills. Soon we would go back to the hall, and the music of the violins would come tripping and tangling out to meet us, and I would dance with Harold, then I would dance with Bob, and for a little while everything would seem all right. But then I would sit out again.

I tried in vain to isolate this phenomenon and regard it objectively. But try as I might it continued to haul on the emotions, till it drew the colour out of my cheeks and dark lines under my eyes. But in the end, laughing and panting, the sets in the last square broke apart. The fiddles were tucked up lovingly into their cases, we shrugged into our coats and stumbled through the darkness towards the waiting cars. The old Plymouth came to life and began to bump obediently over the stony road. I sat small between the boys, who towered on each side, tired and cheerful, not knowing my thoughts.

I remember how, coming home from our last dance, I drooped between them, nearly asleep. And slowly my mind warmed again, and I knew that popularity is like a sky-rocket, vivid and dazzling, but friendship is a stable lantern, and once lighted it will not fizzle out and leave one in the dark. So I sat still between my friends, and thanked them in my heart.

At last, after several weeks of waiting, Bob had his call to go up in the bush. Full of expectancy I scrambled into the old car (which was to carry him as far as the road's end) and away we went. The first night we were to stay at Poplar Dale, a tiny settlement at the end of a road, which wound its way twenty miles into the country of low hills which here lies north of the trans-Canada highway.

We arrived in darkness, but next morning I woke to find that we were staying with a family of Finns in a small farm on the banks of a shallow, violent river. The road we had followed came winding up to the farm, out of maple and spruce forest; then it crossed a bridge and climbed north between other small farms, to cease abruptly in forest-laden hills. The morning lay young and untouched in the early sunshine and the dew hung heavy in the grass when I ran up a little hill to look out on all this. As I looked over the fields to their girdle of forest, I felt that here was a place where I might begin again to write the Canada journal, so long neglected. And, as it happened, this opportunity was to be granted me. For, going down the hill, I was presented to Mr. Schultz, the owner of the timber which was soon to begin its adventurous passage down the Garden River.

He informed me that I had come up too early, for the men would be working at the base camp for a week or two yet, and I could not join them until the drive was well under way. But if I liked, he added, I might stay up here at Poplar Dale while I waited, sleeping in a small bunk-house, and going for my meals to the farm near by. I was delighted at this prospect; so, having returned to Thessalon to collect writing materials, I started out a few days later, with the bi-weekly mail, to go back to Poplar Dale.

But the fearful events of May, 1940, had begun; so that the

journal which I drove myself to write was not of Canada but of Europe. Not the peace of Poplar Dale, but the agony of Belgium, the gallant hopelessness of Holland, was in my heart. I could only write:

. . . the very day that I came bumping up the stony road in the little mail car, Germany marched on the Netherlands. All afternoon came the news over the radio: "Germans at the Hague"—"German warplanes over Brussels"—"Germans beating on the gates of Liège."

I came to Poplar Dale to write about Canada, about the winter and the horses and all that we did. But as I sit on the hill-sides and gaze over the bush, as I watch the maples splashing their hot red buds against the grey-green of the poplars and the birches sparkling white among the sombre spires of the firs, as I walk by the rivers and watch the water folding in chequered patterns over the stones, as I listen to the birdsong and feel the wind tug at my hair—there is one thought, one thought only that beats on my brain, that pounds and hammers and will not let me free—war, war—troops fighting hand to hand in the streets of Rotterdam—warplanes, even now perhaps, roaring over London. . . .

—And a great deal more to the same effect. Day by day we would strain our ears over the imperfect radio at the farm; then I would go back alone to the bunk-house and try to write; but all I could think of, all I could see, were straight, sad poplar avenues, and in every one a fleeing river: people on wagons, people on ox carts, people on foot—the poor people, the real people, the people who have lost every war since the world began.

Meanwhile the swift Canadian spring came racing through Poplar Dale. I walked in the woods among banks golden with dog-toothed violets, and starry with mayflowers. The pussy-willows came out silver-soft by the water's edge, and washes of

"WE HAD ONE FAVOURITE TRAIL"

red and yellow and blue-grey against the hills showed where the maples, birches and poplars were waking from their winter sleep. The sunshine and the rain were warm.

One day, pursuing the road past the last of the farms and into the bush, I followed it for many miles until it led down to the banks of a river and there cheerfully abandoned me. On the other side of the water, a narrow foot-path went winding further into the trees. Intent upon discovering where it ended, I took off all my clothes and swam across, completely forgetting, till I reached the other side, that I should be wanting them to go on in!

So I swam back frustrated, and wandering home I met a porcupine, progressing slowly upon his business among the trees. He was extremely important and absorbed. He was the first I had seen, and I watched him enchanted. I would watch the robins too, newly returned from their journey to the South, and the intricate patterns of the water in the creeks, released at last from its prison of ice. But forever my mind was in travail in Europe.

And wandering desolate through the wonder of the spring, I could see only tragedy. Within nations there is law, but between nations there is anarchy; and the effect of every war is to sow the seeds for the next. There was no question as to what the Allies were fighting against, but what had they to fight for? Even though they won the war, how could they hope to win the peace? What could they do to create a world in which peace might have a chance to grow, to become at last the established order? Whichever way I looked I could see nothing. It was not till many months later, that I was to discover a new hope. . . .

Chapter XX

RIVER-DRIVE

At last one day when the forest was shrouded in rain, and I was shut up alone writing about Canada and thinking about Europe, there was a grinding of brakes on the road outside the bunkhouse and, running out, I found that it was Bob, come to take me up into the bush. So, thankfully abandoning all these frustrating thoughts, I scrambled into the car, and away we went, laughing and ragging.

The logging-camp was north of Sault Sainte Marie, and the Garden River, down which the logs were driving, ran south out of the bush, over a succession of dams and rapids, to empty into Lake Huron some twenty miles east of the city. The logs, Bob told me, had now reached the lowest of the dams, called by the law of opposites the "High Dam." Here the men were camped, working the logs through; and it was arranged for me to stay at Glendale, the highest settlement on the road which led up in the direction of the dam.

After leaving Sault Sainte Marie, the road climbed slowly and steadily into a country of rocks and hills, blanketed more and more thickly with forest. Little Glendale climbed up over cleared fields to the railway, and a waterfall white as lace came diving down a precipice at its back. We reached it in the late afternoon to find it steaming warmly after the rain, and the neat fields laid out around it, clean as a peeled stick. Bob deposited me at the post office where I was to stay, and went on up to the dam.

The postmistress was a little plump woman. I found her with her white hair tied back in a ribbon, and white paint up to her elbows. She was standing on top of a ladder, repainting the kitchen ceiling, which was spotless anyway; but when she saw me she came running down, crying, "Oh, those poor Belgians, did you hear—?" And then I heard that Leopold of the Belgians had surrendered. Leopold, Europe's young crusader! The day died.

I soon knew a good many of the inhabitants of the little settlement. I was glad to talk to every one, so as not to have to think. One Austrian couple, with whom I made friends, had sixteen children and another well on the way. Once I tried to collect the whole family for a photograph; from every barn-door, from every shed and outhouse, children streamed, till the kitchen was packed with an assorted mob. "We don't often get them all in together," explained their mother. They ate in relays; they dressed in relays; I wonder whether it was not in relays that they slept!

I was comforted by the companionship of this family and of the spring village itself, which leant up against the wilderness perfectly unaware of its grace. Its beauty in those late May days was clear-cut and radiant. The sun climbed up at morning into a virginal sky and went down behind the forest in unclouded gold. The shadows of the trees against the houses, of the houses against the ground, cut out dramatic patterns upon the fields of light.

The principal event of the day was the arrival of the southbound train. At the hour of sunset it would come curving down through the rocks, hooting mournfully and clad in red-gold coils of evening smoke. Every day the inhabitants of Glendale would range themselves beside the track, to watch its ritualistic passing.

When Bob was free he came to fetch me up to the camp at the high dam. Into a brilliant morning we set out, bouncing over the rocky road, past lakes and rivers and rocks and goat-footed waterfalls, till, after an hour's ride we reached a small empty shack by the wayside. Here we left the car and plunged on foot into the bush. After walking several miles we reached an arm of the river, and here, tied up under some willows, was a boat with an outboard motor. There was also a wagon full of hay standing beside the water and a small square ferry made of rough boards, which one hauled to the opposite side by means of a wire strung from bank to bank. For both of these I was later to find a use, but meanwhile I passed them without special interest, and Bob and I got into the boat and set off down the river. The stream slid darkly between its forest-haunted shores, till it led us into the vast sheet of water held by the dam.

Leaving the shadows of the bush we shot out straight as an arrow into the sunshine, while nature, supreme master of the higher mathematics, rearranged all the patterns on the glassy lake to accord with the moving line of our boat's passage. Round the edges of the water stood the pale skeletons of drowned trees, and at the southern end, where one could already hear faintly the roaring at the dam, the face of the lake was brown with hundred upon hundred of close-packed logs, waiting their turn to dive into the rapids below. But upon the shore stood the living trees in serried ranks, and I was glad to think of them rolling back, rank on rank, into the mountains, into the North, more trees than there were men to fell them.

So we tied the boat near the dam and went to stand on the bridge above the dam-falls, to watch the great logs come thundering over and go leaping away down the rapids, like dark sea-monsters playing in the troughs of the deep. Above, in the lake, the timber was held in readiness with booms, and the men were running over it agile as cats, pushing the logs about with their hooked peavies, never sliding into the water.

In a small clearing on the west shore stood the camp. At one end was the long white cook-tent, containing all the camp's provisions and the portable cook-stove at which the meals were prepared. Here Tommy the cook and young Victor the "Cookee" reigned supreme. Along the edges of the bush were ranged four other tents, in which the men slept, ten or twelve to a tent. Their beds were blankets and spruce-branches; Mr. Schultz the owner of the timber, curled up with the rest of the river-drivers.

Now as I walked into the camp, he came out with a kindly smile to meet me. But he had bad news; I was not to go down the river with the drive. I think my young and feminine appearance had disconcerted him at Poplar Dale, and now all he could say was, "It wouldn't be right." There was nothing for it but to accept this decision philosophically. However, there was one thing about which I was determined—I would see them break camp in the morning.

By the evening, all being well, the logs would all be over the dam, and next day the camp would move about twelve miles down the river. After a five o'clock breakfast they were to start. If I slept at Glendale, I could not reach the camp in time. For me to sleep at the camp, Mr. Schultz felt, would not be decorous. I therefore decided that I would sleep in the hay-wagon which I had noticed that morning standing by the river. Bob drove me back to Glendale to fetch my sleeping-bag; and, to the accompaniment of gloomy predictions by the postmistress who hauled up from the depths of her memory a perfect library of bear stories, we happily set forth. We reached the river at sunset. Bob helped me to arrange my sleeping-bag on the wagon, climbed into the boat, set its course down the centre of the river and went throbbing away into the silence. I piled on all my clothes and snuggled down into the hay. It was a little damp, but warm and pleasant, nevertheless. Behind me in the shadows a partridge drummed. Over the western bush, the colours died in the sky. I slept. . . .

At a quarter past four, I hauled myself awake. Those who have written poetry about the beauty of the dawn have the right on their side, of course. But any one who, reading such, hastily assumes that to be awake at dawn is an experience invariably idyllic, is entirely mistaken. This particular dawn was of the unpoetical type. As I poked my head out from under the hay, I discovered that there was a light rain falling. Wind went shivering up the river, while a few pale streaks of slate-grey did little to enliven the eastern sky. The bush stood massed in blackness. I combed my hair and washed in the river with extreme perfunctoriness. Then I climbed gingerly on to the raft and hauled myself across.

The trail on the other side led to the lake and round its western shore to the camp. I ran till I was warm and panting. At last I saw the white cook-tent through the trees and, trotting out into the clearing, found them still at breakfast round a welcome fire. The morning began to improve and the pale suggestion of a sunrise glowed above the trees.

Breakfast over, the river-drivers and Mr. Schultz set off into the forest. I should have liked to ask where they were going, but I have long gone on the principle, "Never ask a question; some other fool will." In this instance, however, there was no other fool available, so I contented myself with keeping quiet and watching all that went on.

When the gang had gone, only the cook and cookee and the two Indian boatmen were left, except Bob, who was to stay behind with two old men from Glendale to open and shut the dam. It had to be closed for twelve hours and opened for twelve, so that, at the time when the men were working, there would be a strong flow of water. Each day, as the logs floated further down the river, it would be opened an hour later.

Busily the men set about packing up. Moored beside the cook-tent lay a long heavy boat, pointed at both ends. Into this went first the folded cook-tent, then the supplies. Next the sleeping-tents were struck and stowed away and the rolled-up bedding fitted into the remaining spaces. I talked to the Indian boatmen, took photographs and watched wistfully as the boat got ready to leave without me. It was Fred, one of the Indians, who made the suggestion:

"Why don't you come with us to the next camp?" he asked. "There's a trail through the woods that you can follow from there, right back to this dam. It's only about ten miles."

I needed no second bidding. With the best possible intentions of being back before the evening, I climbed into the loaded boat, and away we went. Like squirrels on a log, the five of us perched on the piled-up luggage. The two boatmen knelt, one each end, steering our course. Tommy sat aft, talking to Fred; Victor crouched rather nervously in the middle, and I sat up in front of him on a high crate. So the heavy boat slipped out into midstream, and my river-drive began.

Slowly we slid between the silent banks. The wind slept. The sun climbed up into a blue and white cumulus sky. The boatmen watched the water. I watched the banks, where the maples and the poplars burnt red and smoked silver against the backcloth of the pines. Tommy and Victor did not watch anything, but shut themselves up happily in a house built of chatter. So we went gliding down the reaches of the river, and forever round every bend there were more pine trees, with more poplars splashing up against them, and more maples against the poplars, and wild white cherry against the maples, and, leaping out from among them all, the birches shouting in shrill green. So, clothed in loneliness and spring, our boat went down the day. . . .

Long hours lapped in silence. Victor had fallen half asleep, Tommy was reckoning up the stores. We drifted into the wilderness as it were into a dream. In flowing patterns the river accompanied us.

Stately Spanish galleon coming from the isthmus,
Dipping through the tropics by the palm-green shores. . . .

Not Spanish, not a galleon, not the tropics—and yet the quality of Masefield's verse was in this effortless, this timeless voyage. Always there were more trees, more rocks, more river, always more patterns along the water. Time stood still. The voyage had been forever and would go on forever. The muted ripple of water against the bows was alone in the liquid silence.

Then we swung round a bend, and there was the gang, tacking about the river in the long low "pointer" canoes, straining to loosen the heavy logs which were stuck against the shores and in the shallows. The boatmen, in no way surprised to see them, brought the boat to land and tied up at the bank. In no time Tommy had a fire crackling in the grass and a cold lunch set out. Bread, "boloney," cookies and pies swiftly disappeared. Nobody appeared to be surprised by my presence, but Mr. Schultz inquired how I was proposing to go back. I replied that I had heard that there was a trail through the bush.

"Oh, that!" said Mr. Schultz. "Why I couldn't let you go back that way; you'd never find it. You'll have to stay with us now."

So I was on the drive after all!

As soon as lunch was over, we set out again, the gang back to work on the logs, and we on the supply boat to drop down to the flats at the head of the Seven Mile Rapids, where we were to pitch our next camp. Early in the afternoon we arrived, to find our camping ground spread out wide and green beside the water, with the bush climbing up steeply behind it, in a protecting wall.

The men carried the supplies ashore and set to work. The great cook-tent ran up quickly, framed upon crossed poles and a horizontal bar. The supplies were stowed inside it, the sleeping-tents were disposed along the shore, and so the little camp was ready for its occupants; whereupon the Indians lay down and went to sleep, and Tommy and Victor arrayed themselves in their white aprons and went into the cook-tent, Victor to peel potatoes and Tommy to make raisin pies, an art in which he was past master. About sunset the gang came in from the river, lighted a fire and hung their wet overalls beside it to dry. Tommy was all ready for them, with supper spread out on a long trestle table —stewed meat, boiled eggs, boiled potatoes, carrots, bread, butter, cookies and raisin pie and tea. It was not for nothing that Tommy had earned a name for being the best caterer the camps could get. The men stood in line to take what they wanted and then carried it away to eat beside the fire.

"MOORED BESIDE THE COOK TENT LAY A LONG HEAVY BOAT"

When supper was over, and Victor and I had washed the dishes, we went into the cook-tent, where I found that kind-hearted Tommy had laid out for me his own mattress and set up his mosquito-net above it. The cook-tent normally acted as sleeping-quarters for himself and Victor, but now they kindly surrendered it to me, joining the rest of the men in the tents beside the fire. I took a last look out as I closed the flap. Very small and lonely the tents looked, snuggling round the dying fire under the pale moon.

Soon all was quiet in the camp, and as sleep slowly descended, fold on fold, I thanked God for the river-drive, which after all I had not missed; and I thanked Him for the gift of not being afraid, for what you are not afraid of does not happen. I have never been afraid of a man or a horse, and so I have never had to be. Our life is a great deal simpler than we make it.

At the sub-human hour of four o'clock, Victor came in to light the cook-stove. I burrowed deeper under the blankets and informed myself that I was still asleep. But it was no use; the day had begun. By five o'clock, breakfast was on the bench, and we were standing in line under a rainy dawn. Through mists of damp, dark and sleepiness, I was vaguely aware that we ate, that the men disappeared down the river, and that Victor and I washed the dishes, after which I dived once more under the mosquito-net, and the world continued without me.

I woke sometime in the middle of the morning, to hear rain pelting down upon the roof of the tent. But a little thing like rain cannot be considered upon a river-drive; so, putting on my moderately waterproof jacket, I set out along the river-bank, for I was anxious to get a look at the rapids, our prospective descent of which was already filling Victor with apprehension. They started suddenly about a mile from the camp. One moment the water was gliding calmly under an unruffled face; the next it was surging downhill with a melodramatic roar, to go swinging round the next bend with such violence that one would expect the outer bank to be dashed to pieces. Near the head of the rapids

I found the men, working on some shallows in midstream, where quite an island of logs was stuck fast. Mr. Schultz called me over to sit in a boat and watch them. He was kindness itself, all through the drive.

"Since you're here," he said, "you may as well enjoy yourself, Mary."

So I sat and watched. Some of the men stood up to their hips in the water; others stood on the logs, hauling and straining at the heavy timber with their peavies. The peavies were about five feet long, with a hook and spike at the end; the men used nothing else for loosening the logs. Every now and then a log would swing free and go whirling away into the rapids. Sometimes a man would be on it, but he was never caught, for he would leap back on to another, agile as a cat. I never saw a man fall into the water.

In a surprisingly short time the great jam of logs had all been released, and the men, although no one had a watch and the sun was invisible behind rain clouds, knew that it was time for dinner. So they tied the boats by the shore and left them tugging at their moorings, while we returned to the camp. There, sure enough, was Tommy all ready, with the table set—bacon and eggs, boiled beef, potatoes, turnips, bread, butter, cookies, stewed prunes, apple pie, and tea black as the night. Tommy certainly knew how to feed us! Dinner over, the men went back to the river, and I arrayed myself in a pair of grey flannel slacks, kindly provided by Victor, and spread out my own to dry by the stove.

When they had steamed for a little while, I climbed into them again and set off to see what the gang were doing. I found them working some way down the rapids, tacking from shore to shore. I climbed into one of the boats, and we were instantly whirled away. By rowing with all their might, the men were able to keep their pointer at an angle to the current, so that it drove them at speed on to the opposite bank. Here they laboured till they had set free any logs caught up against the trees and rocks at the water's edge, and when they had all been pushed out once more into the current, we climbed into the boat and were swept back again to the opposite shore.

This was always an anxious passage, for if the pointer had once succeeded in turning into the stream, it would have been hurled to the foot of the rapids or dashed to pieces on the way. Even though all went well, our arrival at the bank was somewhat adventurous, for we made contact at such speed that the boat was in danger of overturning. However all went well, and personally I got no more of a wetting than that which the rain and the dripping forest administered. But so generous were their contributions, that I believe I reached camp that evening scarcely drier than the men, who had been wading all day among the timber. As we walked homeward, however, the sky cleared, and we stood in line for our supper under watery blue.

By this time I was beginning to know the men. They were not in the least what I would have expected lumberjacks to be. I had vaguely imagined men of the build of Bob Gordon, long-legged broad-shouldered giants. But they were mostly small and weedy looking, and it amazed me that they had the power to wrest the heavy logs free from the entangling shores. Nearly all were Indians or half-breeds; there were only three white men among the drivers.

Of these the foreman, Pete, was a French Canadian. He had a firm body and eyes deep-set in a lined handsome face. He had the rock-founded assurance of one who knows perfectly a dangerous trade. The best of the drivers would occasionally become excited in a moment of exceptional difficulty, but Pete never. Of the other whites, one was a small red-haired, weak-faced fellow, and the other was no more than a boy, a thin long-limbed lad, with brown spaniel's eyes, and a clever unhappy face. He reminded me constantly of somebody else, and a whole circle of events connected with this other person would stir, tantalizing and irretrievable, in the pit of my mind. I wonder to this day who the other person was.

Of the Indians, only a few stood out. There was one who had

slanting eyes like a Chinaman, and was extremely fat and top-heavy looking; he was the best of the whole gang for running over the floating logs; his name was Pegi. Another was remarkable for the fact that his dark Indian face was surmounted by a crop of tawny hair, exactly the colour of a lion's mane; and there was another who drew the eyes continually, for he had the impudence and the tiger-grace of a story-book buccaneer. The weathered blue overalls could not hide the lean arrogance of his perfect figure. One could not but feel that his natural habit would have been a doublet and hose and a crimson sash and a dagger between the teeth. His name was Jake. To me the rest of the gang were a sombre-eyed dark-faced ebb and flow of indistinguishable taciturnity. All, that is, except Fred the boatman. Fred was a full-blooded Indian, but he was unlike any other Indian I have seen. He had an eager intelligent face, and his talk was of education, and the chance his children were to have because he had not. How he had come by such an Anglo-Saxon attitude remained a mystery.

"Canadians think," he would remark without rancour, "that there are two kinds of people in this country, 'men' and 'Indians.' The Indians have got to fix that different."

That evening some of the gang sat talking in the cook-tent. Their talk was of bears and the river, but mostly of bears. Jake, flashing his eyes and teeth, told me I was brave to sleep alone. Then his stormy eyebrows drew down like a thunder-cloud, as he expatiated on the fearful propensities of bears. I knew well that these tales were told simply in order that the assembled company might be entertained by the sight of my shivering, and that they were founded on the very minimum of fact. Nevertheless, such was Jake's power of lurid presentation that I crawled into bed that night with a small seed of apprehension in my mind.

I do not know how long I had slept when the noise woke me. It was the sound of methodical scraping, followed by a sort of chattering. Then there would be a short silence, after which the scraping would be resumed. I lay still in the dark, explaining to myself in detail why this could not be a bear, and why, if it *were* a bear, there was nothing whatever to be afraid of. I went back to the beginning and explained again. The scraping continued. I became aware that I was sweating.

Finally, seizing my torch, I flashed it against the wall of the tent, and there he was—a diminutive porcupine, busily gnawing at the corner of a crate. I went over to him. He ceased to gnaw and began to chatter his teeth, regarding me unabashed with his beady eyes. Then he turned his attention to the crate again. I had evidently entirely failed to strike terror and inspire respect. I stood for some time beside my visitor, completely at a loss. At last, using the butt end of the flashlight, I administered a poke. The porcupine turned his back upon me in a perfunctory manner and set his bristles. I continued to prod. Finally he turned once more and, with the utmost deliberation, preceded me to the door of the tent and solemnly disappeared into the darkness.

The next day dawned cloudless and, since it was Sunday, the men did not go to the river. They slept in the sun and played horseshoe, while Mr. Schultz looked anxiously at the water. For a drive is not without dramatic tension. The timber must ride out on the spring flood, and if the water level drops too far before it reaches the lake, it will be stranded, and the fruits of a whole winter's work are lost. No wonder Mr. Schultz and Pete watched the river.

As for me I was occupied for a good part of the day in chasing away the porcupine. He was still around, prospecting for the crate, and I knew that if the gang found him it would be the end of him, for the temptation of a porcupine is too much for an Indian; he cannot leave it alone until it is dead. Accordingly much tact and discretion had to be exercised in returning him to the bush. I had to walk behind his slowly retreating form in the nonchalant manner of one who is merely taking leisurely exercise. Occasionally my small friend would grow tired of our progress and would entrench himself, drawing his face and paws in tightly and sticking up his bristles in an arch. I had no choice then but to become absorbed in the contemplation of some near-by object and to continue my scrutiny until the small person in the grass graciously consented to proceed. Thus I persuaded him many times back into the forest. But the unfinished work on the crate evidently weighed on his mind, and I would almost invariably return from any small excursion on my own account to see the small figure solemnly wending his way towards the cook-tent.

Apart from myself, only Victor knew about the porcupine. Victor had formally adopted me as his young lady. When I walked in the bush, Victor accompanied me; and when Victor went fishing, I was politely invited to assist. It was pleasant to sit on the sunshiny beach, dangling our improvised lines in the water. But we caught nothing, which seems to be the invariable result when I go fishing. I do not know what makes me such a bad fisherman, unless it be that one half of me does not really want to catch the fish and sits there mutely warning them, while the other half repines at our failure. Be this as it may, I have assisted at many fishing-sessions, but I have never had the pleasure of seeing so much as a minnow flapping at the end of the line.

So we loitered about the camp, and Sunday went gliding by. As we stood in line for our supper, I could feel the wind of tomorrow already blowing to meet us; for tomorrow we were to take the supply-boat down the rapids. Every one was a little excited. For this run down the Seven Mile Rapids was the dramatic climax of the whole drive. The gang, who would not be on the boat, expatiated happily upon the difficulties we should encounter. Victor, listening, rattled the dishes nervously; Tommy fell silent, which was not his habit. Only Fred the boatman, upon whom our safety would depend, remained completely unmoved.

The rest of us retired to bed in quivering expectation. I listened for my little porcupine, but he did not come again. Only the wind went winnowing through the trees and the river streamed by in the dark. I listened till my thoughts streamed with it, melting into dreams.

Next morning dawned fair. The men seemed to take hours over their breakfast, but as soon as they had finished, and disappeared down the river-bank, we set about packing as fast as we could. Soon the tents were stowed away in the great red boat, the bedding was rolled into corners, and the supplies were piled in the middle, all ready for our accommodation. When we were finally disposed, Fred guided us out into midstream. Steady as a swan, our boat went gliding down the river. In a slow rhythmic curve, we rounded the first bend. And then before us the glassy water smashed suddenly into a surge of white. The boat slid toward the line, gathered speed, and we were away. With the spray in our eyes and the wind snatching our breath, we hurtled between the banks. We reached the point where the men were working and passed before we could catch our breath to hail them. The forest rushed by us in a solid mass; the water stormed beside the boat. As we sped onward, I realized what a superb boatman Fred was. With perfect control, with regal confidence, he held us on our course. His eyes never wavered; the lines of his face never changed.

And then, rushing to meet us, came the corner. Not a blunt curve or a wide bend, but a solid right-angled corner. Just above it the water swirled up into a heap, then scooped into a hollow below. Our bows shot out an instant into nothing, then dropped with a quiver. For a fraction of time it seemed that we should follow the water that went crashing against the bank, and ram the rock-bound shore with all our force. But seizing the second which could save us, Fred and his helper wrenched the stern of the boat across the current, and headed us dead centre down the stream again. We were round the hook!

So we tore on headlong down the river, till at last we shot out into calm water. We had run seven miles in eighteen minutes

Chapter XXI

LAST DAYS AT DAYTON

THE camping ground at the foot of the rapids could be reached from a road, so Bob fetched me with the car. Bidding a regretful farewell to the camp and the river, I climbed in beside him and went bumping away.

I reached Dayton that evening, thrilling with my stories of the bush, to be plunged once more into the news from Europe. The brilliant and terrible retreat from Dunkirk had just been completed. The Maginot Line was smashed, and the German army was pouring into France.

I remember very little of what we did in Dayton during those days. I know that the year stood suddenly in high summer. I know that the grass was starry with ox-eyed daisies, and that the bad, beautiful devil weed spread in burning sheets across the rising hayfields. I know that I went on milking Sally and grooming the horses, and that Jonty still looked lovely as a dream striding over the pasture. But what was really happening was that the Germans were taking Armentières, were taking Abbéville, were taking Amiens, and that the distance separating them from Paris was growing daily less and less.

And the sun shone dazzling every day, till I grew brown as a nut, and people said, "Doesn't she look fine?" And I was enraged at myself for looking fine when the Germans were taking Abbéville, were taking Amiens, were taking Rouen.

At about this time the berry-picking started, and we would go out for long days, armed with pails, and bend down in the woods to pick the strawberries which shone ripe and red beside their white-faced flowers. Or we would push in among the tangled trees to where the raspberries fattened under their leaves, and later we would make our expedition to rock and muskeg country, where the bloom-clouded blueberries clustered on graceful bushes. Searching for the blueberries we would climb high up on rocky hill-sides, till we could stand and look over lakes and forests away to the northern wilderness from which I was so lately returned. I was a bad picker, for I would be always stopping to fill my hands with the sweet red and purple berries which we called sugar-plums, and which grew on rough bushes among the stones, or to pull down delicate red clusters from the wild cherry trees, or to discover belated raspberries along the edges of the bush. And as these were not the treasures we were seeking, they would be no good at all, so I would sit down upon the hill-side to eat them myself, and my pail would sit beside me neglected. The friendly smell of the sumac would come quivering up to me through the heat, the sunshine would hit the rocks and bounce off again, and I would wriggle into the shade of the bush-fringe and lie down. As I lay under the leaves, my body would seem to stretch away from me like a mountain range, and my spirit would grow so small that I could go adventuring with the ants and spiders among the forests of the grass.

In the midst of these wanderings, Mum's voice would come ringing down the hill-side: "Bob!" "Mary!" And I would leap to my feet and fling myself with belated urgency upon the blueberry bushes. Perhaps after a while Bob would come wandering by, and take a look into my pail. Filling the bottom with leaves, he would artfully dispose the berries upon the top; then labouring under the imagined weight, we would return to Mum. So home, and blueberries with cream for supper. . . .

And this would have been a perfect summer if the Germans had not been taking Amiens, been taking Rouen, been taking Mantes.

Only in the warm evenings, when I rode through the bush with Harold or Bob, life would be whole again; and I would know that out of this waste and tragedy men would yet make something,

something for which it would be worth-while to work and suffer, a new step in the world plan. I did not know then what to hope for, but I knew even then that I should find it.

I can remember nothing lovelier in my life than those evenings. The shadows would be lengthening already over the grass when we went cantering up the fields towards the bush. We would part the trees and brush our way in, on to a tiny trail. The lights of the sunset would shine gold and green and purple through the leafy roof. There was a clearing deep in the bush, where the horses stopped for a little while to graze. From the clearing we would often walk, and the horses would follow obediently, striding big and beautiful behind us in the dusk. But one evening, I remember, they left us and went cantering away, kicking up indifferent heels. So we walked on without them, and when we came out upon the farm road which would lead us home, night had fallen. The sky was starry, the night hung black; and fire-flies were weaving patterns into the curtain of the dark. There was no sound of the horses, for they had gone home; so we walked on into the velvet silence.

"You don't belong to houses," said Harold; "you belong to out-of-doors."

So entwined with the darkness we went home together, and the fire-flies danced before our eyes.

Next day Paris fell.

I know that by this time I was a trial. Mum was magnificent, never losing patience. Bob and I still fought affectionately with pails of water; Harold and I still rode in the bush; we still worked, visited and went fishing. But the fever of my mind burnt into the sunshine of the peaceful farm. Over and over my thoughts went. To return to England was absurd, when women and children were being sent out to North America as fast as ships could carry them. To stay in Dayton was distracting; to go on with the ride would be worse. So the days went on. The shadows in the bush were cool as water, the hayfields flowered in the sun.

"Too bad to see those weeds," said Harold, watching the ox-eyed daisies shine.

So we watched the rising grain and swam in the lakes and chased the neighbours' sheep out of the wheat-field.

And on June the seventeenth, France capitulated.

Then I knew what I would do. I would go to Toronto, Montreal —anywhere—and find work to do for the English refugee children who were coming over every week under the government plan.

But before I went I wanted to paint and repaper the farm. So I bought paint and paper and, with the help of an efficient neighbour, we set to work. We made curtains too, and began upon bedspreads.

And Britain fought the French fleet in the Mediterranean.

Then, on the first Sunday of July, a girl came down from Toronto to stay with her mother. She bought an excursion ticket and, since she was staying for a month, she offered me the return half. But to use the ticket I must leave that very night. Throwing what clothes I had into a suitcase, I left.

And at that point, not because I cared about it, but simply as an outlet for pent-up emotions, I began again to write the journal:

Sudbury. Cloud-rack over a night sky. Dazzle of lights, the clang of a railway-bell, dismal hoot of a freighter approaching the station. Close to me but infinitely remote, passengers walk up and down the platform. A black, beautiful sleeping-car attendant cracks a cheerful, impersonal grin. In a curious suspension of all thought and feeling, I follow the other passengers up and down, up and down.

I do not know whether reason is driving me, or pure blind

emotion. I have abandoned the ride and the horses and all the people I have learnt to love, and I am going east to look for work—any work that will help the refugees, that will have some connection, however remote, with the millions in agony in Europe. I do not want to go. There is no joy, no adventure any more. I go because I cannot stay. Already the quiet fields of Dayton seem infinitely far away. I can no longer bear their beauty and peace.

Toronto. The roof-garden of a girls' hostel. Plants in boxes, growing bravely into the city sky—roses, petunias, creeping jenny and nasturtiums in yellow pots. The nasturtiums will be out at home now, surging in splendour round the roots of the apple trees. "Good to keep the pests down," says Dunford. And the family are clearing the attics for fear of incendiary bombs. For fear of incendiary bombs.

Centre Island. No work. None of those to whom I have applied seem to be in need of paid workers. And I must earn enough to live on, for I have not very much money left. "*So nice if you could arrange to come in three evenings a week and knit.*" "If you could arrange to be free on Wednesday and Friday afternoons to meet the war guests at the station." This is all I can get.

I am now staying with some distant cousins called George and Nelly at a hotel on this small pleasure island; they are extremely kind. I go in every day to look for work.

There are crowds of young in the house, rather tensely occupied in having a good time. Unremitting talk of benders and boyfriends, tireless display of sun-suits and cigarettes. The popular conception of a good time has never greatly appealed to me; now the futility of it appals me. Iceberg sense of aloneness. Nelly tells me I am tired, that four or five days' rest will set me up. Only it should be a week she says.

Three weeks since France capitulated. Germany still crouches for the spring. When will she attack? How? What is she preparing?

If I could find work. . . .

I am on the road back to Dayton. From the very beginning I was afraid. It was too complete, too much like a novel, or the dénouement of an uplift film. For on the fifth day in Toronto I found work more perfect than anything I had dared to pray for.

I knew, from hearing my mother speak of the last war, that the Quakers, who are pacifists themselves, are always in the forefront of constructive work in war-time. I went to see them. Their leader, Raymond Booth, was just back from Philadelphia. His eyes shone. One could almost see the clouds of glory trailing. He looked at me, and I think knew at once what I could do. He began to talk. For he was back from the United States with a plan; brand new, red hot. The American Quakers had decided to take a number of refugee children; but, owing to government restrictions, it was not possible to convey the children direct to the States. This being so, the Canadian Quakers were to start an independent self-supporting settlement for the children until permanent arrangements could be made for them. As Mr. Booth saw it, it might be much more than a settlement—an experimental Christian state, of value whatever the future held. In neat beautiful English, Mr. Booth outlined the plan. Together we held in our hands the infinitesimal seed of a brave New World.

In Mr. Booth's mind there was no question but that I was needed. "In about six weeks, as far as we can tell," he said. For four days I was radiant. A thousand lights shone in my body and mind. The willows and lawns of Centre Island seemed to me dazzling in their beauty. And then came the meeting. It was a meeting of young Quakers at which was to be discussed, among other things, the settlement.

It was a little depressing from the beginning. A good many

plainish young men came drifting in, and a few girls. The destructive side of my critical faculty (always stimulated to excess by observation of the members of any religious gathering) began to fight the bit. I held it in with an iron grip, but still it jiggled and cavorted impudently under the saddle. At last Raymond Booth arrived, and the meeting began. I waited, taut as a fiddle-string, for the subject of the settlement to come up. At last it came. In a voice grown suddenly tired and prosaic, Mr. Booth spoke:

"I am both happy and sad to have to tell you," he said, "that the restrictions which prevented the children going direct to the U.S.A. have unexpectedly been swept aside, and there will therefore be no need for the settlement in Canada."

Raymond Booth sat down. The lights in my body and mind went out.

So I am going back to the farm, and, when the haying is over, I shall take Jonty and finish the ride; I shall give Timothy to the Gordons. I might as well face the fact that just now I am not needed.

I am hitchhiking back to the farm, because, if I am to finish the ride, I cannot afford the train fare. I bought a pair of shorts and a little rucksack and sent the suitcase by rail. Then I set out on the road for North Bay. The country north of Toronto is rolling and venerable; one could imagine it England. Sometimes I walk a long way without being offered a ride. What I ought to do, of course, is to look round when a car comes and signal with my thumb; but I cannot bring myself to do this, so I just walk along the road, and after a time somebody stops and asks how far I am going. I had three rides yesterday and two today. The last was with a young commercial traveller. He said nothing for a long time, then, looking straight out of the window, he said, "Your legs put ideas in my head."

"Oh, dear!" I said.

"What do you mean, 'Oh, dear'?" he asked.

LAST DAYS AT DAYTON

"I meant, 'Oh, dear, perhaps I should have worn a skirt.'"

"Not at all; you would not get half so many rides if you wore a skirt," replied the young man.

Tonight I am in North Bay, staying at a tourist home. I can just afford this, if I do not have any breakfast. Tomorrow night I hope I shall be home on the farm.

And sure enough, next day, though the journal does not say so, I reached the farm and flung myself into the outstretched arms of Mum.

"Goodness me, child," she cried, pushing me out to arm's length; "you're as thin as a rail! Sit down till I boil you some eggs!"

And indeed I was hungry, having eaten nothing since the day before.

I do not believe that any return in my life was sweeter than this one—to have left behind the barren heat of the city, the frustration of work not found, the loneliness of the road; to have determined to finish the ride; to settle down for a few last precious weeks on the farm, and to realize gradually, as the days went by, that the staggering blow against England was not to fall.

Two weeks later I began once more to write the journal.

August on the farm and the haying over. As I sit in the hay-mow, I can watch the horses grazing on the hill. Big Timothy, little Jonty, so soon to be parted.

Two neat complete and perfect weeks are gone. Weeks of sunshine and hungry health, and the pleasure of achievement. I have cut forty acres of hay. I have learnt to drive the rake and the hay-fork and to build the strange rounded Canadian hay coils. New days, full of summer adventure. Starting, with a tiny shiver of apprehension, to block out the next acre of hay; driving the steady old team into the virgin grass; straight as we can down a deadfer, keeping a distant pine tree between the horses' heads.

Beside us the hay falls, falls—daisies, clover and slender grass, all alike. An instant's tremor as the knives strike, and then it lies. It sets me thinking of the suddenness and finality of death and the appropriate symbolism of the mediaeval mower and his scythe. In the west end of the field the men work at the coiling, their sunburnt bodies bare to the waist, beautiful and unconscious as the horses on the mower. At the turn of the block I stop for a drink, water full of hay-seeds out of the side of a milk pail. Harold holds it up for me, and some of the cool drops run down my breast, and I think that, when the haying is done for the day, we shall go swimming, and our brown bodies will be green and cool under the evening water. . . .

So the cutting is done, and the coiling, and now we are hauling in. I drive the team in the field; two men pitch on; one builds the load. Then load after load bumps into the barn, the hay-fork comes into play, and I have two mares to drive at the end of the pulleys. Ropes are stretched along the angle of the barn-roof. The man on the load hauls the fork towards him, digging it deep into the tight-packed hay, then locking it, ready for its journey along the roof to the stack which Harold is building against the north wall. I lean sleepily against the door and watch the rhythmic line of the rope streaming down out of the barn-roof and snaking in liquid coils over the dusty floor. Outside the sunshine is yellow as a flower, the sky is infinitely blue, bluer than we can ever deserve. . . .

"All right, Mary," shouts the man on the hay-fork. "Git up," I translate to the mares, and we walk out solemnly across the barn-yard.

At last comes the end of the week, and we are building a stack in the east field. They are using the gin-pole, a high triangular erection, to which are attached the fork and pulleys. There are four teams working, eight men and I. By evening the last coil is stacked. So the haying ends, with the teams bumping their empty racks down the great field, and behind them the moon rising in cloud-rack, and a wet wind shrilling from the lake shore. That night I lie in bed and listen to the rain drumming on the roof and remember the two weeks so quickly gone—remember the day when Harold's load stuck fast in the barn-door, and he had to unhitch the team and drag it out again backwards; and the day he fell down the front of the towering load and landed astride the tongue, to the astonishment of the team; and how once Bob found me taking a well-deserved drink and drove up behind me with the hay-rake, upsetting me head first into the pail, to which I had replied by throwing the remains of the water down his front. But Bob, unabashed, got in the last word:

"Don't look now," he remarked shamelessly, "but I think I've wet my pants."

Last of all, before I go to sleep, I remember how the dragon of the spy rumours gave a last lash of its tail before it died. It seems that some one had written to the Canadian Mounted Police in Sault Sainte Marie, advising them to make investigations concerning me. One afternoon I had just finished cutting several acres of hay, and Harold had blocked out a new island for me to begin upon. To celebrate this achievement we had plunged for a few minutes into the shady creek, which went winding along the edge of the field. Harold wore only a pair of trunks for the haying, and I wore a cotton sun-suit, so we jumped in as we were. When we came out, shaking the water from our eyes and blinking in the sun, it was to see a surprising shiny motor car driving down into the middle of the field. Out of it climbed a beautifully groomed young man who strode down to meet us and inquired:

"Is Miss Bosanquet here?"

"What did you want?" asked Harold, in the manner of one preparing to do battle.

"It was a private matter concerning Miss Bosanquet," replied the young man imperturbably.

So with the water running out of my hair and down my legs, I went and sat on the running-board of the shiny car. The young man had a sturdy face; there were surprise and kindness in his wide-open brown eyes.

"We're the Royal Canadian Mounted Police," he said, and I became aware of another man dim in the background, armed with a note-book. "We have to ask you a few questions as a matter of routine."

"Would the routine have anything to do with rumours of my being a spy?" I asked.

As a matter of fact, admitted the young policeman, it had. So we went exhaustively into the subject of my father's occupation, the purpose of my visit to Canada, my home in England, and all the rest of it. Then I discovered that the mounted policeman was English and had been born at a village near Cambridge where I had often stayed. So we sat and talked of Cambridge, while the water trickled in patterns down my muddy legs, and the young man looked at me seriously with his melting eyes. Finally, assuring me that I should not be troubled again, he turned the car in a wide curve and went bumping away back to the road.

Ten minutes later Mum came whirling down into the field, swinging a pail of ice-cream in one hand, and waving to me with the other.

"Eat that!" she commanded, setting me down against a hay coil and plumping the pail of ice-cream on to my knee. "Whoever sent that complaint to the police ought to be locked up themselves!" she cried in a perfect spate of indignation, "but *I* told them! I showed them your passport and that letter you have to Lord Tweedsmuir; and I told them what *we* thought of you, and I'm glad you couldn't hear that, because I'd hate to make you vain!"

So ended the spy stories; with a brown-eyed young man talking about England, and Mum running down to the field to comfort me with ice-cream. And so most of our troubles would end, if we left them alone.

Last things, last things, how they hurt! Last milking of Sally, last grooming of Timothy, last trip to the post office, last trip to town—and worst of all, last ride over the bush-trail that the boys and I had learned to love so well.

When we first rode the trail there had been snow on the ground, and the trees were fast in their winter sleep. Then month by month we had watched them swell into bud and scatter into leaf, and at last spread wide in the lush completeness of summer.

Then on the long Sunday afternoons we would plunge into the bush and bathe in the green shade, or we would come at evening when the mists lay white on the fields, and the slim bewitching whippoorwills cried strangely among the trees. I can remember many such days and many such evenings, but one evening above the rest, when we stood still by one consent in the midst of the trail; and I remember, as we watched the poplars rounding their leaves in black patterns against the sky, how our hearts ached for fulfilment, for a work splendid enough to be worthy of this exquisite world which we so briefly inherit.

And now, on this last evening, as we lay in the clearing and watched the horses grazing together, so happy and unaware, I remembered these things; and suddenly my eyes were blinded with tears, and the horses, the trees and the sky swam together into the trembling flower face which is the pattern of all partings. Then I thought of Jesus Christ, and the saddest words he ever spoke: "Little children, it is the last time." . . .

Chapter XXII

THE ROAD AGAIN

So Jonty and I are on the road again, and overnight I have turned back into the girl who is riding across Canada. I am Mary Bosanquet, temporarily famous, cool, self-contained and unattached, infinitely different from the lonely dependent Me, who lay in the clearing and cried, because I must leave the bush and the broad fields and the people I had learned to love.

The Dayton life lies behind me, finished. It is like a rare book, discovered, read to the end with delight, and put back in the shelf with a sigh and a sense of loss. Vaguely one longs to discover it again, to go on with it, to go back—but the experience is complete and not to be recaptured. Already the Dayton life is rushing away from me into the past, and my heart strains back to it in vain.

The Gordons took Jonty and me with a trailer as far as Whitefish, where we stopped last year. So we started off again from the home of the Finns.

They are a splendid family, those Finns. I remember them on the wild winter night when I first came to their farm, how they brought me in blinking out of the dark with the rain running out of my hair. There they were—the big blonde mother and the five boys. I thought them splendid then—when they were all bundled up in winter clothes and had mud on them, and the two youngest had snuffly colds—but now, in high summer, they are magnificent. Great sun-browned bodies, eyes blue as the water and butter-bright hair.

I can see them now at the creek, diving in one after the other in that soul-satisfying arc which I strive after always in vain.

I can see them swimming far down into the water, then breaking surface again, trumpeting like young sea-lions, with the bright hair smoothed on to their foreheads like the edge of a golden bowl. The middle one of these boys is different from the others. He is slighter than they are and has the look of a greyhound among mastiffs. There is a quality about the lift of his head, the breadth of forehead and the almost too gentle line of the chin which must have come down to him from some far-away Finnish nobleman, slipped somehow into the long-forgotten ancestry of this sturdy family.

The day we left the farm at Whitefish, summer seemed to turn the corner towards autumn. We left Sudbury some days later under a lowering sky; behind us the great mining town smouldered gloomily; before us, over the naked rocks, the naked road stretched grey and desolate. I got down and walked. Jonty, wanting Timothy, trudged behind me sadly. I felt so sorry for him that I was ready to cry.

That night we reached a belt of farming country and stayed with a large and hilarious Irish family. I counted fifteen in the house at one time, but there must have been more in all. The house was not very large or very waterproof, but they found me a little sofa to lie on and some of the dampest bedding it has been my lot to encounter, and I slept dreamlessly all night.

Next day the pony and I were catapulted again into a completely different environment. For early in the afternoon we reached Warren, where we had been invited to stay with "Bis" Warren, the son of the founder of the little town. Dismounting in the street, I asked a storekeeper if he knew Bis. "Why sure," he replied; "there he comes now." Down the street a tall thin man was driving at considerable speed in an improbable looking sulky. "Bis!" cried the storekeeper, as the equipage drew alongside. Instantly the pony stopped dead, precipitating her driver unceremoniously on to her fat little quarters.

"Don't mind her," remarked her lord and master, recovering

his seat without the smallest loss of dignity; "like every one else in this place, she knows my name."

So away we drove to his pleasant farm, and then began three delightful days for both me and the pony. Bis has three horses who might have come straight off a ranch in the West, and five jolly daughters running up in a rather gap-runged step-ladder from two years old to twenty.

We are at North Bay.

I am gradually deciding to take an extra month and go down to New York. I should like to meet some Americans before I go home, and to learn a little of how they think and to see their great capital. In Montreal the last fifty pounds which the family were able to send me, and which I have scrupulously avoided touching, are waiting to take me down.

I understand that I have now reached the summit of experience, for I have seen the Quints!

On Sunday afternoon, anxiously punctual, my hostess and friends hustled me into the car, and we joined the stream of traffic which was bound for the same destination as ourselves. The curly road to Callander, in marked contrast to four-fifths of the trans-Canada highway, is paved right out to the edge, and in superb repair. From the moment we leave North Bay city limits, garages, pop stands and tourist cabins line our route in unrelieved succession. The road winds through them for ten miles. At last we reach a supremely magnificent burst of cabins, and behold, we are in Callander!

The first thing which greets us, as we drive in, is a hilariously blatant placard, bearing the legend: "Madame LeGros, Aunt and Midwife to the Quints!" I understand that if we go in and cross this lady's hand with silver—quite a lot of silver—we may secure the inestimable privilege of seeing and even touching the absolutely genuine basket in which the Quints were laid at the hour of birth. There are, however, in other parts of Callander, at least two other absolutely genuine first baskets; for it seems that not even nails from the True Cross were ever reduplicated with a more carefree abandon, or subsequently regarded with a more ecstatic devotion.

Callander itself is a cross between a miniature World's Fair, and Banff-without-the-mountains. There is hardly a house which does not sport a filling station, pop stand, or "Accommodation for Tourists."

We turn north and climb a gentle hill, upon the top of which stands the residence of the Quints themselves. Opposite to us, as we reach the summit, stands an imposing edifice of the World's Fair type, inscribed: "Portrait Gallery of the Five Most Famous Babies in the World." On our right stands a vast restaurant and store, entitled "Oliva Dionne's Booth," and crowned with portraits of the Quints in gigantic relief. I understand that, to maintain the exterior decoration of this edifice, Borden's Dairies cheerfully disgorged two thousand dollars a year. Next to it is a shop devoted exclusively to the sale of English woollens and having no special reason for existence, beyond the generally accurate assumption that the average tourist can be induced to buy anything.

In the extensive parking lot behind these buildings, expensive cars are standing in serried ranks. Having wriggled our own into place, we hastily cross the road and find that some three or four hundred pilgrims are already gathered at the shrine. We take our place at their rapidly lengthening tail; and I strain my ears, hoping against hope that I may hear the proverbial lady tourist gurgling ecstatically: "Just imagine, *five* little girls! Isn't it adorable? Isn't it just too cute for words?" To be answered by the grimly adjacent stranger: "Cute nothing! I've got ten of my own."

However, no such conversational exchange takes place; instead a man concealed in a small hut suddenly begins to speak into a powerful amplifier, admonishing us that when we pass before the Quints we must keep moving, and must on no account speak or take photographs. He concludes by informing us with impressive severity that our co-operation in every respect is essential.

Guiltily we surrender our cameras to an attendant and move on in hushed expectancy towards the gates. Finally they open and we crowd in, pushing decorously. We enter the wooden cloisters which surround the play-yard; half of us turn to the left, half to the right; we turn at right angles again and—We Are in the Presence!

There they are, exactly as advertised, five plump, black-haired little girls, wearing today blue coats and white gloves and digging in the sand with such a dazzling spontaneity that one feels sure this act must have been rehearsed over and over again— as indeed it has, daily from 9:30 to 10:30 and from 3:30 to 4:30, ever since the infants were old enough to crawl.

There is one illusion which a visit to Callander must forever dispel; this is the pleasantly maintained fiction that each little Quintuplet lives exactly the same normal life as any other little girl of six. One visit to Callander, and *that* bubble bursts with a bang! Of all the houses in the place, I noticed only one which seems to have remained entirely unaltered since the arrival, six years ago, of the little human gold-mine.

It is a plain red brick house, nestling behind five maple trees, and on the door, if you take the trouble to look, you may see a worn metal plaque bearing the name of Dr. Allan Roy Dafoe. He alone refuses to swell with swelling Callander. His news value is so tremendous that a reporter once paid him a dollar to pull a perfectly sound tooth, and considered his autograph on the receipt cheap at the price. But the little Doctor's sturdy common sense remains unshaken by his meteoric rise to fame. If any one can succeed in giving the Quints' lives even a semblance of normality, it will be their humorous, four-square, both-feet-on-the-ground little guardian. But he will have an uphill struggle.

For the Quintuplets, as one press man enthusiastically remarked to me, are the greatest human interest in the world today. Poor little girls—Cecile, Emilie, Annette, Yvonne, Marie —the greatest human interest story in the world—but who wants to be?

The first town we struck after leaving North Bay was Mattawa. I remember the warm thrill of surprise when the road led up on to the brow of a hill, and I looked down to see the little town snuggling up against the western end of the Laurentians. North of Mattawa, under the hills, ran the Ottawa River, broad and bright; and south, on the rolling uplands, little white farms sparkled in the sun.

We trundled down toward the town but were waylaid on the outskirts by a little French Canadian girl, who invited me to go in and visit her mother. In a few minutes the pony and I found ourselves being the life and soul of a huge party of sisters, brothers, mothers, aunts and neighbours. Jonty stood patiently while innumerable women and children were hoisted on to his back, photographed and hoisted down again. I dispensed autographs, answered questions, and finally was persuaded to stay the night. So I bought Jonty some oats, turned him into a fine pasture, and settled down for the evening.

This was the first French Canadian family we encountered, but as we go east along the borders of Quebec, there begin to be more and more. These Habitant families are very interesting. The change of environment seems to have changed their racial characteristics very little. They are light-hearted, thrifty and remarkably efficient farmers; and they remain Latin to the last degree.

The other day I was resting a little while at a filling station, where I met a young French schoolmaster waiting to be conveyed to a Catholic Church picnic. He was dressed for the occasion in the palest of pearly grey flannel suits, a white shirt with a stiff collar and most exquisite tie, a brown velour hat, and dazzling white buckskin shoes.

We soon get into conversation and, although he knows fair

English, it is his pleasure that I talk French, a language which he assures me I speak perfectly. The enormity of this mis-statement would be apparent to any one who has ever heard my flounderings in that exquisite and much-abused tongue. We have not been talking long before the witching word *amour* begins to worm its way into the conversation. Resolutely I steer our discourse back to more mundane topics, but in vain. In no time my friend is asking me how many young men have fallen in love with me, indicating, with a wealth of gesture and a flattery which again rather misses its mark, that he feels sure they could not begin to be counted upon the fingers of our combined hands.

"*Choses comme ça,*" I reply, in French which I feel is more stately than idiomatic, "*ne sont pas pour raconter.*"

However he is not one whit abashed by this stately rebuke, and goes on to suggest that I might come home and stay with him for a few days. I ask him whether this is likely to be convenient for his wife, to which he blandly replies that he is a bachelor living alone. Absurd, of course. But somehow the French have such a charming and childlike way of saying these things that one is incapable of being properly outraged.

Soon after, I get on the pony and ride away, whereupon my young friend calls after me in a final crescendo of French-ness, that I had better stay a little longer, for there is a thunderstorm coming up, and I shall undoubtedly be killed by the thunder. . . .

The character of this part of the country is as different from the district around Dayton as is the character of its inhabitants. The road from Mattawa to Pembroke leads mostly along the Ottawa River, and the Laurentians run roundly down to the water, quiet and kindly looking and solid with bush. The river is wide and steady and dotted with tufty islands. To the south the country is rolling and prosperously farmed. Pembroke itself is a pleasant little town, enriched with avenues of fine matured maples and with the company of the ever-changing river along its northern edge. Beyond the river, in the background but eternally present, run the hills. "The low, lovely, lounging Laurentians," says Wilson MacDonald.

In Pembroke I planned to stay for two nights, but in the end I stayed for eight days, and was loath to leave even then. For I stayed with the Williams family, who, in addition to being charming, have a stable of hunters.

Mr. Williams' groom is an Englishman; but "groom" is the wrong word for him. He is a man for whom horses are such a passion that he must have work for them or perish of emptiness. I have never since I left England seen such a well-kept harness-room or three horses in more perfect condition. In my many months in the West and on the farm, I had almost forgotten that things could be like this. But my hands slipped naturally back over the double bridle, and my mind over the familiar words: "head-collar," "flexion," "collection," "conformation," "well let down," "well ribbed up," and all the rest. I was almost in England again.

Mr. Williams himself (although he is over seventy, perfectly absurd) is a splendid rider. He did not learn till he was forty-three—a slap in the eye for those who say that a good rider cannot be made after the age of twenty! Mr. Williams still breaks his own horses, and makes a first-rate job of it.

On the eighth day after my arrival, he picked up the entire stable, plus Jonty and another horse, and transported them to Renfrew Fair. I was delighted, as it would be the first Fall Fair I had seen.

Renfrew fair grounds are large and pleasant, with good buildings for the accommodation of the horses and cattle. The atmosphere of these Fall Fairs is jolly and informal to the last degree, and the organization is a little vague. This is in complete contrast to an English horse show, where the organization is perfect but the atmosphere is tense, so that I for one ride a good deal worse than usual as a result.

At Renfrew they exhibit everything, from honey to workhorses. I did not have time to see much, as Ward (Mr. Williams' man) and I were working all the time on the horses; but I know very little about poultry, preserves and whatnot, anyway. I came to know most of the work-horses, though, and fine stuff some of them were. The showing of the saddle-horses was as pleasant and unorthodox as everything else. Mr. Williams, the principal exhibitor, put up the jumps, while the judge and committee looked on.

I found that, in the Ladies' Hunter Class, I had to ride all the entries, as there was no other girl. One of the ladies' hunters charged head first into the stone wall and landed me neatly the other side, on the back of my neck, to the delectation of the populace. Mr. Williams' bay mare, as usual, jumped superbly, for which I most unfairly got all the credit. I showed Jonty in two classes, and he took a first prize and a second, though whether they were awarded entirely on the strength of his "conformation and way of going," or whether the fact of his having brought me across Canada, which was being announced with disconcerting blatancy over the loud speaker, had anything to do with it, I do not feel competent to judge. Either way I felt he deserved them, bless him.

On the last day they had the stock parade, which I thought more beautiful than any regal procession. First came the work-teams, shining like satin in beautifully studded harness. Then there were the peerless stallions, with the look of eagles in their eyes, dangling their insignificant owners at the end of their haltershanks; there were heifers and bullocks, young and strong and bouncy, and solemn dairy cattle, rich and generous-looking. Almost last came the brood-mares, with their baby-eyed foals curvetting around them, and after them the bulls in rugged magnificence.

They all walked slowly round the fair ground, a very splendid company. So the fair was over.

Almost the last to go were Jonty and I. I put on him the unaccustomed saddlebags; Mr. Williams' unemotional Englishman bade us good-bye with tears in his eyes; and we were away.

The most exciting part of this unmeditated journey is that there are so many treasures to discover, treasures of sudden surprising people at the ends of lonely days.

Two evenings ago, Jonty and I came all alone into Arnprior; and in an hour I was sitting down in a grey house with windows over the river, sitting down to dinner with candles before me and with the strenuous scent of chrysanthemums upon my senses, sitting down with a family that I had never seen, but seemed to have always known, and pouring out the thoughts which had been struggling in my mind for many months. Soon we were sharing the certainty that an ungoverned world must at last destroy itself, sharing the certainty that Britain and America must unite, sharing the burning necessity to find one's part in all this, to find the job for the future which was one's own.

For we must bring out of this war not only victory, but an ordered world, a governed world; otherwise we fight in vain.

Chapter XXIII

NEW FRANCE

AFTER nearly a year and a half, I am in the Dominion's capital, and have spent my first day in exploring its geography.

Ottawa is a fresh and kindly city. The Parliament Buildings are dignified and well-balanced and have the advantage of a perfect situation, on the crest of a gentle hill, with a steep drop on the north side towards the river. I have never before been in a town which is focused to such an extent by one point. It seems impossible to go anywhere in the centre of the city, without gravitating naturally towards the Parliament Square.

I am now busily engaged in preparations for the ride to New York; for I have decided to make it before I go home. It will be exciting to discover the States, about which I have heard so much, and know so little! Only out of my half-conscious mind, dim pictures arise: the sky-line of New York, which I feel I have already seen; Palm Beach, which I hope I never shall see; and somewhere the weary, wide Mississippi, curving through endless plains. . . .

In Montreal, my last fifty pounds are waiting. At Six Hundred and Twenty Park Avenue, some cousins are living. They have written a charming letter inviting me to stay with them. The idea of cousins is comfortable, but the idea of arriving on Park Avenue with my entire luggage in a pair of saddlebags is not!

However, formalities for my visa go forward, and I do not doubt that in about four weeks we shall be crossing the border.

We left Ottawa yesterday and crossed over the river into the Province of Quebec. We stayed last night at Buckingham, and

NEW FRANCE 231

today brought us to Montebello. In the morning we followed small roads among the hills, but this evening we were winding our way again along the lazy reaches of the river. The trees by the water are already burning into autumn; red-hot Virginia creeper runs wild among the rocks, and in another week the hills will be on fire. Autumn again, and we are still on the road!

We are indeed in Quebec. Today I met nobody at all who could speak English. I am now staying with a charming and distinguished Habitant family, who are no exception. My elderly hostess has been telling me about the lands in this district which still belong to the Seigneurie of Papineau, and for which fiefs are paid. Quebec is still under Roman Law. Remarkable to find the Holy Roman Empire stretching out its tentacles into this new world of the West!

I said good-bye to my white-haired hostess in a pale September mist. She held both my hands in hers and asked me to pray for her husband, who had lately died. Then she said, very slowly, so that I might be sure to understand: *"C'est bien evident que la Providence vous garde."* I have no particular illusions about the Roman Catholic church, but there is something about a faithful Catholic which is entirely charming.

Already we are half-way to Montreal. How I wish I had longer to ride through Quebec! It is old France and new France; it is the Middle Ages and the New World; it is mediaeval Europe and modern America meeting.

The villages have a character which is theirs alone. The great silver-steepled church by which each is dominated bears witness to the old-established power of the Catholic religion. Below, against the forest or the sky, stand out the bell-cast roofs of the cottages or the mansard roofs of the larger houses, which are allied to the Canadian barn-roof, but hipped at more sharply contrasting angles. Down the sleepy street, the Habitant farmers go driving their French Canadian horses. Deep copper red is the predominant colour of these little creatures, and their lean, large-jointed bodies seem not unlike those of the Barbary horse, which, with the Arab, formed the light saddle-horse of the later Middle Ages.

Passing the small solid houses in the country, set four-square into the ground and built of great squared logs, I cannot help thinking of Champlain and his sturdy seventeenth century settlers, who built for the future, as we do not. Riding by the boundaries of some still-surviving seigneurie, I thought of the curious history of the Feudal System, which, as it died in Europe, was to find a short rebirth upon the wild borders of a half-discovered continent. I imagined the feudal figure of Frontenac, cruel, picturesque Frontenac, setting forth through the forests to do battle with the Iroquois, like a Crusader seeking the Saracens. I wish I had time to ride on and see Quebec, centre of French Canada, to see the precipitous city where Montcalm—because of the genius of Wolfe, and not from his own lack of it—lost New France to the British.

I am spending Sunday with a family whom I met in Calgary. They have left the West and come back to their old home in the Province of Quebec.

I left Jonty last night in a stable in Lachute, and the Readings met me with the car and brought me out in the pitch dark. I stumbled, half asleep, into the lighted island of the house, not knowing in the least where we were. This morning I woke to find that we were perched on a rounded shoulder of the Laurentians, with grassy slopes before us, and behind us maple trees, burning in red and gold, climbing up the hill-side into the pines.

Now I am sitting high up in the autumn hills, looking across the distance at Mount Royal, and trying to realize that tomorrow we shall be in Montreal. The horses and I have done without any difficulty what people said was impossible, but I find there is no sense of achievement, only a great thankfulness for the gift of this last year. I have been given the experience of innumerable friendships, but beyond even this has been the sacramental experience of aloneness. I have been alone in happiness and alone in pain, alone in peace and alone in fear, alone in the mountains and in river-valleys and on the burning range, beside boiling creeks and under giant trees and on the naked prairie; alone I have felt the grip of the snow-mantled wilderness and known the veiled solemnity of a forest in the rain.

My deepest love, my deepest gratitude of all, is to the horses, for this journey is their gift to me. With them I have been alone but never forsaken, for companionship with animals is the most precious aloneness there is.

Chapter XXIV

END OF AN ADVENTURE

So we have reached Montreal.

The Ogilvies, with whom I am staying, live out in Saraguay beside the Rivière des Prairies. They have a stately, grey stone house, with long lawns running down to the water. My bedroom is curtained in flowered chintz; over my bed hangs a misty greygreen Corot in perfect reproduction. I wake every morning and run to the window to see the early-morning sun on the elms, which are brightening into daffodil yellow, and on the maples which are burning into red. As their home is, so are the Ogilvies.

My arrival here is one more of the delightful accidents of the ride. Upon the Douglas Lake Ranch, where I found Timothy, I found also Hugh Ogilvie, visiting his friend, Mr. Ward, and running horses with the cowboys. He invited me to stay with his parents when I reached Montreal, and a year and a half later I arrived.

So once more I am one for a little while with the life of a city. I have climbed to the top of the mountain, and looked out over tidy homes and smoking factories. I have walked down Saint Catharine Street, and gazed into the brilliant windows of the palace of merchandise which is Morgan's, and stood in Burton's amid the luxury of books—books ranged high up the walls, books standing on the counters, books spread out before me wherever I turned—fresh, fascinating, packed with treasure. In Burton's book shop I am home again, and the ride for that hour forgotten.

But yet, as my Irish cousins might very well say, the best parts of my visit to Montreal have been the days when we left it to go into the mountains.

Before I knew them I used to allow myself a quiet smile at the persistence with which every one described the low, quiet Laurentians as "mountains." But I smile no longer, for they *are* mountains. There is that about their weathered maturity which, to me at least, is quite as satisfying as the smack-you-down magnificence of the Rockies.

I remember the first day when we drove up in the fading evening light. Engraved on my mind is the liquid line of the North River Valley, with the lean fields running down to the water, and the flaming bush running down to the fields, while before us the mountains unfolded spur on spur.

Then, just a week ago, the autumn was at its peak; it lapped us round in a flaming red-gold dream. The air was still, with that poised stillness which comes sometimes at the peak of the old year, before the winds come tearing down the valleys to strip the trees for their winter vigil. Now we are in the mountains again, and there is a great change. Already the trees stand half naked, in a cooler, less exuberant beauty. Already we may look up and see the shining limbs of the silver birches perfect and unadorned against the sky. Best of all I love to stand on an open hill and look into the mountains.

Yesterday we rode out and gazed far away to the north, watching the hills roll on and on towards lonely Hudson's Bay. Above us a tough wind out of the west was riding herd to the clouds, chasing them helter-skelter across the sky, so that their fleeing shadows came gliding towards us over the hills and crossed the forest behind us, to lose themselves in the hidden valley upon the other side. And gazing upon it all, again I thought how the young of our generation *must* work to make a world in which the nations will have peace, for only so can we earn the right to enjoy this beauty which now we love with pain, feeling that we have no right to peace and happiness, while others, as young as we, fight their way through fire and blood.

At long last all is in order for the journey to New York. I have signed innumerable papers with regard to Jonty. I have stood in innumerable queues and sat in innumerable consular ante-rooms. I have trotted obediently from room 915 to room 910, and back to room 915, and on to room 920. Every time I came into the presence of a new official, he invented a new way of mispronouncing my name, and asked me how old I was, what I did, why I wanted to go to the States and how long I proposed to stay there. Then he wrote all this down on a form and I signed it. This afternoon, when I had almost given up hope of ever coming to the end of this ritual, I was told to go to room 921 to receive my visa. In 921 a brand-new official young man regarded me across a desk. Having remarked, "The name's Bozzankay, is it not?" and asked me how old I was, what I did, etc., he suddenly said, "I have to put down your race—French, I suppose?"

"No, English!" I replied, horrified.

"French name," said the young man.

"Huguenot," I answered wearily.

"Must be French extraction," observed the young man, to whom Huguenot meant nothing.

"Oh, well yes, but . . ."

"Race—French," wrote the young man.

"As a matter of fact," I cried, outraged, "the Bosanquets were British before the States were even United!"

In the next second I realized that this is exactly the sort of remark that the Americans expect from the English, and I wriggled my toes in anguish, while the hot blood mounted out of my neck and ran up into the roots of my hair. But the young man looked at me with an amused twinkle and, deciding to humour me, crossed out "French" and put down "English." Then he stamped my passport, wished me good luck, and away I went. So I have my visa.

It was a cold, cruel day when we left Montreal. I rode shivering between the blank fields which bordered the road. Wistfully I remembered the lovely leisurely house at Saraguay; I missed the kindly presence of the Ogilvies; I thought of fire-light and tea. Almost I wished we had no further to go.

It was pleasant at last to see the silver church steeple of Chambly, where I was to stay the night with friends of the Ogilvies, who had maps and a first-hand knowledge of the state of Vermont, into which I proposed to set out. I reached the Rosses early in the evening, and who should arrive soon after me but Hugh Ogilvie, his car piled high with the things which I had forgotten to pack in my saddlebags. It was not long before we were all kneeling head to head upon the floor, poring over maps on which bridle-trails, marked in green, went winding their way among the exciting contour lines of the Green Mountains, which ran from north to south down the romantic page. The prospect of going into unknown mountains is always exciting, to ride into them with a horse is eternal adventure.

Once more the mysteries of the road had me in thrall. The cold ride from Montreal was forgotten. One more mountain range to discover, one more month to ride through the autumn— one more mountain range, one more month! As we bent our faces over the map, the love of riding and mountains burnt in us all, till the Rosses were ready to take their horses out of the barn and go with me; but, because they could not, they said to Hugh: "Why don't you go and ride down to the border anyway? We'll lend you Dawn."

So next morning we set out—Jonty with his tail flying, bounding up into the bit, and Dawn striding beside him on her fine thoroughbred legs. Hugh was in no way provided for the journey, not having so much as a tooth-brush with him, but neither he nor I care much for the amenities of travel, so we rode southward in high spirits while the wind skirled behind us and the sun shone down upon the fields, cold and brilliant.

At midday we stopped at a French Canadian farm, where they allowed us to tie the horses in the barn while we ate our lunch. The family had a remarkable machine for drawing water; it was a treadmill composed of a hollow wheel. At a word from his master, a large collie dog leapt into the wheel and, with much tail-wagging and self-congratulation, ran upon the same spot, turning the wheel underneath him until released by a word from the farmer. Later in the same day we met a boy with a dog neatly harnessed to a four-wheeled cart, and I was reminded of my childhood in France, when my greatest desire (after a pony) was to own a cart and a dog to draw it, such as the country children had.

So we rode southward all day, and the outlines of hills began to appear. The White Mountains south-east of us, south-west the Adirondacks, and at last between them, fairy-pale, the Green Mountains of Vermont.

Late in the afternoon of the second day, we reached the border village of Sainte Armande where Hugh left me; and that night Jonty and I reached St. Albans, our first town in the states.

Next day, in dazzling sunshine, we left the little town and began to climb up into the mountains. First the road streamed wide and open over gently sloping grassland, but by midday we were already on rough rocky trails, winding our way among the hills. Just now the Green Mountains are not green; in the pale colours of the dying autumn, silver and copper and old gold, the hill-sides wait for the winter. Yesterday was one of those days when one looks and looks, afraid to miss anything; one seizes sudden pictures and says, "I must remember this."

I remember how, as we went up between the wide fields, I looked west and saw a farm-house dark against the vivid sky, with a sculptured line of maples beside it, and behind it the blue Adirondacks running southward beyond Lake Champlain. I remember later another house, very small against a wall of bush, clad in the white smoke from its chimney, and looking like the back-set for an opera. And there was the strange mountain. We came out of the woods, and there it was, all of a sudden among the little rounded hills—a mountain of naked rock cutting up into the sky.

When the sunshine was reddening already towards the afternoon, we came down into a valley in which a little lake lay nestling under the shoulders of the hills. The road came winding down out of the trees and crossed the river which fed the lake, upon a white bridge. I stopped on the crest of the bridge to talk to a plain kindly faced woman with a little girl.

"That's a beautiful horse," she said, looking at Jonty, who was shining in the sun.

"There isn't another horse like that one in the world," I replied happily, for what must have been the several hundredth time. "I'm wondering," I added after a little more conversation, "where we shall stay the night."

"Oh, I should think any one would be tickled to death to have you," replied the little woman.

Her predictions, however, proved to be over-optimistic. At sunset we were wending our way along a small road bordered by comfortable-looking farms. I went to the door of one and asked if we might stay the night. But the lady of the house looked at me forbiddingly from behind the screen-door, and replied that she had not a spare bed. I went on. Four farm-houses turned us down. Feeling small and negligible as a leaf in the wind, I wandered on into the gathering dusk, trailing Jonty behind me and wishing I were either child enough to cry or adult enough not to want to.

At last we reached a farm-house where, after considering us carefully, they took us in. But it is evident that the women of

Vermont are more surprised than delighted by the appearance of a solitary girl on a pony.

It seems that the first night did not provide a fair sample of the reception which one may expect to receive in Vermont. For on the next evening I was gladly welcomed into the first house at which I knocked, the only concern of the Polish family who inhabited it being that their spare bedroom was not heated. Soon I was sitting down with them to a huge supper of veal, potatoes, carrots, cream cheese and delicious rye bread; and, having done full justice to this repast and milked seven cows, I went thankfully to bed.

Next day the weather was stormy. The little hills glowered at us from under beetling clouds, and behind them the mountains were half-hidden in shadow. Bucking a strong south wind we wound our way down through the valleys and under the shoulders of the hills. In the evening we reached Middlebury and the government farm on which they raise the sturdy, graceful little Morgans, famous Vermont breed of all-purpose horses. Here Jonty stayed in state in a palatial box stall, and I stayed with a charming family whose farm was only half a mile away. They were the most interesting family I had met so far.

The children were enthusiastic members of the "Four H Club," which is a nation-wide club for the young people of farming communities. The four H's stand for Head, Heart, Hands, and Health, and the society is run largely by the young people themselves. Extensive competitions are organized, in such subjects as stock-raising, horticulture, cooking, and dress-making. Those of the members who can, go to Four H camps in the summer and so meet Four H youngsters from other communities.

The Jewett children took me out to the barn to see the calves for which they had lately won a prize, and in the house we turned over enormous scrap-books into which had been stuck newspaper cuttings describing Four H activities in which they had taken part—photographs of camps, patterns of dresses for

"ONE MAY RIDE FROM DAWN TILL DARK WITHOUT EVER TOUCHING A HIGHWAY"

END OF AN ADVENTURE

which the girls had won prizes, recipes for which they had been commended, and a really impressive collection of blue ribbons. As for the children, their club work was the delight of their life and stimulated a vivid interest, not only in the various aspects of their own work on the farm, but in the work of young people in other communities. I believe that such a club as this would be invaluable in any country, old or young.

Next morning I woke to find that it had rained all night, but now the wind was rolling back the curtain of the clouds from a backcloth of blue sky. Jonty and I put down our heads and half closed our eyes and went battling up the road with our tail and rain-coat flapping behind us. We saw little till suddenly I heard a shrill whinny; I looked up, and behold, a dazzling white horse, cantering towards us down the middle of a field, and behind him a bank of grey and copper trees smouldering in shadow, and behind *them* rain and sunshine hunting each other across the mountains. Then I thought of the people who write fairy stories, striving to create something more wonderful than reality, when there could be nothing more wonderful than reality in the mind of any one on earth.

Meanwhile the horse began to canter along the fence, hooting and jeering, while Jonty ignored him with regal disdain. Jonty has perfect manners with regard to other horses. No matter what demonstrations they make, he goes on unmoved, looking solemnly straight ahead of him, like a good little girl who gets winked at in church. His behaviour is just as exemplary when dogs bark at him. Timothy would lash out at them furiously, and I would shut my eyes and ride him up hard, expecting any minute to hear the yells of a shattered dog. Actually he never did hurt one, but it was not for lack of evil intent. All Jonty does, on the other hand, is to make an innocuous pass with the off hind, as if to say, "Any other horse would kick you, so mind!"

Jonty's extreme virtue on the trip almost worries me sometimes. One of the factors which make a long-distance ride very hard on a horse is the fact that he has so little fun. A healthy horse, like a healthy human being, enjoys physical self-expression. He likes to go prancing out in the morning, play up a little, show off to the other horses, collect himself, play with the bit, use all his paces, perhaps go over a few jumps, and come home, as the writer of Job puts it, still "pawing in the valley and rejoicing in his strength." But on a long-distance trip he cannot do these things. He finds that it does not pay to waste his energy pawing in the valley. He must buckle down to the road and go steadily, from the moment he starts out, if he does not want to be dead tired by the evening.

That is why I have always tried to make my longer stays at places where the horses could have not only rest but recreation. In the West we would stay at ranches, and I would give them runs after cattle. Now that Jonty is alone, it is doubly important. I try to find a place where there are other horses, and where he can have pleasant and varied exercise in company. I do not stop for long, unless there is a good field. Even in the depths of winter when the grass is covered, it does a horse good to run out, to roll, buck round and feel for a little while that he is a free horse, and nobody in the world can gallop faster than he.

Thanks to the fact that he has never gone very long without relaxation, and thanks to the great heart which is packed into his neat little body, Jonty's temperament has not suffered from the ride. He is as solemn as a judge on the trail, but after a couple of days' rest, he begins rejoicing in his strength again to such an extent that I have both hands full to ride him. So I know that really I need not worry.

I have not ridden a day in Vermont when I have not been grateful to the Green Mountain Horse Association. For they have the trails through the mountains so systematically blazed and mapped that one may ride from dawn till dark without ever touching a highway. Sometimes the road will wind among the smaller hills, snuggling against their warmly wooded sides, or curving along the banks of a rough little river. At other times

END OF AN ADVENTURE

it will lead out into a wide valley and continue uneventfully between level meadows, and then on either hand one may see the tops of the higher mountains, standing back, lonely and remote. Often it will climb up and run along a western ridge, and then one may look across the plains to see the stately Adirondacks running south beyond Lake Champlain. It is tantalizing to be so consistently accompanied by these other mountains. When we ascend a ridge and look westward they are always there, yet to me they seem as lonely and unreal as the mountains of the moon. It is not till the south-bound trail leaves Brandon that we climb really high into our own range.

We reached Brandon late in the afternoon, and, turning east, began to wind our way up into the forest. Up and up we went; I walked ahead and Jonty followed busily behind me. Suddenly we came out into a country of apple orchards, where we drifted pleasantly along the road, picking up the heavy red apples and eating them as we went. So we passed once more under the roof of the forest, and climbing for hours through the trees, we came out once more on to an open hill-side. And then I saw how high we were, for we could look right into the intricate pattern of the hills, as they went weaving away fold on fold into the sunset. As I gazed into them my thoughts went back, as they so often do, to this problem of government for peace. For to fight this war for anything less than a world order is to fight in vain. This time, government which keeps the peace within nations must be extended till it can keep the peace between them. Here, I believe is our greatest hope.

In Bennington, near the border of Vermont and Massachusetts, I devoted half a day to sight-seeing. Obediently I admired the oldest church in Vermont, the oldest inn and the oldest cemetery, and the highest memorial of a battle in the world. We also drove past Bennington College, where they have the biggest or the best or the oldest or something college dancing school in America.

It certainly appears that to lay any claim to interest in the

United States, an object or edifice has to establish a record in some way. To be the largest of something seems to be the best, but failing that to be the oldest will do. But perhaps all this is just myself, being English!

I found in my mail at Bennington a letter from a friend who informed me, among other home truths, that I had gone to sleep at the age of three, and that it had taken a little thing like a war to wake me up. Riding down the by-ways of Massachusetts, I have been considering this. I think it might more accurately be said that, in common with many others, I have been squeezing my eyes shut while the car which carried me drove headlong towards a precipice.

For as long as I can remember, our generation had been carefully conditioned to see nothing whatever beyond the outbreak of this war. There was only one thing we were sure of: this next war would mean "the Destruction of Civilization." Meanwhile we rushed towards it. There was nothing we could do. The League of Nations was a gallant failure; appeasement was an absurdity; pacifism was logical but useless. Of what use was it to occupy our minds with social problems or to concern ourselves in the battle between capitalism and socialism? Of what use was anything, when we were charging full tilt towards the Destruction of Civilization?

Then the war broke out; the Destruction of Civilization did not immediately ensue. And gradually our minds were set free; or, to pursue the original metaphor, our car dived over the precipice. We reached the bottom and were still alive. We opened our eyes. The car was smashed. And then we realized that if we left it and began to climb the precipice again, slowly, dangerously, forgetting all else, we *might* reach the top.

We have passed through Massachusetts and into Connecticut, and now I am sitting in bed in a white house on a hill-side, watching the dawn coming over the Berkshire Hills.

In a few days now we shall be in New York, and the ride will

Courtesy Clifton Nugent, Manchester, Vt.

"JONTY'S TEMPERAMENT HAS NOT SUFFERED FROM THE RIDE"

END OF AN ADVENTURE

be finished. Watching the mists lying white in the valley, I have been sliding my mind back and realizing how many of the unhurried impressions of the last eighteen months will go with me into the years, helping to create day by day the person who is me. Wherever I go from here these things will go with me. Always in my mind there will be mountains running down to the Pacific, great trees and tiny trails and deer, and packers lighting fires and pitching tents and hauling up the slack on a diamond hitch; there will be year-old snow and black tea out of billy cans and rain in the mountains; but no rain on the scorching range of the dry belt, only cactus and sage-brush and sunflowers burning down the hill-sides.

Rain and sun in the foot-hills though, rivers and ranches, great fantastic Western saddles on little lean broncos, steers bucking to heaven at stampedes, ten-gallon hats and high-heeled boots and close-fitting overalls on bandy legs, horses milling in high corrals and little ranch-houses filling with unexpected guests. After that, sunsets over the wheatfields and northern lights arching up into the sky, and straight sandy roads which go on almost forever, and elevators and cottonwood trees and the rare delight of river-valleys.

Then Winnipeg, and the wilderness beyond, and tamaracks burning gold out of the blue-black swamps, naked rocks and lonely lakes shivering in the wind. Then the vast expanse of Lake Superior, and so winter on the farm—lamplight in the early morning kitchen—milking time in misty barns—teams labouring out of the bush—spring and syrup-boiling under budding maples, daisied hay standing high, and a boat floating down a river on the trail of a timber drive.

Autumn again under the shoulder of the Laurentians, and so at last this gold and silver journey through the Green Mountains of Vermont. And always, through everything, the horses with me, tireless and kind, giving me their unchanging companionship, their unbroken trust. Remembering Canada, I remember too the majesty of Vancouver, standing between the mountains and the sea, Calgary and Winnipeg on the borders of the prairies, Ottawa with the Parliament Houses standing upon their hill, and Montreal grouped round its royal mountain.

But when seas divide me from her, Canada will live for me, not in the memory of her cities, but of hip-roofed barns and snake fences and stout corrals, of the dark flash of a red-winged blackbird and the snort of a little branded bronco, of mountains and wheatfields and the wilderness. For the soul of Canada is not in her cities. And I do not believe that the soul of the world is in cities either, or ever can be.

All these last days, following large scale maps, Jonty and I have been winding down the by-ways of Connecticut. Tomorrow our journey together will be over.

It is terrible to love horses like this, to love one horse like this, and to have to part with him. Often in these days I get down and walk, because then Jonty follows along with his head close to my shoulder, and so I seem to be nearer to him. Whatever people say, a horse does not often become deeply attached to a person. But this has happened to Jonty. To part with a horse who will not miss one is bad, but to part with a horse who will miss one is as bad as anything I know.

Sometimes I put my arm round his neck and fit my face into the hollow behind his cheek. But this surprises and annoys him, and he shakes his head impatiently. So there is nothing to do but walk beside him, as I have walked so many times before.

So we have made it. Encouraged by an escort of mounted police, little Jonty carried me in undaunted—through Harlem, through the Bronx, down the narrow length of Central Park, down Eighth Avenue and into the Mounted Police barracks on Forty-eighth Street, where he is temporarily installed.

It is evening now, and I sit to write at the window of my cousins' thirteenth storey flat. Far below goes by the muted roar of the traffic upon Park Avenue. Before me the lighted windows of the sky-scrapers tower into the dark.

So ends the journal of an experiment in adventure.

And now I shall go home and join the Land Army, and take my part in the adventure which is England.

END

Some of the other titles in the Equestrian Travel Classic series published by The Long Riders' Guild Press. We are constantly adding to our collection, so for an up-to-date list please visit our website:
www.thelongridersguild.com

Title	Author
Tschiffely's Ride	Aime Tschiffley
The Tale of Two Horses	Aime Tschiffley
Bridle Paths	Aime Tschiffely
This Way Southward	Aime Tschiffely
Bohemia Junction	Aime Tschiffely
Through Persia on a Sidesaddle	Ella C. Sykes
Through Russia on a Mustang	Thomas Stevens
Riding Across Patagonia	Lady Florence Dixie
A Ride to Khiva	Frederick Burnaby
Ocean to Ocean on Horseback	Williard Glazier
Rural Rides – Volume One	William Cobbett
Rural Rides – Volume Two	William Cobbett
Adventures in Mexico	George F. Ruxton
Travels with A Donkey in the Cevennes	Robert Louis Stevenson
Winter Sketches from the Saddle	John Codman
Following the Frontier	Roger Pocock
On Horseback in Virginia	Charles Dudley Warner
California Coast Trails	J. Smeaton Chase
My Kingdom for a Horse	Margaret Leigh
The Journeys of Celia Fiennes	Celia Fiennes
On Horseback through Asia Minor	Fred Burnaby
The Abode of Snow	Andrew Wilson
A Lady's Life in the Rocky Mountains	Isabella Bird
Travels in Afghanistan	Ernest F. Fox
Through Mexico on Horseback	Joseph Carl Goodwin
Caucasian Journey	Negley Farson
Turkestan Solo	Ella K. Maillart
Through the Highlands of Shropshire	Magdalene M. Weale
Wartime Ride	J. W. Day
Across the Roof of the World	Wilfred Skrede
The Courage to Ride	Ana Beker
Saddles East	John W. Beard
Last of the Saddle Tramps	Messanie Wilkins
Ride a White Horse	William Holt
Manual of Pack Transportation	H. W. Daly
Horses, Saddles and Bridles	W. H. Carter
Notes on Elementary Equitation	Carleton S. Cooke
Cavalry Drill Regulations	United States Army
Horse Packing	Charles Johnson Post
Mongolian Adventure	Henning Haslund
The Art of Travel	Francis Galton
Shanghai à Moscou	Madame de Bourboulon
Saddlebags for Suitcases	Mary Bosanquet
The Road to the Grey Pamir	Ana Louise Strong
Boots and Saddles in Africa	Thomas Lambie
To the Foot of the Rainbow	Clyde Kluckhohn
Through Five Republics on Horseback	George Ray
Journey from the Arctic	Donald Brown
Saddle and Canoe	Theodore Winthrop
The Prairie Traveler	Randolph Marcy
Reiter, Pferd und Fahrer – Volume One	Dr. C. Geuer
Reiter, Pferd und Fahrer – Volume Two	Dr. C. Geuer

The Long Riders' Guild
The world's leading source of information regarding equestrian exploration!
www.thelongridersguild.com

Lightning Source UK Ltd.
Milton Keynes UK
UKHW04f0627260918
329553UK00001B/197/P